BLACK CAT
INFINITY SCORE

Felicia Hardy is the world's greatest thief, known to some as the **Black Cat**. Recently, she pulled off a string of high-stakes heists backed by her crew, **Bruno and Doctor Korpse**, at the behest of her former mentor and father figure, the **Black Fox**. But when the Fox revealed that his true plan was to sink New York City into an extradimensional vault in exchange for immortality, Felicia was forced to betray him to save the city, condemning him to the vault instead.

With New York saved and the Black Fox gone, Felicia needs some time to grieve her loss. But when a shiny new mark comes her way, she won't be able to say no...

collection editor **JENNIFER GRÜNWALD** ♦ assistant editor **DANIEL KIRCHHOFFER**
assistant managing editor **MAIA LOY** ♦ assistant managing editor **LISA MONTALBANO**
vp production & special projects **JEFF YOUNGQUIST** ♦ book designers **SARAH SPADACCINI** with **JAY BOWEN**
svp print, sales & marketing **DAVID GABRIEL** ♦ editor in chief **C.B. CEBULSKI**

BLACK CAT VOL. 6: INFINITY SCORE. Contains material originally published in magazine form as BLACK CAT (2020) #8-10 and GIANT-SIZE BLACK CAT: INFINITY SCORE #1. First printing 2021. ISBN 978-1-302-93138-4. Published by MARVEL WORLDWIDE, INC., a subsidiary of MARVEL ENTERTAINMENT, LLC. OFFICE OF PUBLICATION: 1290 Avenue of the Americas, New York, NY 10104. © 2021 MARVEL No similarity between any of the names, characters, persons, and/or institutions in this book with those of any living or dead person or institution is intended, and any such similarity which may exist is purely coincidental. **Printed in Canada.** KEVIN FEIGE, Chief Creative Officer; DAN BUCKLEY, President, Marvel Entertainment; JOE QUESADA, EVP & Creative Director; DAVID BOGART, Associate Publisher & SVP of Talent Affairs; TOM BREVOORT, VP, Executive Editor; NICK LOWE, Executive Editor, VP of Content, Digital Publishing; DAVID GABRIEL, VP of Print & Digital Publishing; JEFF YOUNGQUIST, VP of Production & Special Projects; ALEX MORALES, Director of Publishing Operations; DAN EDINGTON, Managing Editor; RICKEY PURDIN, Director of Talent Relations; JENNIFER GRÜNWALD, Senior Editor, Special Projects; SUSAN CRESPI, Production Manager; STAN LEE, Chairman Emeritus. For information regarding advertising in Marvel Comics or on Marvel.com, please contact Vit DeBellis, Custom Solutions & Integrated Advertising Manager, at vdebellis@marvel.com. For Marvel subscription inquiries, please call 888-511-5480. **Manufactured between 10/22/2021 and 11/23/2021 by SOLISCO PRINTERS, SCOTT, QC, CANADA.**

10 9 8 7 6 5 4 3 2 1

BLACK CAT
INFINITY SCORE

writer	**JED MacKAY**
artist	**C.F. VILLA**
color artist	**BRIAN REBER**
letterer	**FERRAN DELGADO**
cover art	**PEPE LARRAZ**
	WITH **MARTE GRACIA** (#8 & GIANT-SIZE)
	& **ALEJANDRO SÁNCHEZ** (#9-10)
assistant editor	**LINDSEY COHICK**
editor	**NICK LOWE**

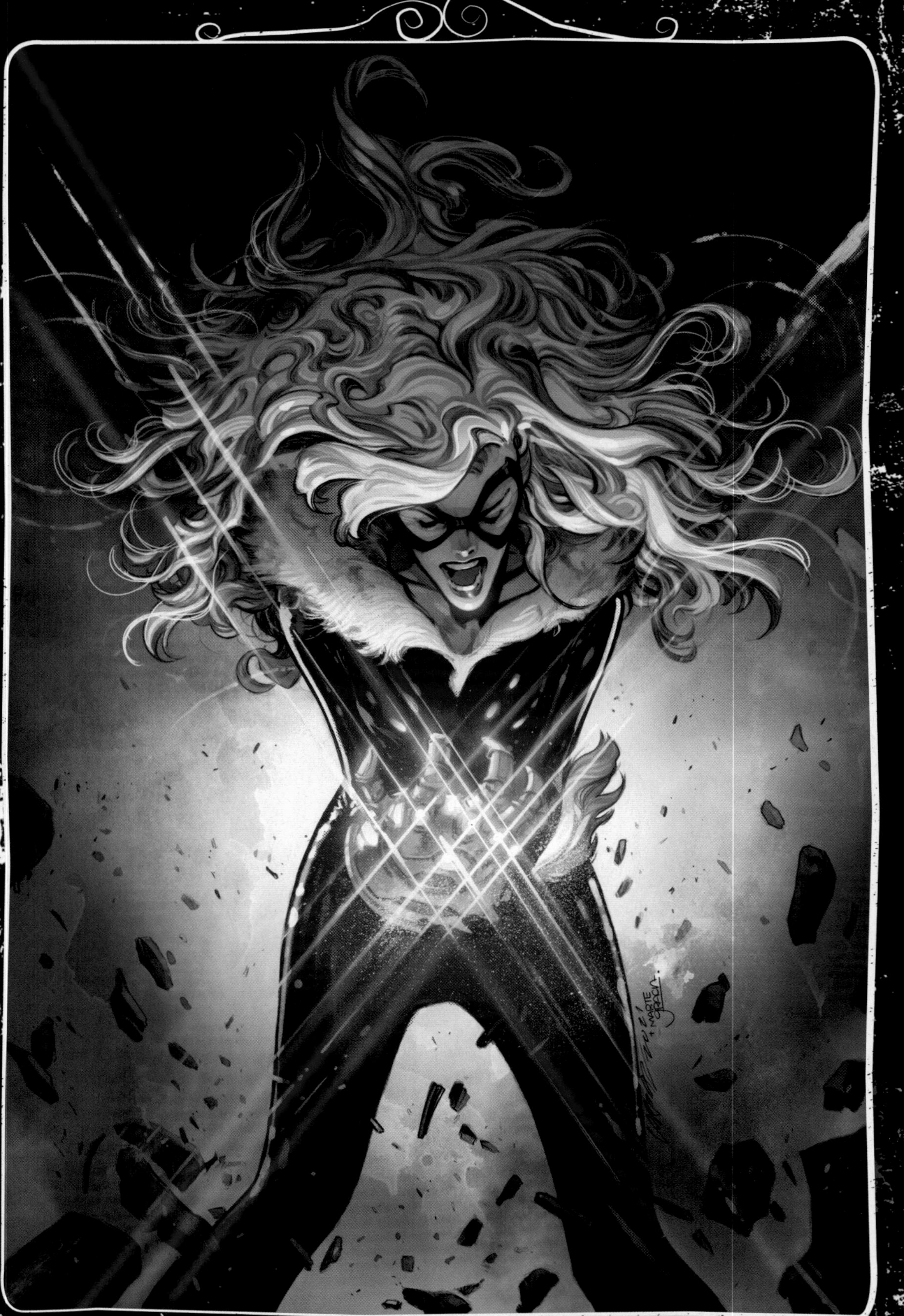

8 • INFINITY SCORE PART ONE

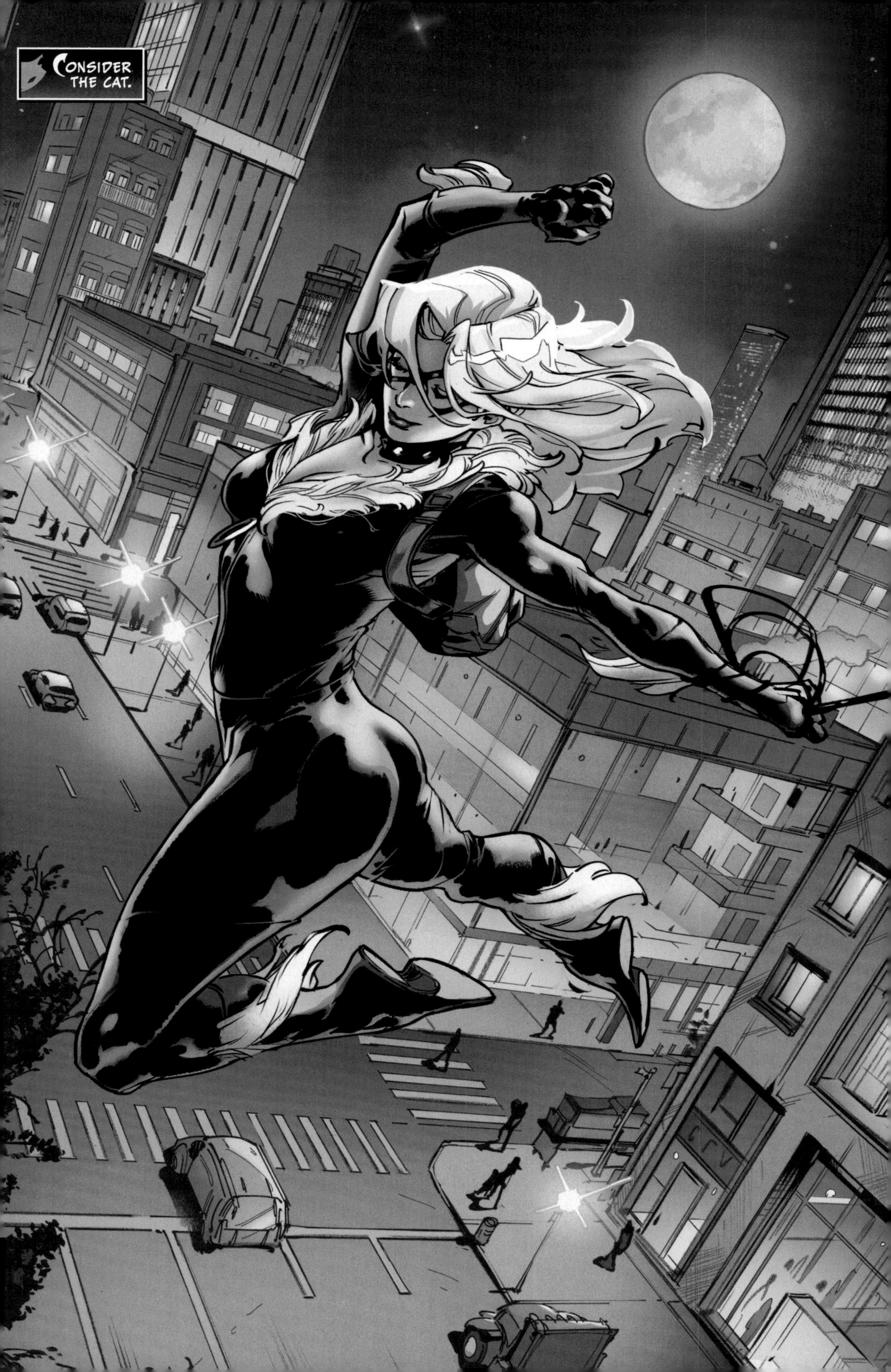
CONSIDER THE CAT.

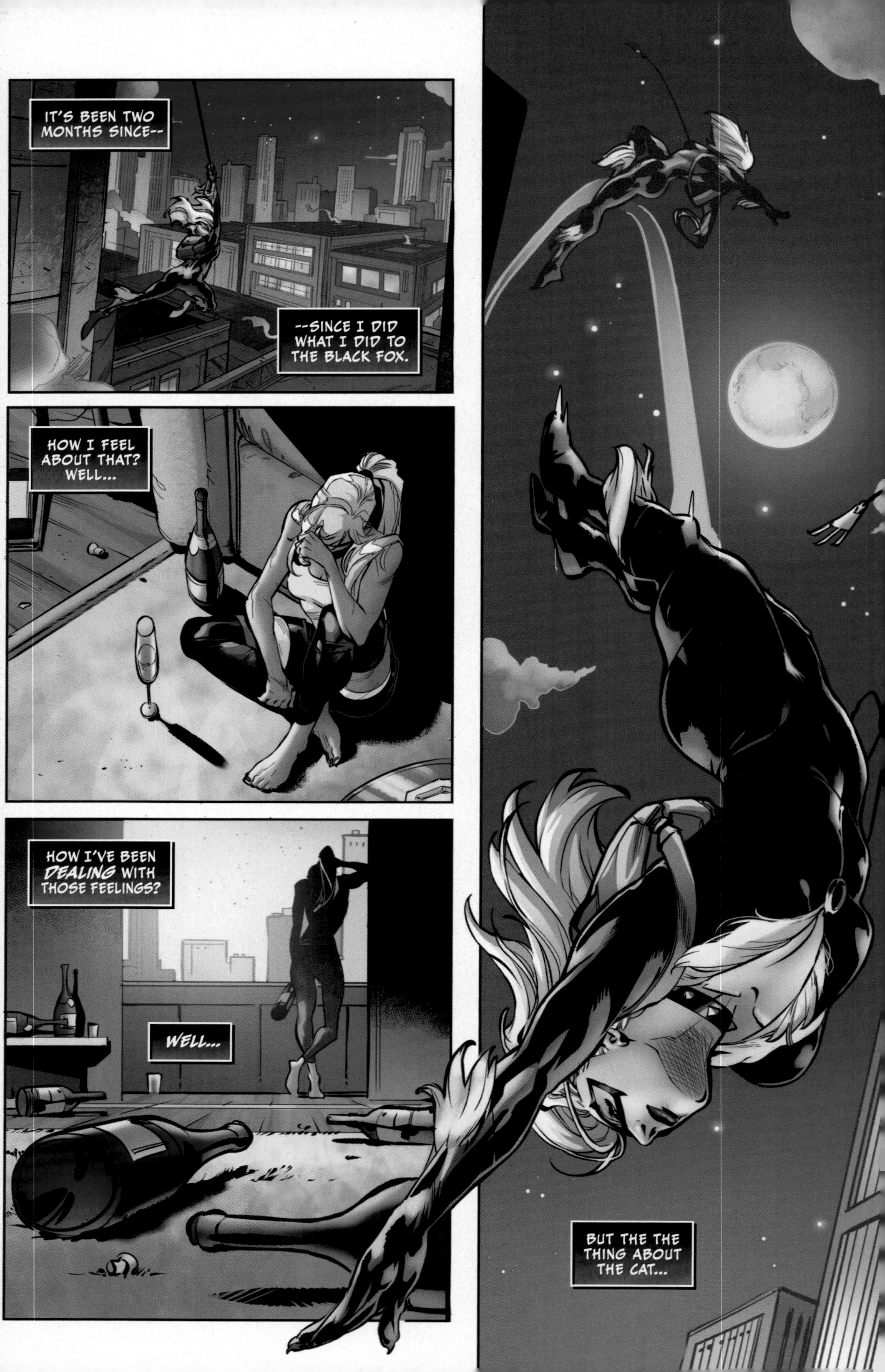
IT'S BEEN TWO MONTHS SINCE--
--SINCE I DID WHAT I DID TO THE BLACK FOX.
HOW I FEEL ABOUT THAT? WELL...
HOW I'VE BEEN DEALING WITH THOSE FEELINGS?
WELL...
BUT THE THE THING ABOUT THE CAT...

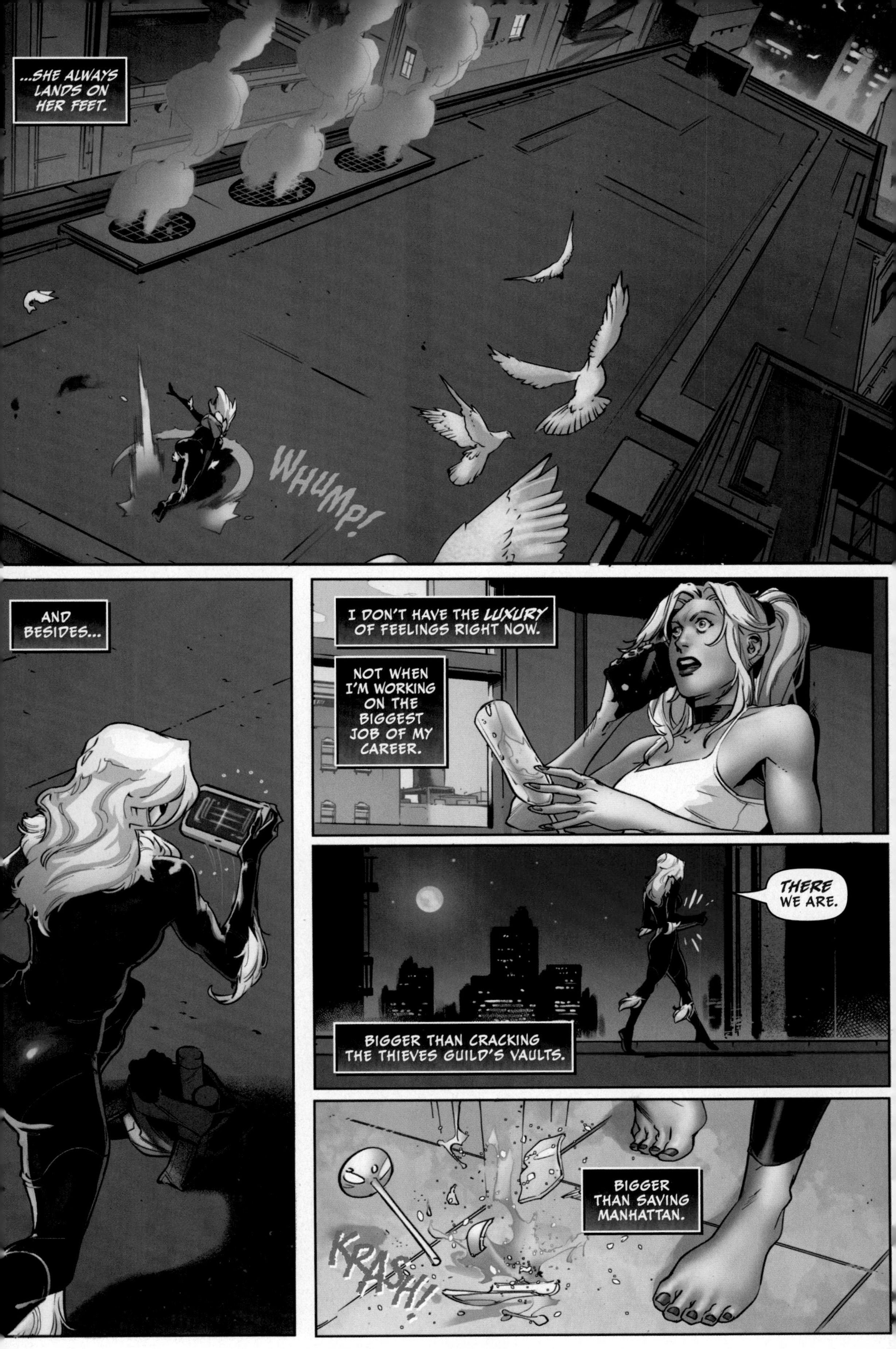
...SHE ALWAYS LANDS ON HER FEET.
WHUMP!
AND BESIDES...
I DON'T HAVE THE LUXURY OF FEELINGS RIGHT NOW.
NOT WHEN I'M WORKING ON THE BIGGEST JOB OF MY CAREER.
THERE WE ARE.
BIGGER THAN CRACKING THE THIEVES GUILD'S VAULTS.
BIGGER THAN SAVING MANHATTAN.
KRASH!!

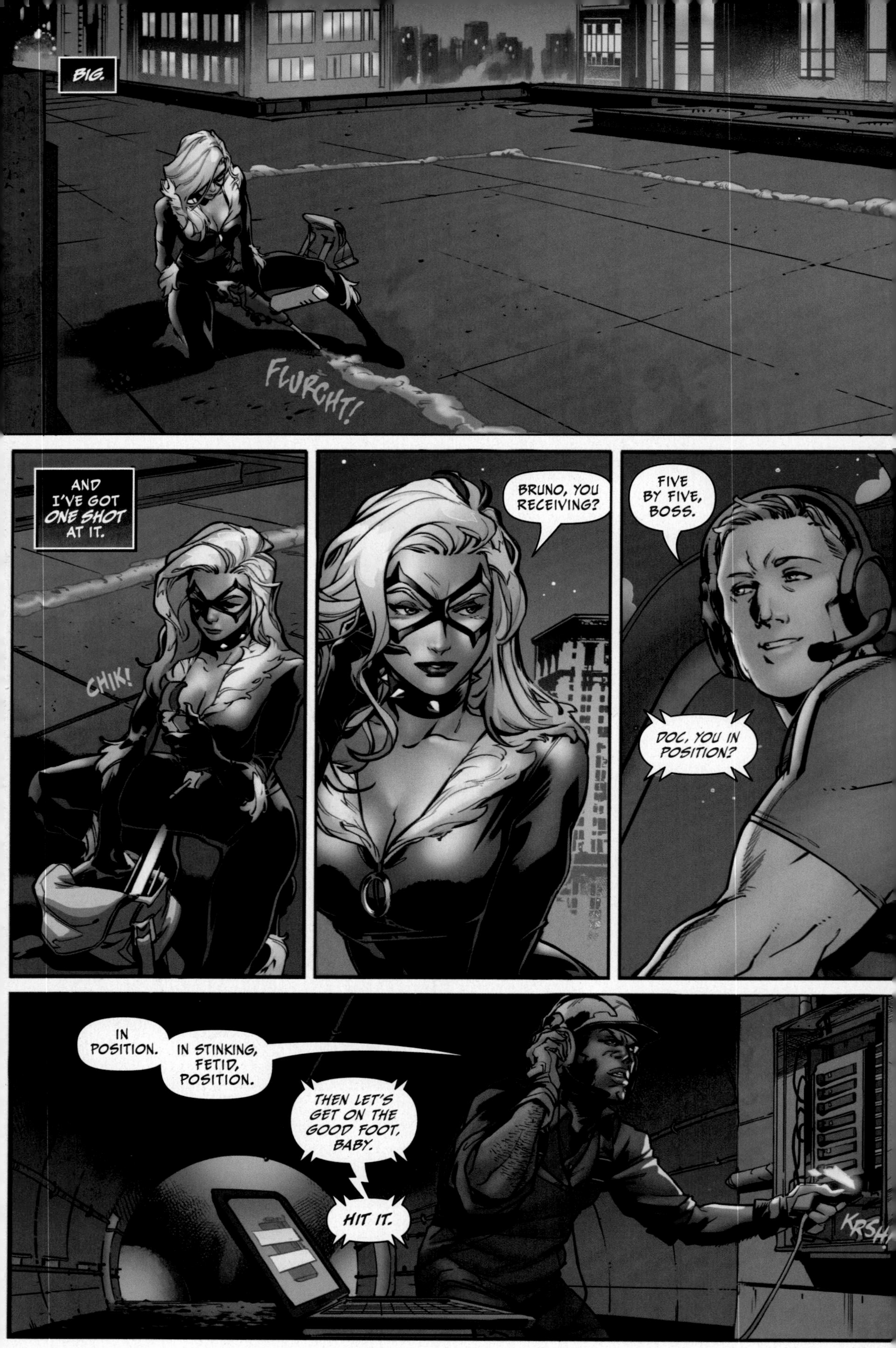
BIG.
FLURCHT!
AND I'VE GOT ONE SHOT AT IT.
CHIK!
BRUNO, YOU RECEIVING?
FIVE BY FIVE, BOSS.
DOC, YOU IN POSITION?
IN POSITION.
IN STINKING, FETID, POSITION.
THEN LET'S GET ON THE GOOD FOOT, BABY.
HIT IT.
KRSH

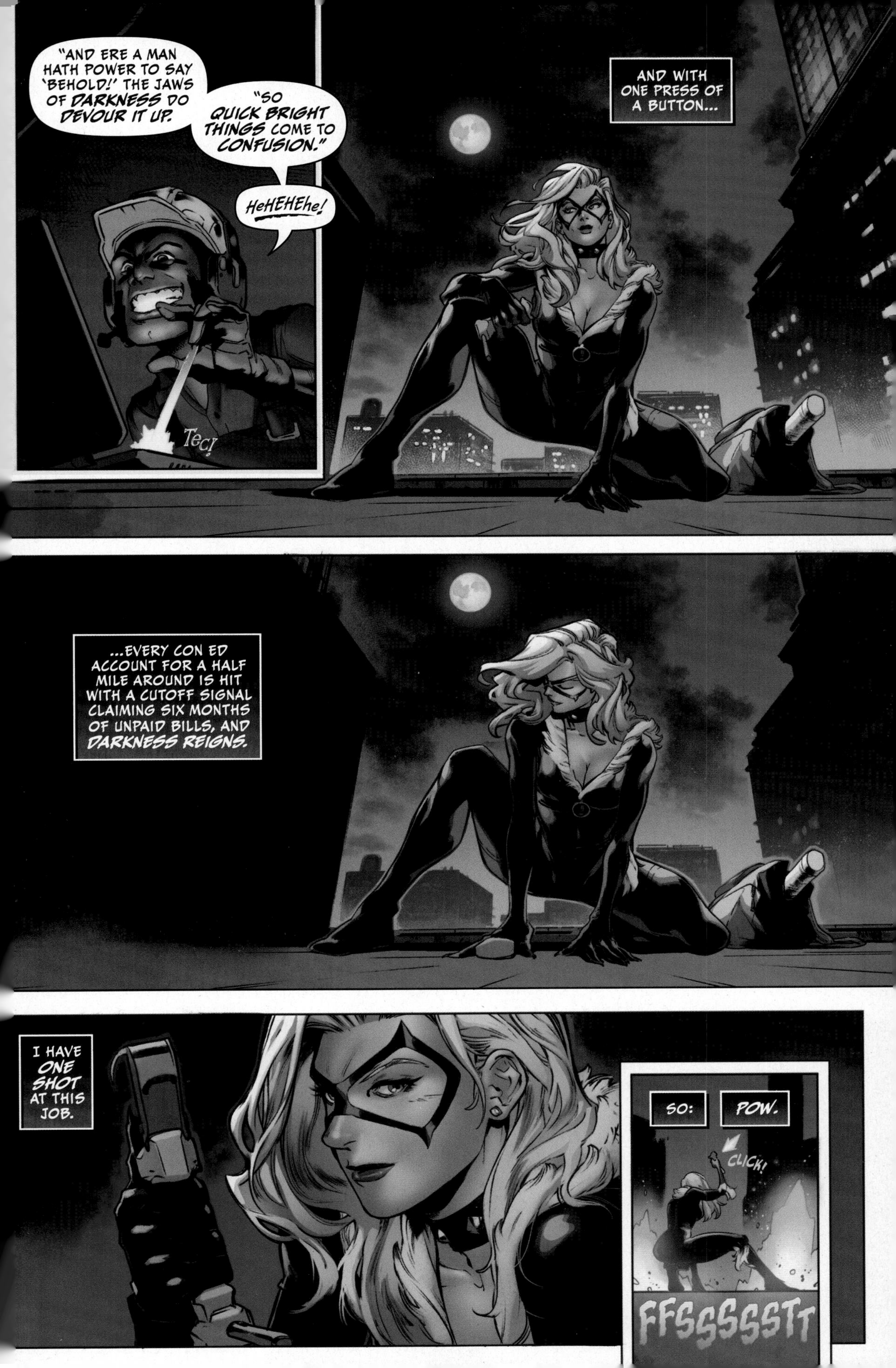
"AND ERE A MAN HATH POWER TO SAY 'BEHOLD!' THE JAWS OF DARKNESS DO DEVOUR IT UP.
"SO QUICK BRIGHT THINGS COME TO CONFUSION."
HeHEHEHe!
TEC!
AND WITH ONE PRESS OF A BUTTON...
...EVERY CON ED ACCOUNT FOR A HALF MILE AROUND IS HIT WITH A CUTOFF SIGNAL CLAIMING SIX MONTHS OF UNPAID BILLS, AND DARKNESS REIGNS.
I HAVE ONE SHOT AT THIS JOB.
SO:
POW.
CLICK!
FFSSSSSTT

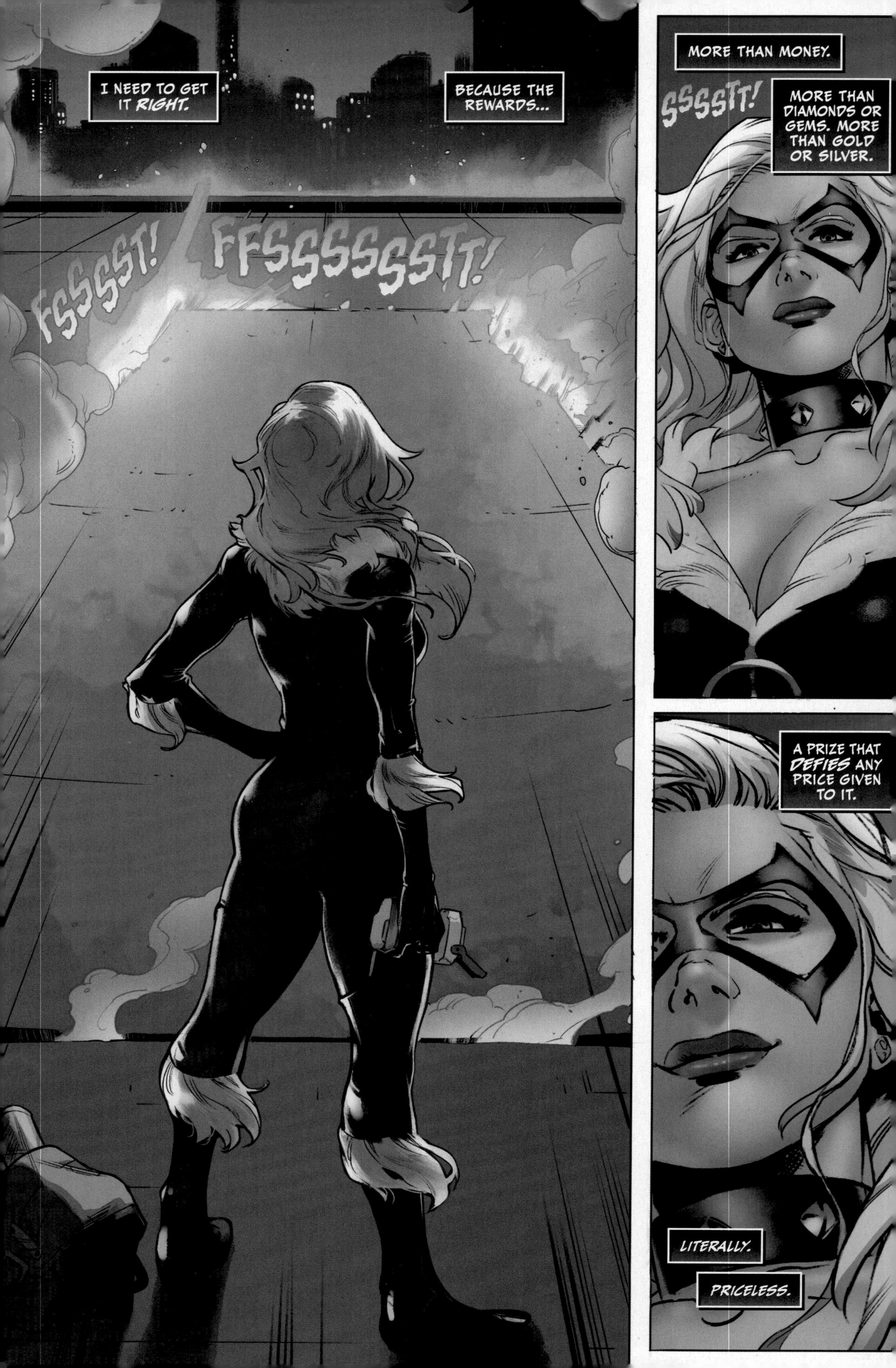
I NEED TO GET IT RIGHT.
BECAUSE THE REWARDS...
FSSSST!
FFSSSSSSST!
MORE THAN MONEY.
SSSSTT!
MORE THAN DIAMONDS OR GEMS. MORE THAN GOLD OR SILVER.
A PRIZE THAT DEFIES ANY PRICE GIVEN TO IT.
LITERALLY.
PRICELESS.

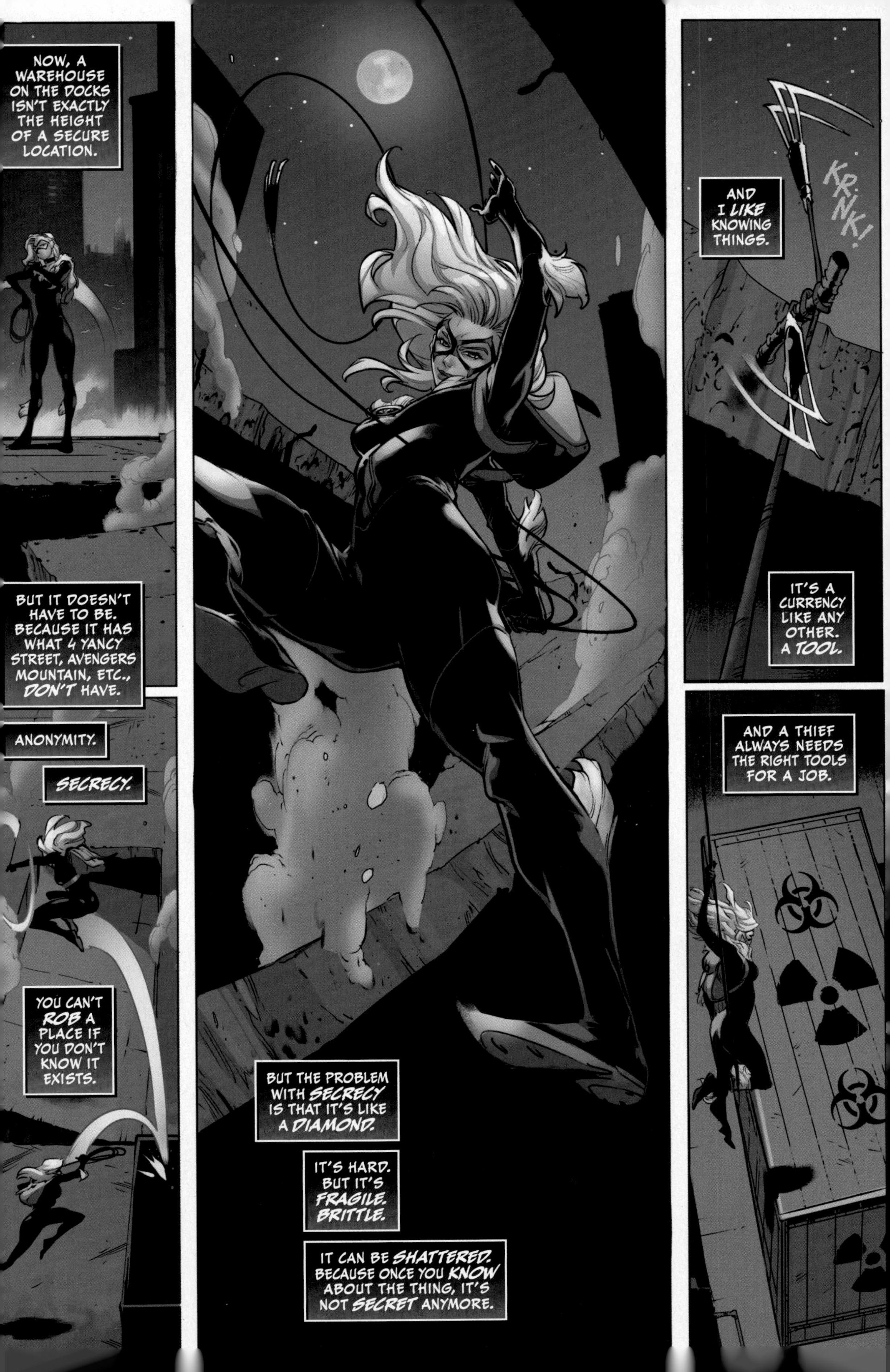
NOW, A WAREHOUSE ON THE DOCKS ISN'T EXACTLY THE HEIGHT OF A SECURE LOCATION.
BUT IT DOESN'T HAVE TO BE. BECAUSE IT HAS WHAT 4 YANCY STREET, AVENGERS MOUNTAIN, ETC., DON'T HAVE.
ANONYMITY.
SECRECY.
YOU CAN'T ROB A PLACE IF YOU DON'T KNOW IT EXISTS.
BUT THE PROBLEM WITH SECRECY IS THAT IT'S LIKE A DIAMOND.
IT'S HARD. BUT IT'S FRAGILE. BRITTLE.
IT CAN BE SHATTERED. BECAUSE ONCE YOU KNOW ABOUT THE THING, IT'S NOT SECRET ANYMORE.
KRINK!
AND I LIKE KNOWING THINGS.
IT'S A CURRENCY LIKE ANY OTHER. A TOOL.
AND A THIEF ALWAYS NEEDS THE RIGHT TOOLS FOR A JOB.

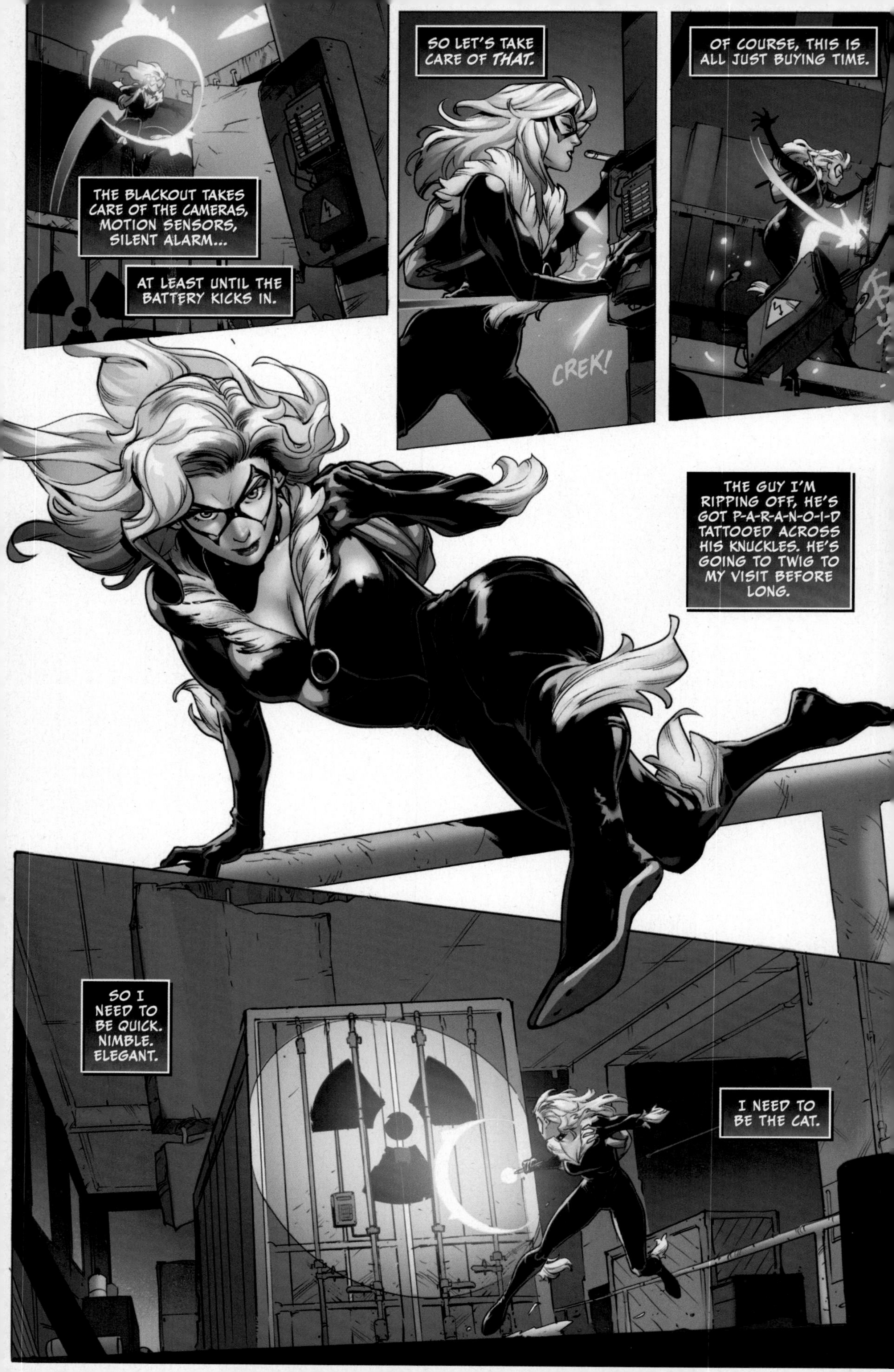
THE BLACKOUT TAKES CARE OF THE CAMERAS, MOTION SENSORS, SILENT ALARM...
AT LEAST UNTIL THE BATTERY KICKS IN.
SO LET'S TAKE CARE OF *THAT.*
CREK!
OF COURSE, THIS IS ALL JUST BUYING TIME.
THE GUY I'M RIPPING OFF, HE'S GOT P-A-R-A-N-O-I-D TATTOOED ACROSS HIS KNUCKLES. HE'S GOING TO TWIG TO MY VISIT BEFORE LONG.
SO I NEED TO BE QUICK. NIMBLE. ELEGANT.
I NEED TO BE THE CAT.

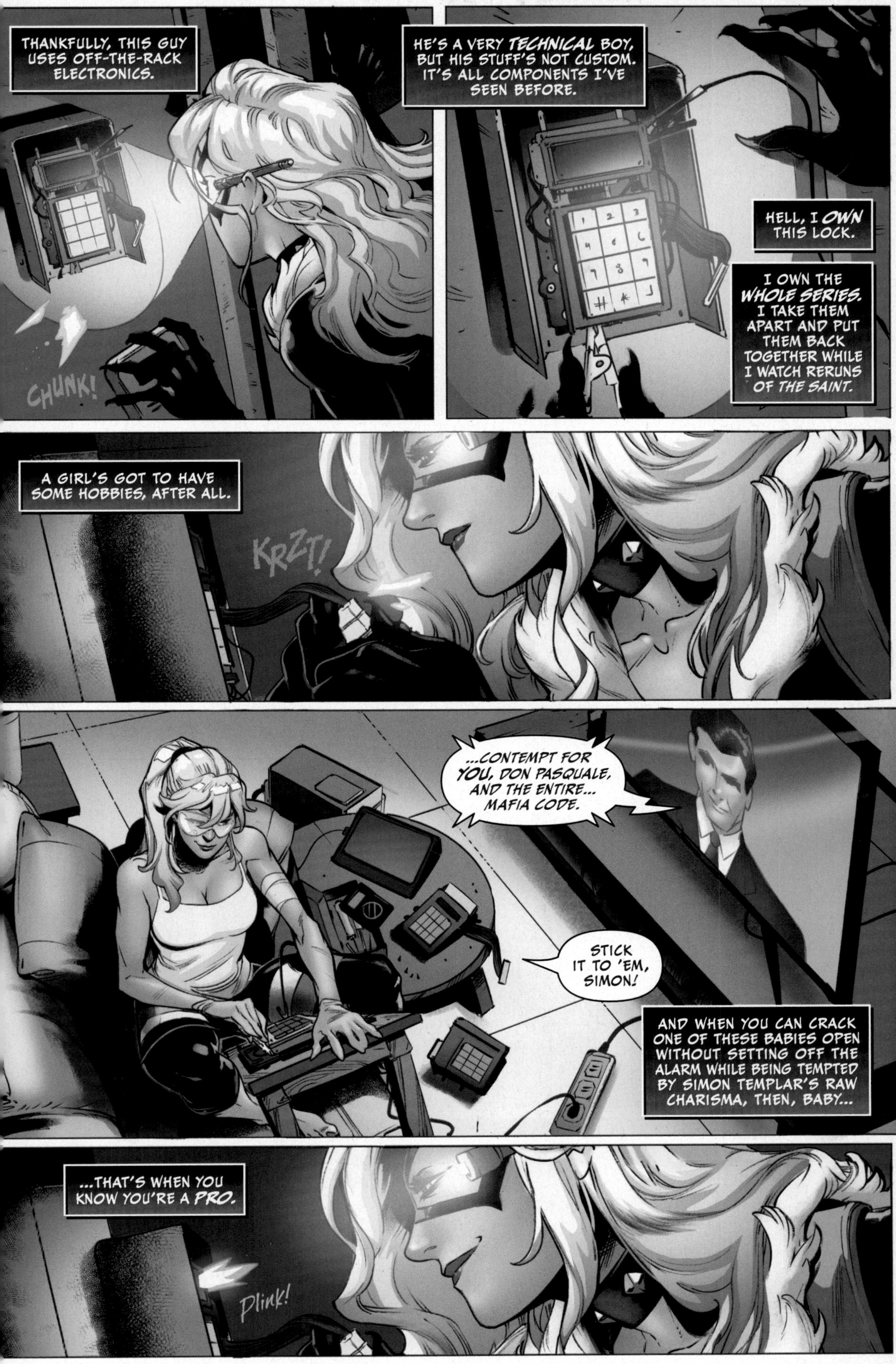
THANKFULLY, THIS GUY USES OFF-THE-RACK ELECTRONICS.
CHUNK!
HE'S A VERY TECHNICAL BOY, BUT HIS STUFF'S NOT CUSTOM. IT'S ALL COMPONENTS I'VE SEEN BEFORE.
HELL, I OWN THIS LOCK.
I OWN THE WHOLE SERIES. I TAKE THEM APART AND PUT THEM BACK TOGETHER WHILE I WATCH RERUNS OF THE SAINT.
A GIRL'S GOT TO HAVE SOME HOBBIES, AFTER ALL.
KRZZT!
...CONTEMPT FOR YOU, DON PASQUALE, AND THE ENTIRE... MAFIA CODE.
STICK IT TO 'EM, SIMON!
AND WHEN YOU CAN CRACK ONE OF THESE BABIES OPEN WITHOUT SETTING OFF THE ALARM WHILE BEING TEMPTED BY SIMON TEMPLAR'S RAW CHARISMA, THEN, BABY...
...THAT'S WHEN YOU KNOW YOU'RE A PRO.
Plink!

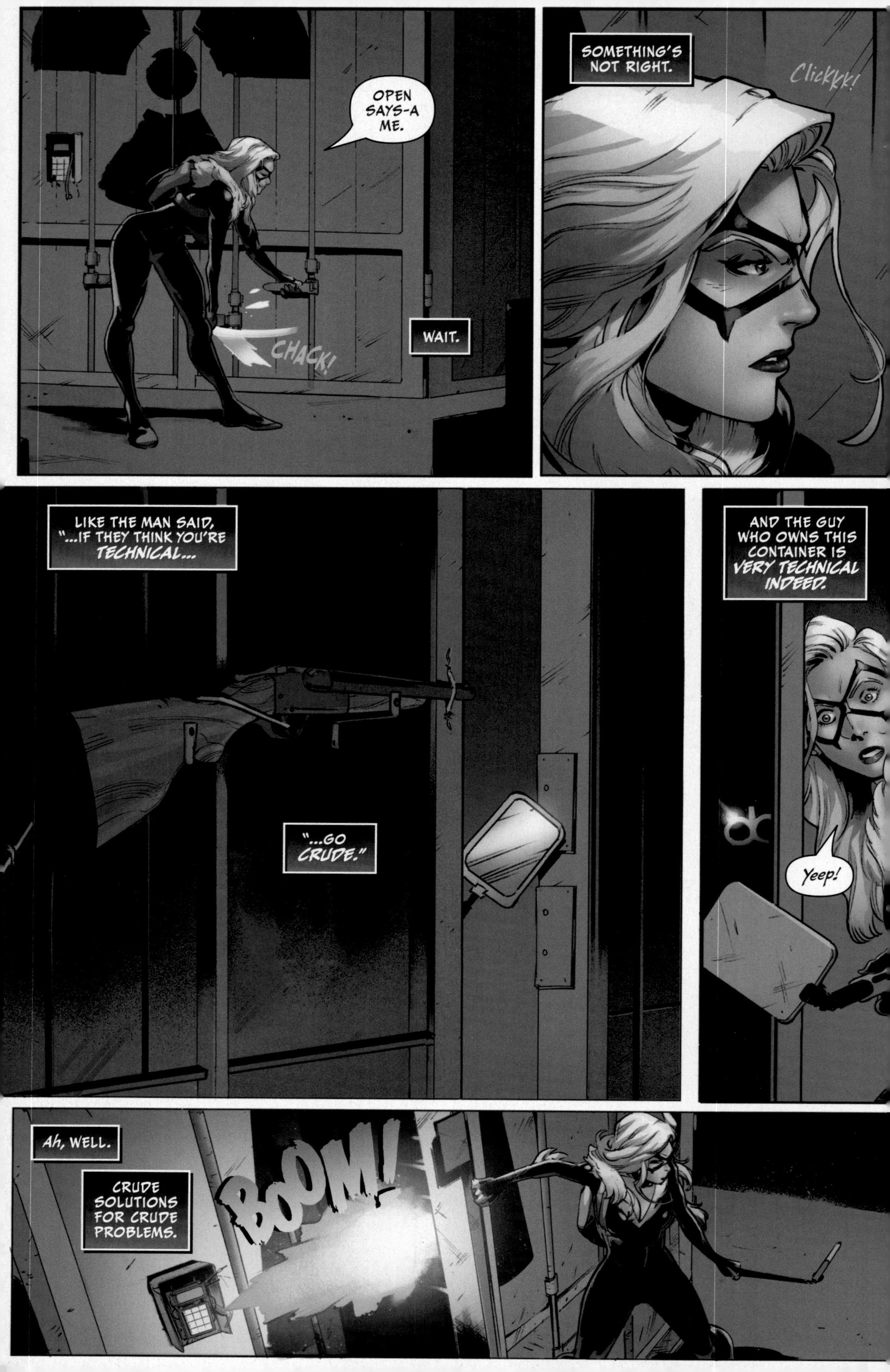
OPEN SAYS-A ME.
CHACK!
WAIT.
SOMETHING'S NOT RIGHT.
Clickkk!
LIKE THE MAN SAID, "...IF THEY THINK YOU'RE TECHNICAL...
"...GO CRUDE."
AND THE GUY WHO OWNS THIS CONTAINER IS VERY TECHNICAL INDEED.
Yeep!
Ah, WELL.
CRUDE SOLUTIONS FOR CRUDE PROBLEMS.
BOOM!

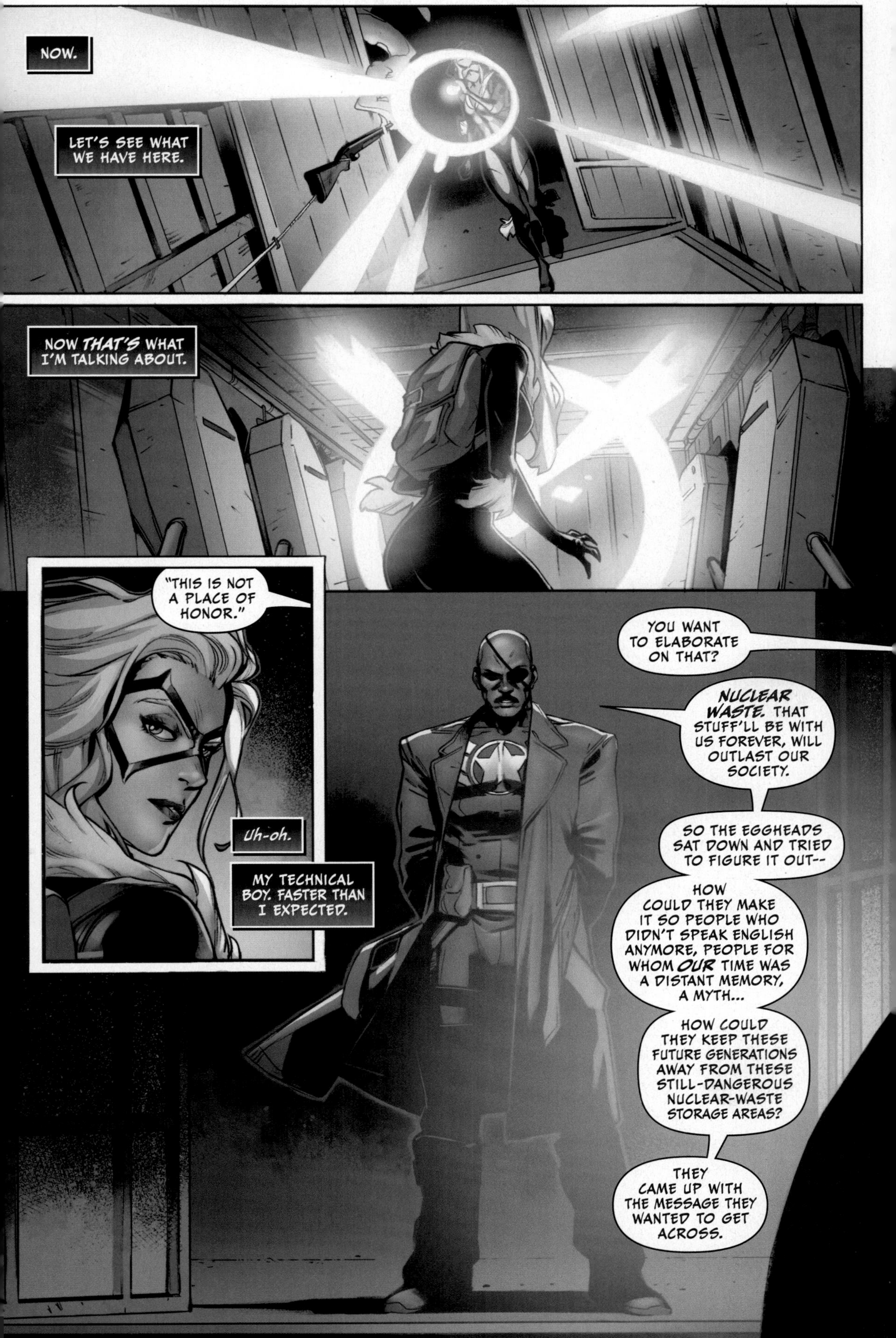
NOW.
LET'S SEE WHAT WE HAVE HERE.
NOW THAT'S WHAT I'M TALKING ABOUT.
"THIS IS NOT A PLACE OF HONOR."
Uh-oh.
MY TECHNICAL BOY. FASTER THAN I EXPECTED.
YOU WANT TO ELABORATE ON THAT?
NUCLEAR WASTE. THAT STUFF'LL BE WITH US FOREVER, WILL OUTLAST OUR SOCIETY.
SO THE EGGHEADS SAT DOWN AND TRIED TO FIGURE IT OUT--
HOW COULD THEY MAKE IT SO PEOPLE WHO DIDN'T SPEAK ENGLISH ANYMORE, PEOPLE FOR WHOM OUR TIME WAS A DISTANT MEMORY, A MYTH...
HOW COULD THEY KEEP THESE FUTURE GENERATIONS AWAY FROM THESE STILL-DANGEROUS NUCLEAR-WASTE STORAGE AREAS?
THEY CAME UP WITH THE MESSAGE THEY WANTED TO GET ACROSS.

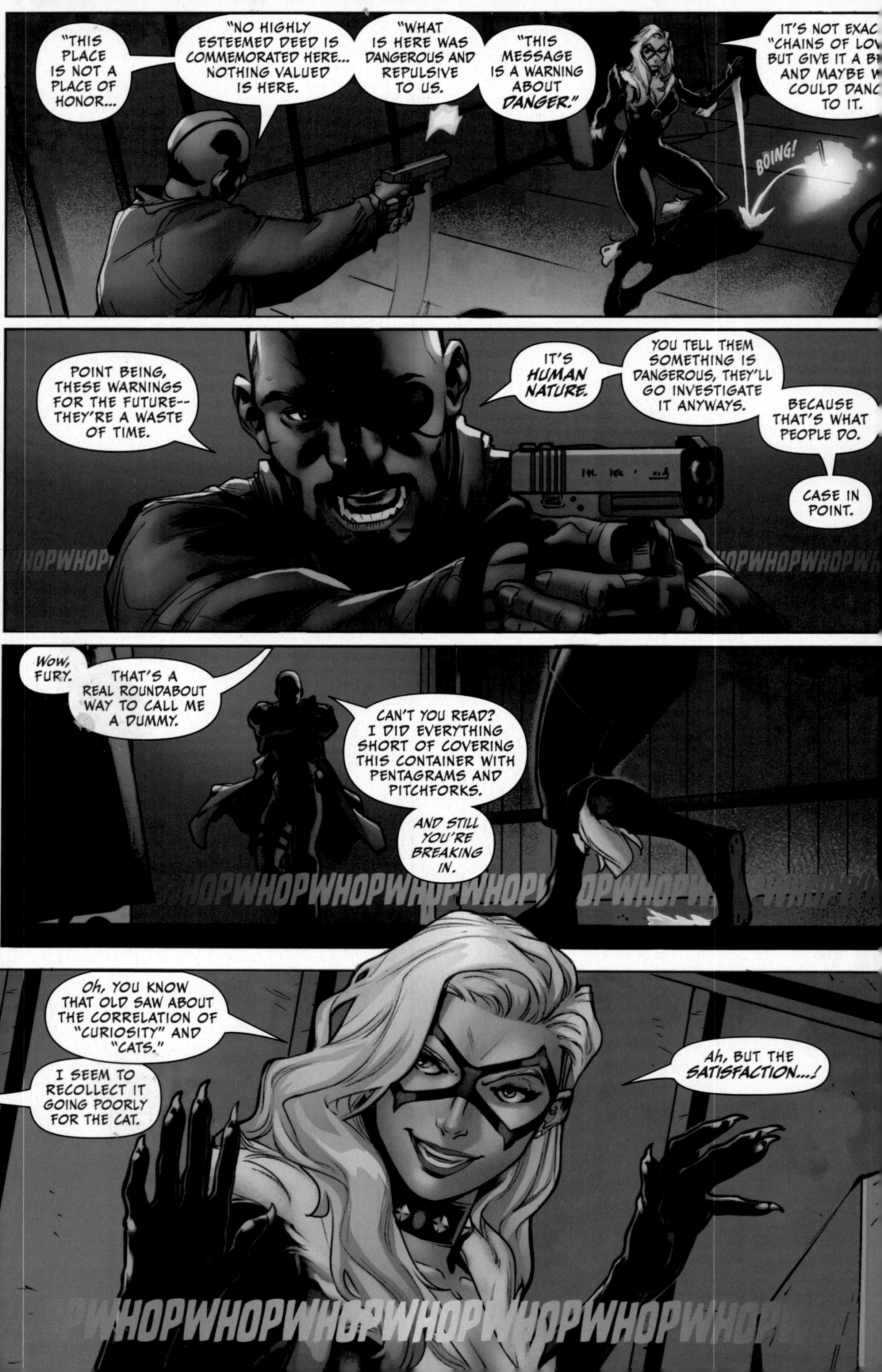
"THIS PLACE IS NOT A PLACE OF HONOR...
"NO HIGHLY ESTEEMED DEED IS COMMEMORATED HERE... NOTHING VALUED IS HERE.
"WHAT IS HERE WAS DANGEROUS AND REPULSIVE TO US.
"THIS MESSAGE IS A WARNING ABOUT DANGER."
IT'S NOT EXAC "CHAINS OF LOV BUT GIVE IT A B AND MAYBE W COULD DANC TO IT.
BOING!
POINT BEING, THESE WARNINGS FOR THE FUTURE-- THEY'RE A WASTE OF TIME.
IT'S HUMAN NATURE.
YOU TELL THEM SOMETHING IS DANGEROUS, THEY'LL GO INVESTIGATE IT ANYWAYS.
BECAUSE THAT'S WHAT PEOPLE DO.
CASE IN POINT.
WHOPWHOPWHOP
Wow, FURY.
THAT'S A REAL ROUNDABOUT WAY TO CALL ME A DUMMY.
CAN'T YOU READ? I DID EVERYTHING SHORT OF COVERING THIS CONTAINER WITH PENTAGRAMS AND PITCHFORKS.
AND STILL YOU'RE BREAKING IN.
WHOPWHOPWHOP
Oh, YOU KNOW THAT OLD SAW ABOUT THE CORRELATION OF "CURIOSITY" AND "CATS."
I SEEM TO RECOLLECT IT GOING POORLY FOR THE CAT.
Ah, BUT THE SATISFACTION...!
WHOPWHOPWHOPWHOP

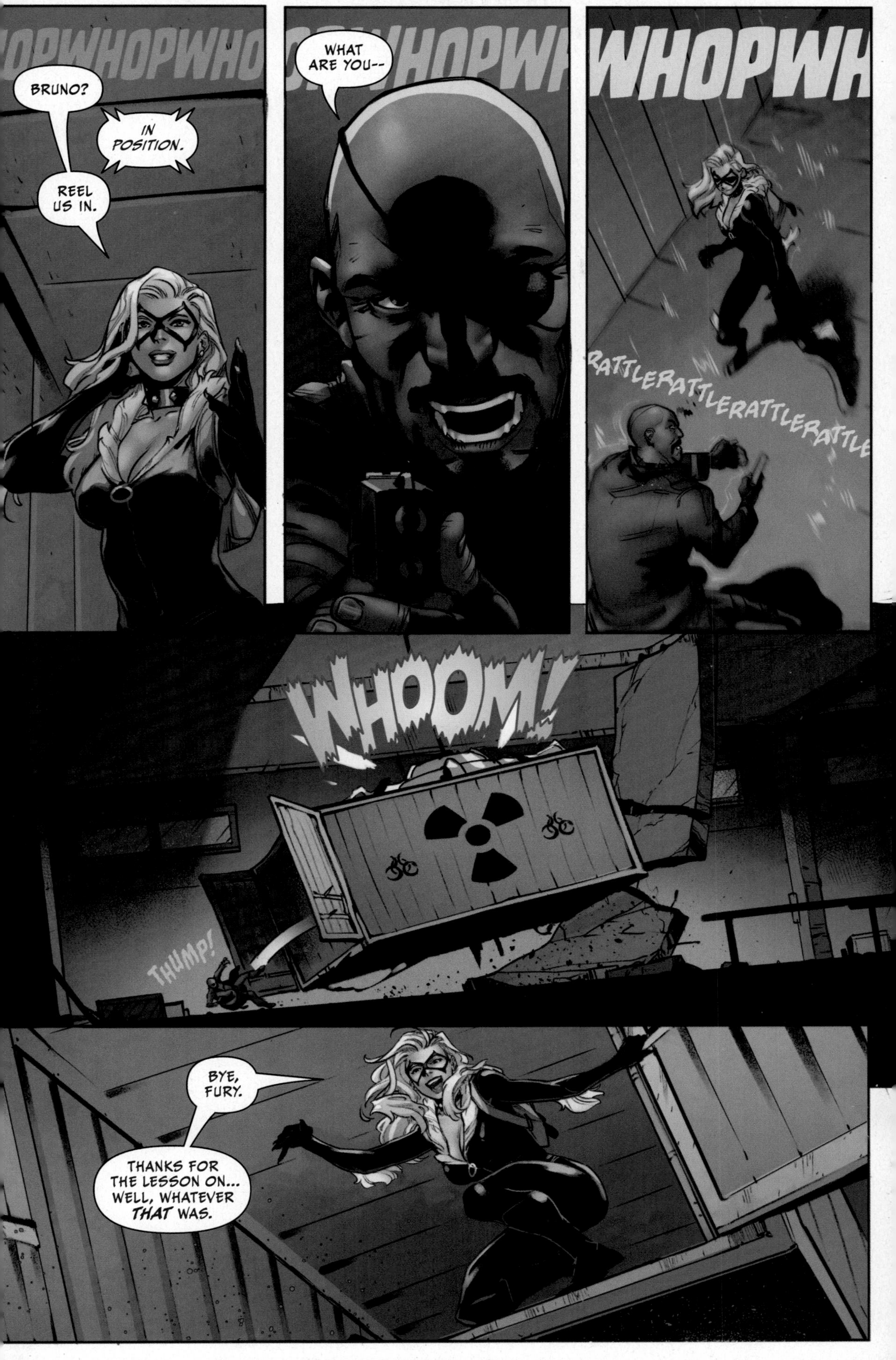
WHOPWHOPWHO
BRUNO?
IN POSITION.
REEL US IN.
WHAT ARE YOU--
WHOPWH
RATTLERATTLERATTLERATTLE
WHOOM!
THUMP!
BYE, FURY.
THANKS FOR THE LESSON ON... WELL, WHATEVER *THAT* WAS.

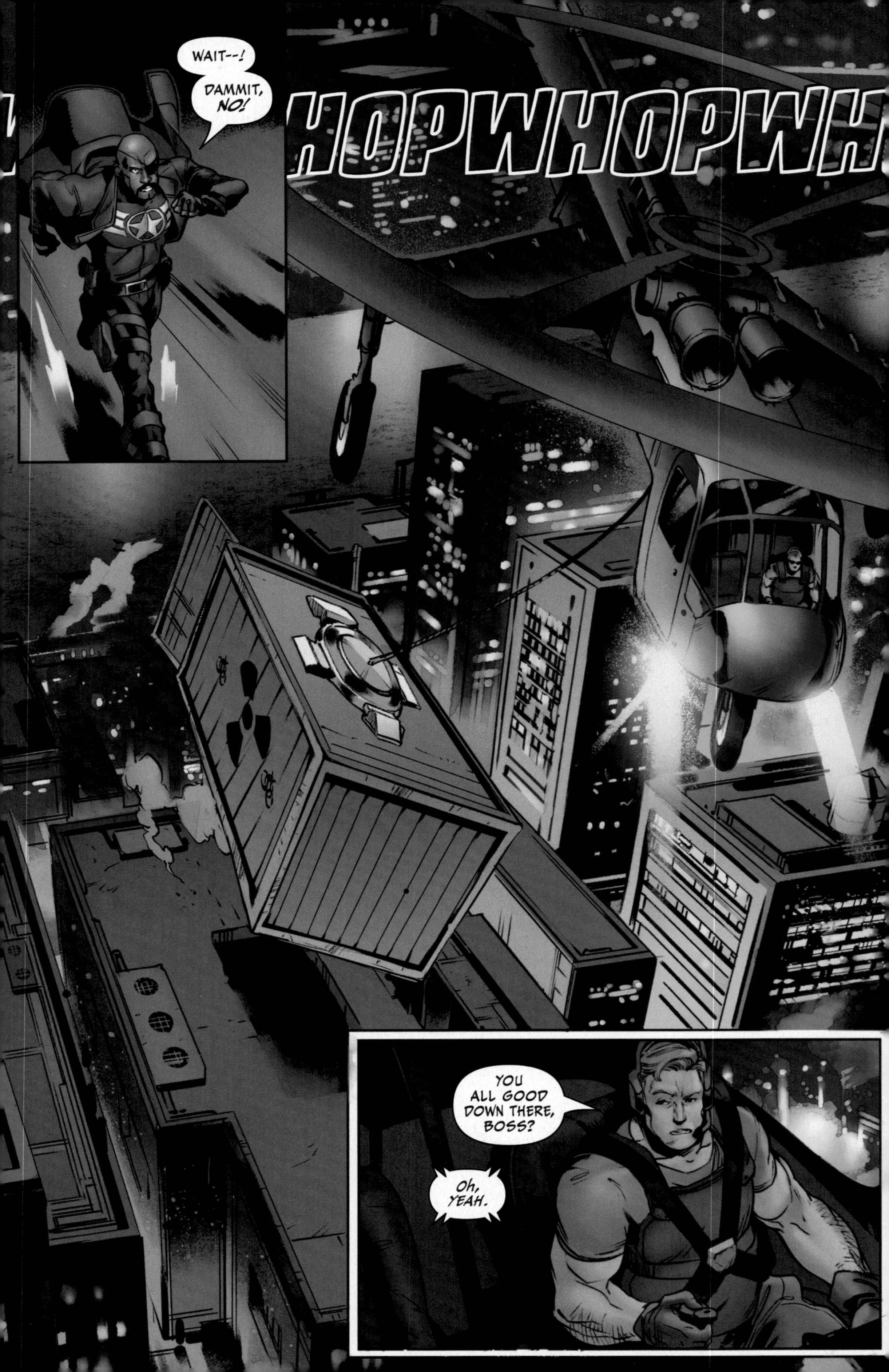
WAIT--!
DAMMIT, NO!
WHOPWHOPWHOPWH
YOU ALL GOOD DOWN THERE, BOSS?
Oh, YEAH.

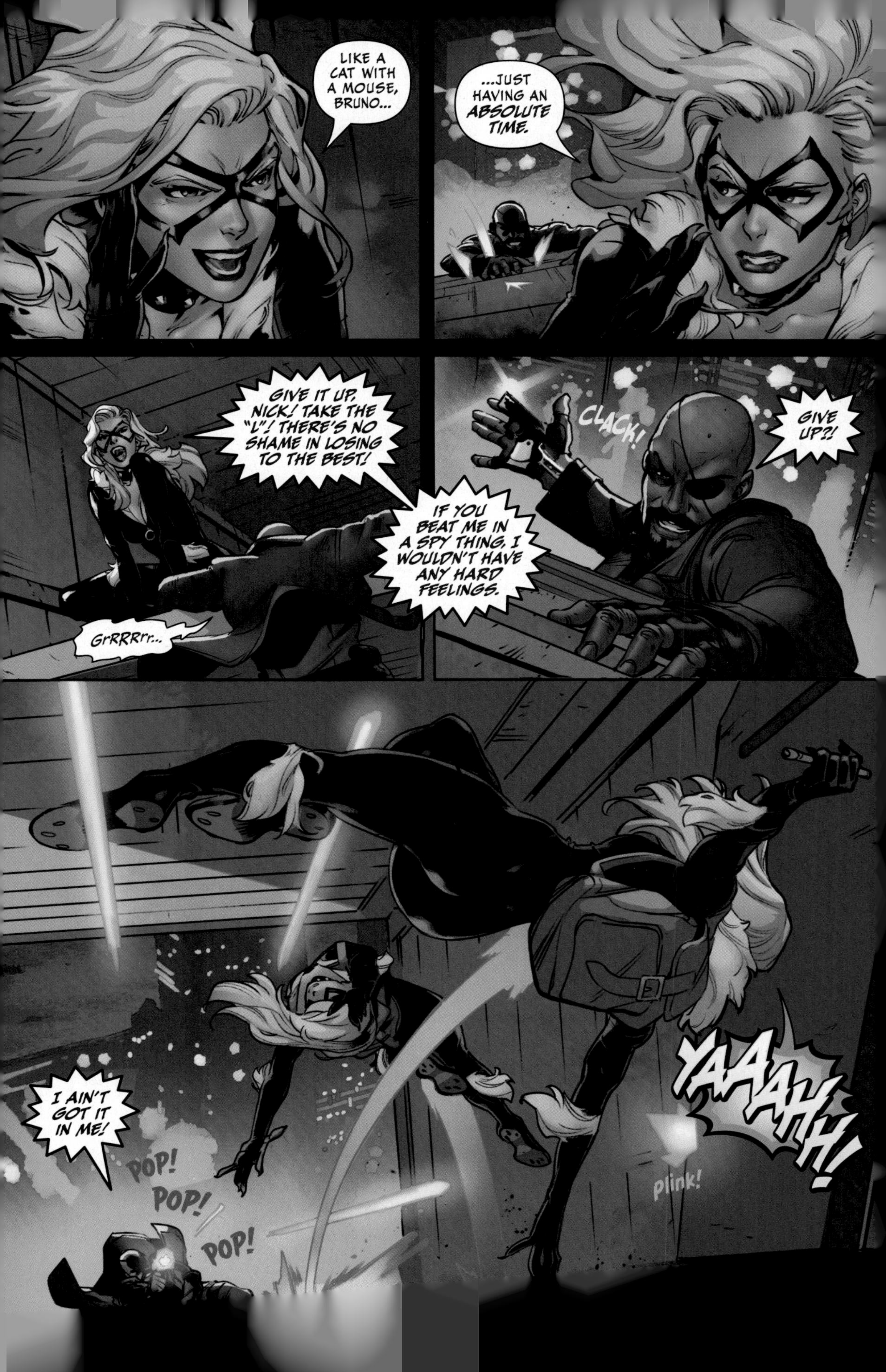
LIKE A CAT WITH A MOUSE, BRUNO...
...JUST HAVING AN ABSOLUTE TIME.
GIVE IT UP, NICK! TAKE THE "L"! THERE'S NO SHAME IN LOSING TO THE BEST!
GrRRRrr...
CLACK!
GIVE UP?!
IF YOU BEAT ME IN A SPY THING, I WOULDN'T HAVE ANY HARD FEELINGS.
I AIN'T GOT IT IN ME!
POP!
POP!
POP!
YAAAHH!
Plink!

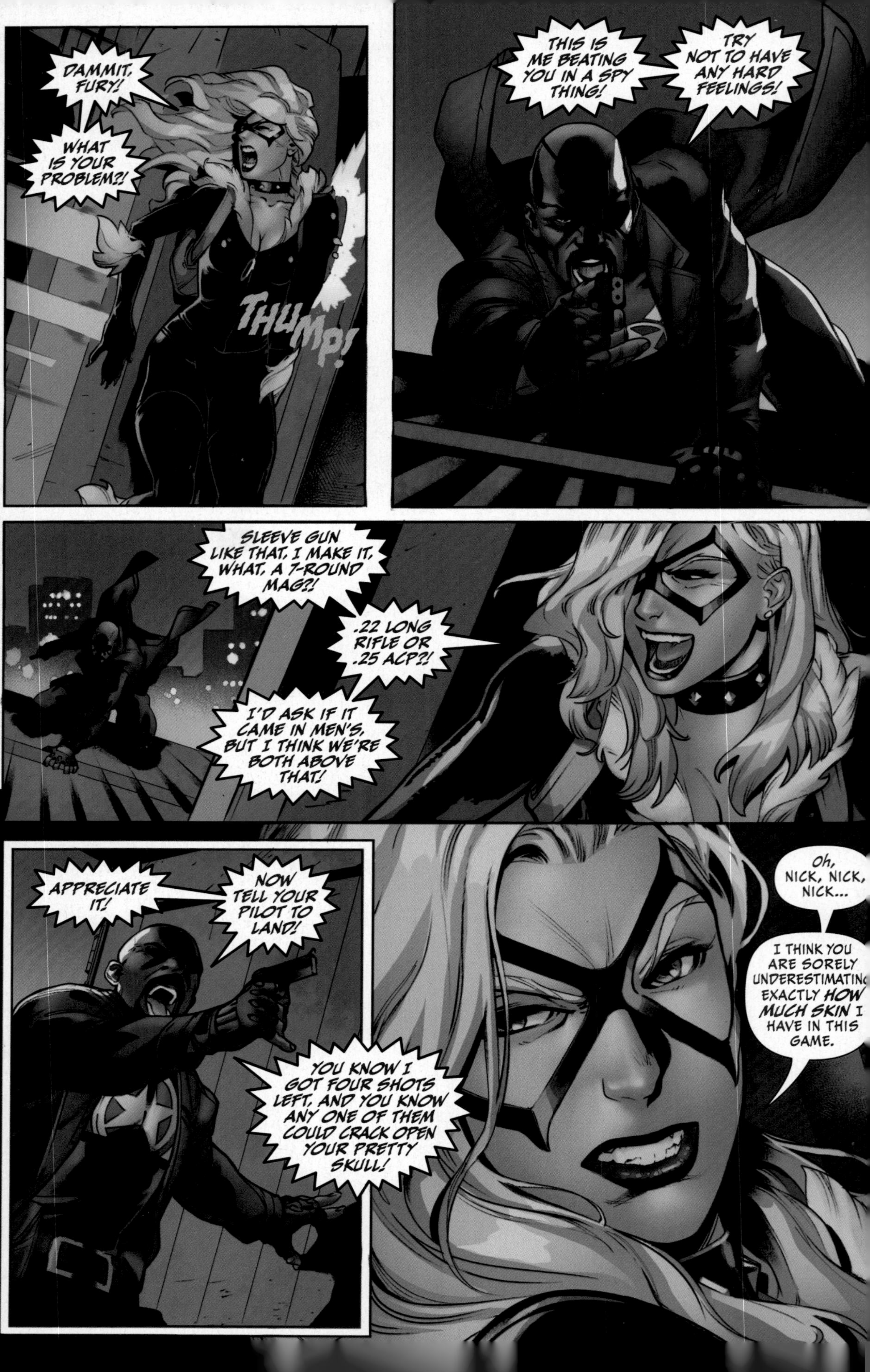
DAMMIT, FURY!
WHAT IS YOUR PROBLEM?!
THUMP!
THIS IS ME BEATING YOU IN A SPY THING!
TRY NOT TO HAVE ANY HARD FEELINGS!
SLEEVE GUN LIKE THAT, I MAKE IT, WHAT, A 7-ROUND MAG?!
.22 LONG RIFLE OR .25 ACP?!
I'D ASK IF IT CAME IN MEN'S, BUT I THINK WE'RE BOTH ABOVE THAT!
APPRECIATE IT!
NOW TELL YOUR PILOT TO LAND!
YOU KNOW I GOT FOUR SHOTS LEFT, AND YOU KNOW ANY ONE OF THEM COULD CRACK OPEN YOUR PRETTY SKULL!
Oh, NICK, NICK, NICK...
I THINK YOU ARE SORELY UNDERESTIMATING EXACTLY HOW MUCH SKIN I HAVE IN THIS GAME.

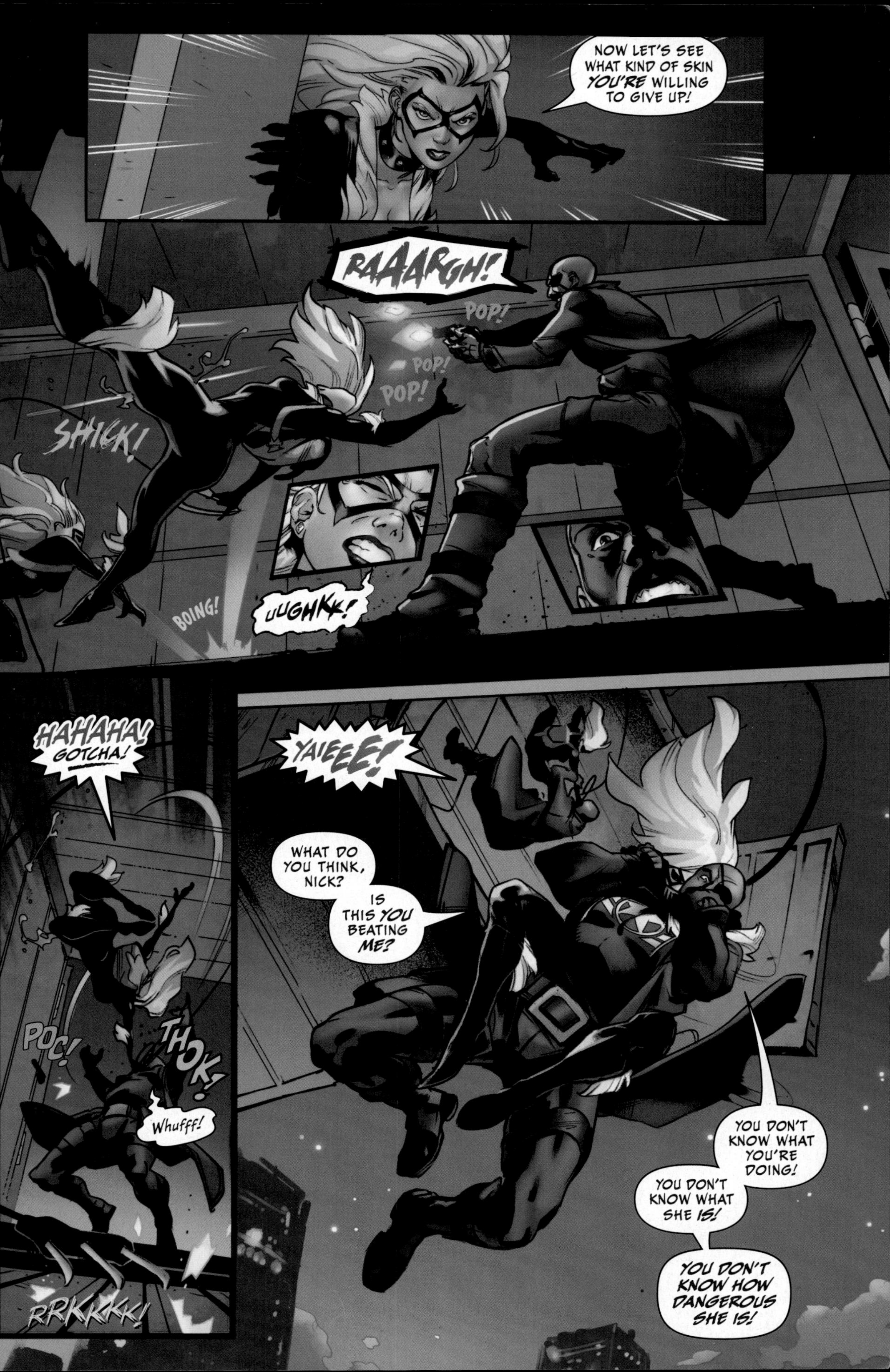
NOW LET'S SEE WHAT KIND OF SKIN YOU'RE WILLING TO GIVE UP!
RAAAARGH!
POP!
POP!
POP!
SHICK!
BOING!
UUGHKK!
HAHAHA! GOTCHA!
YAIEEE!
WHAT DO YOU THINK, NICK?
IS THIS YOU BEATING ME?
POC!
THOK!
Whufff!
RRKKKK!
YOU DON'T KNOW WHAT YOU'RE DOING!
YOU DON'T KNOW WHAT SHE IS!
YOU DON'T KNOW HOW DANGEROUS SHE IS!

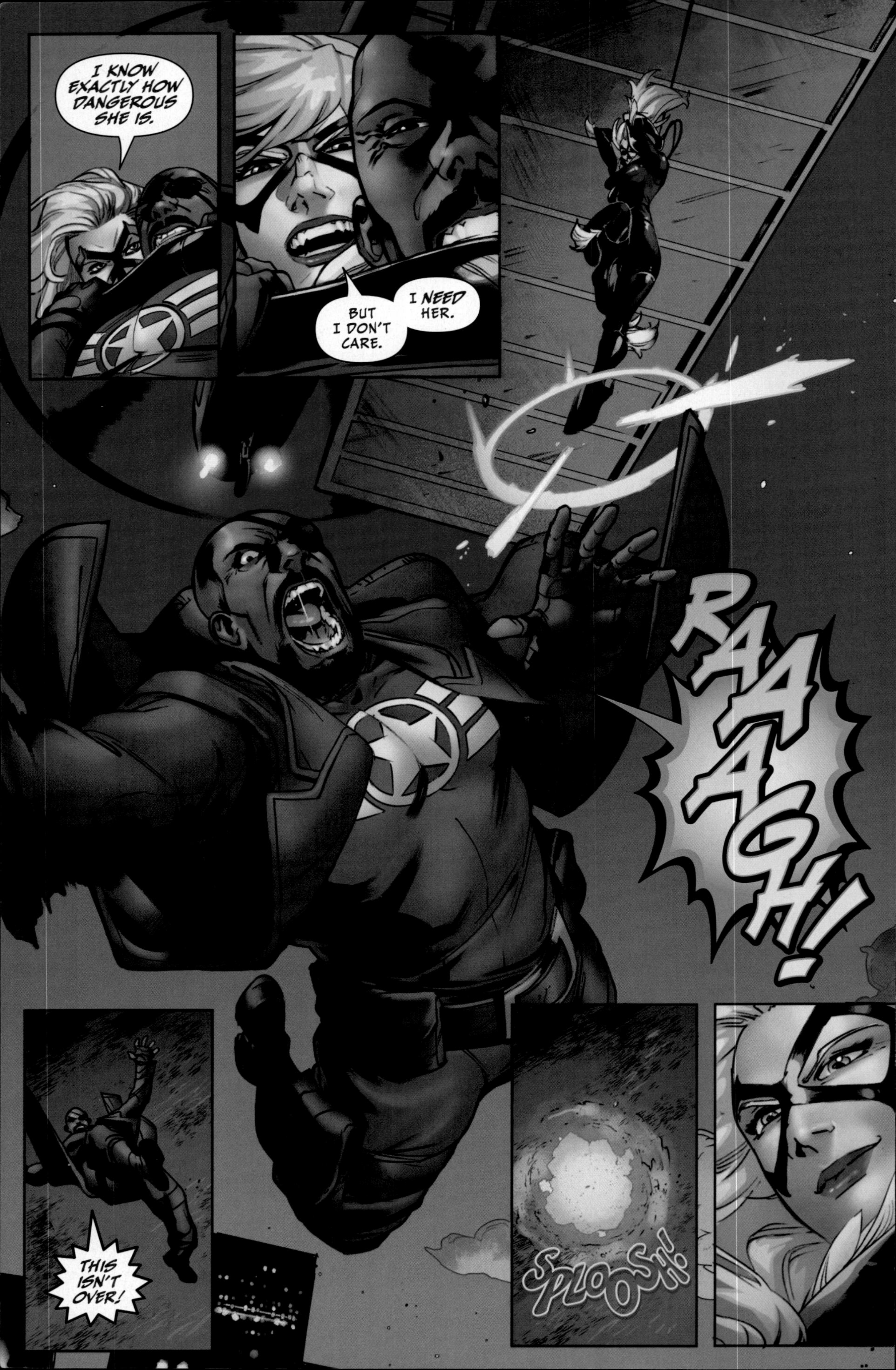
I KNOW EXACTLY HOW DANGEROUS SHE IS.
BUT I DON'T CARE.
I NEED HER.
RAAAAGH!
THIS ISN'T OVER!
SPLOOSH!

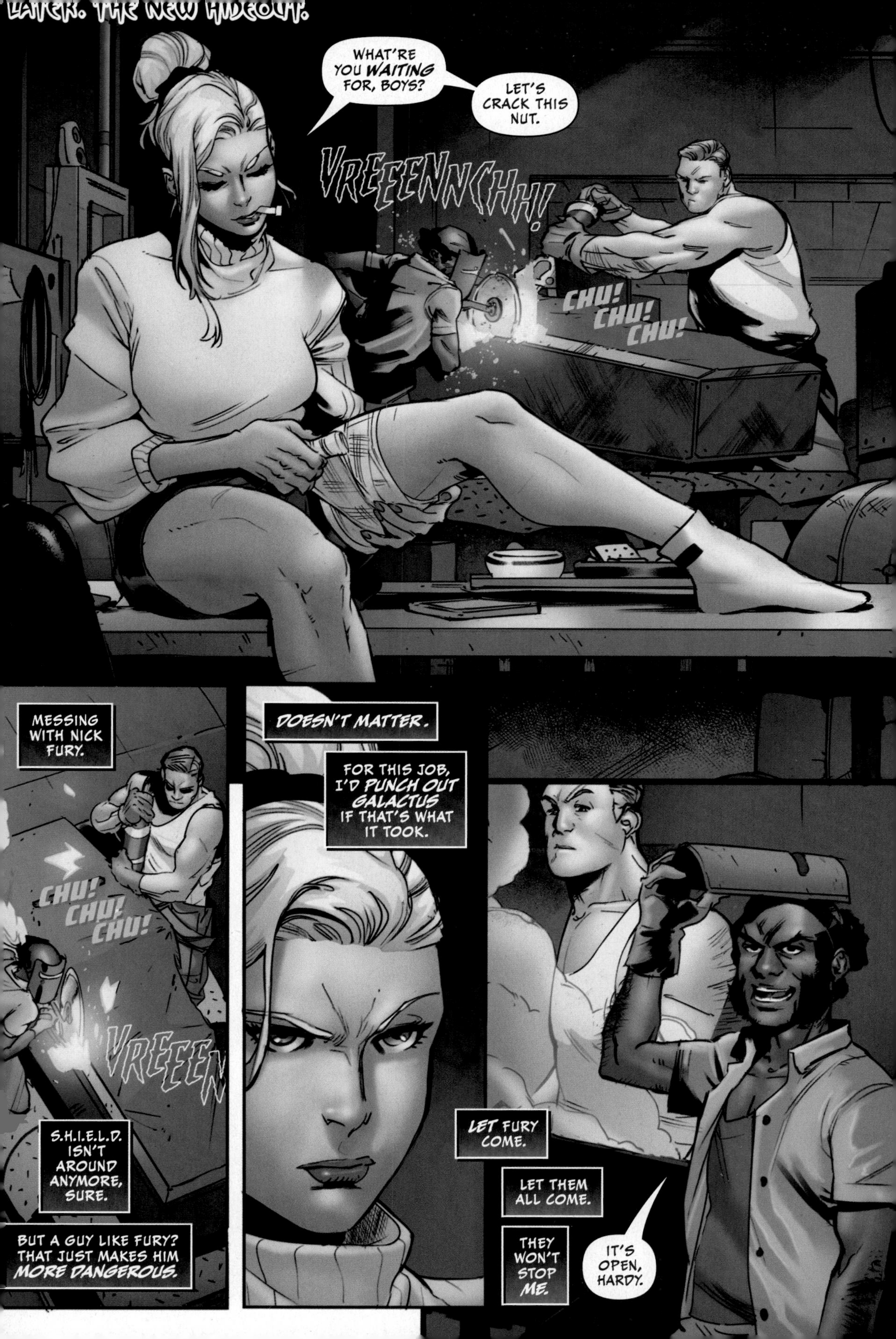
LATER. THE NEW HIDEOUT.
WHAT'RE YOU WAITING FOR, BOYS?
LET'S CRACK THIS NUT.
VREEENNCHH!
CHU! CHU! CHU!
MESSING WITH NICK FURY.
CHU! CHU! CHU!
VREEEN
S.H.I.E.L.D. ISN'T AROUND ANYMORE, SURE.
BUT A GUY LIKE FURY? THAT JUST MAKES HIM MORE DANGEROUS.
DOESN'T MATTER.
FOR THIS JOB, I'D PUNCH OUT GALACTUS IF THAT'S WHAT IT TOOK.
LET FURY COME.
LET THEM ALL COME.
THEY WON'T STOP ME.
IT'S OPEN, HARDY.

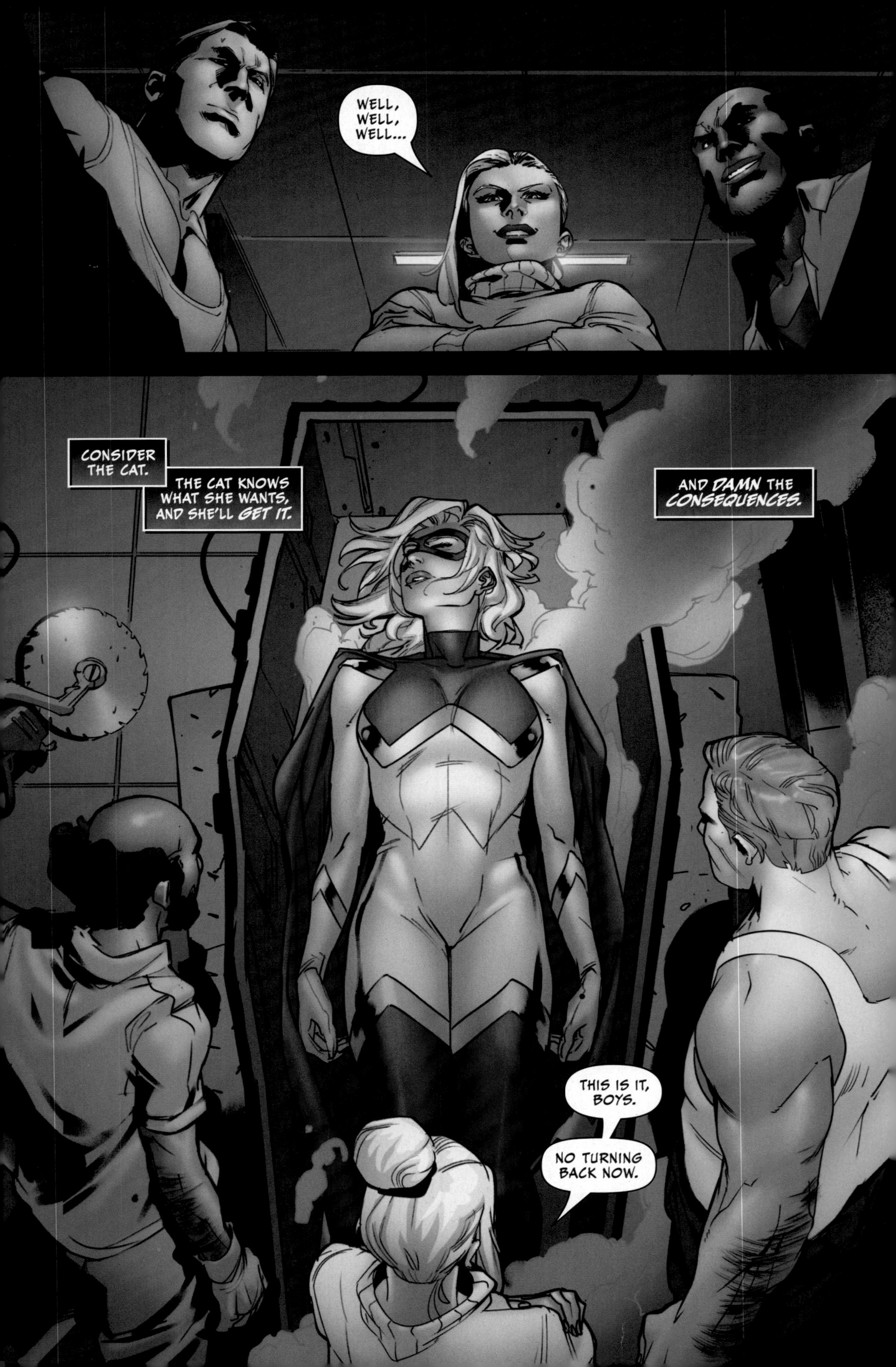
WELL, WELL, WELL...
CONSIDER THE CAT.
THE CAT KNOWS WHAT SHE WANTS, AND SHE'LL *GET IT*.
AND *DAMN* THE *CONSEQUENCES*.
THIS IS IT, BOYS.
NO TURNING BACK NOW.

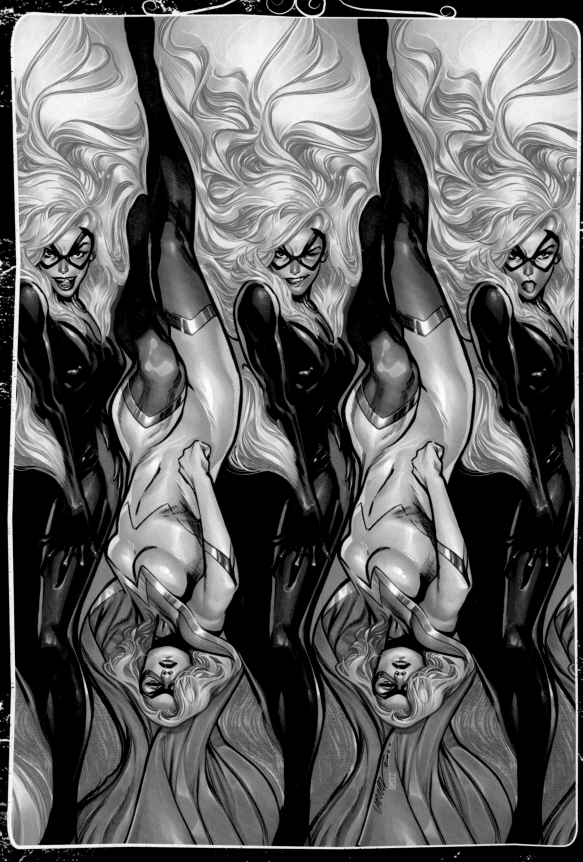

9 ◆ INFINITY SCORE PART TWO

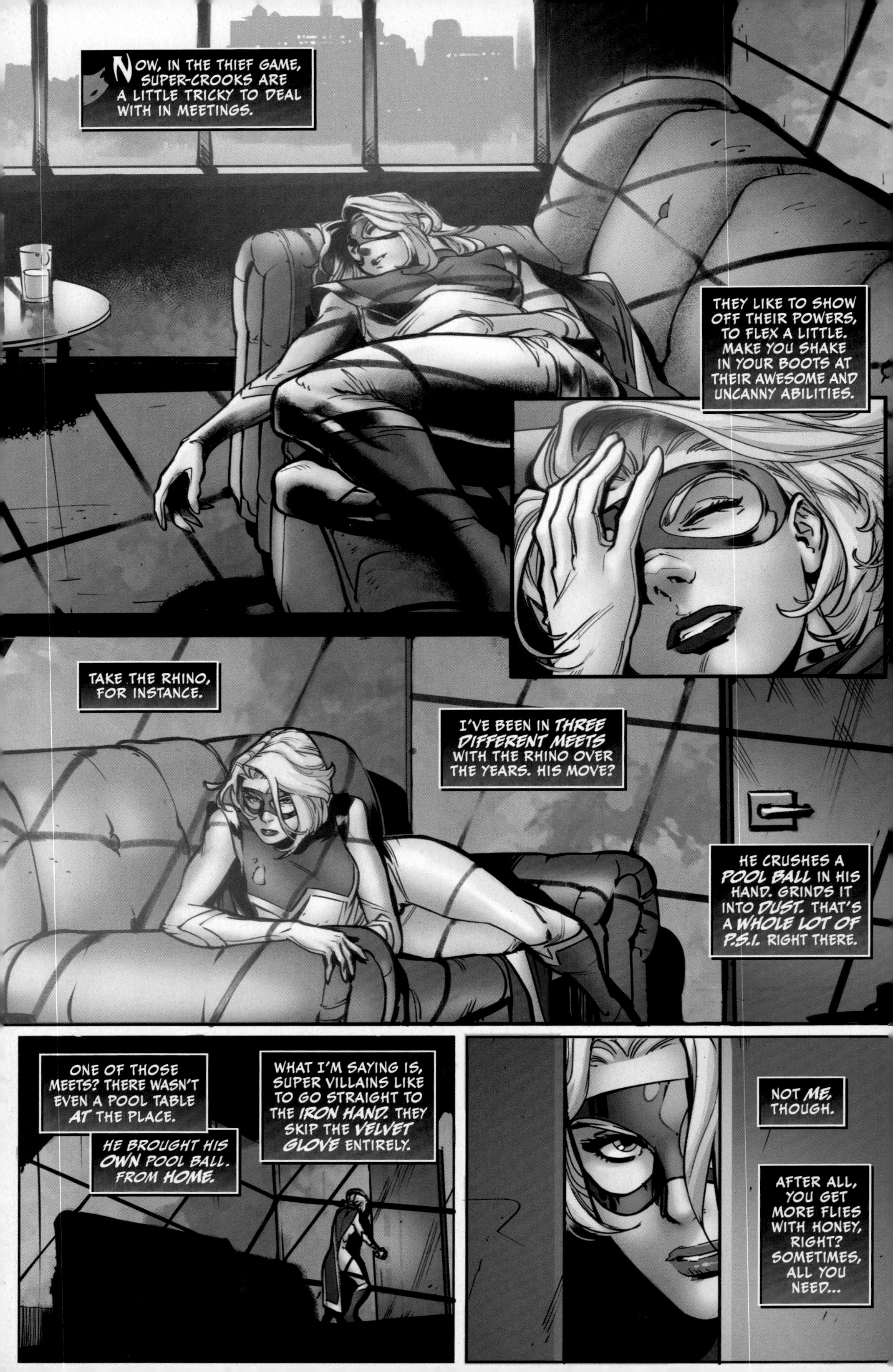

NOW, IN THE THIEF GAME, SUPER-CROOKS ARE A LITTLE TRICKY TO DEAL WITH IN MEETINGS.
THEY LIKE TO SHOW OFF THEIR POWERS, TO FLEX A LITTLE. MAKE YOU SHAKE IN YOUR BOOTS AT THEIR AWESOME AND UNCANNY ABILITIES.
TAKE THE RHINO, FOR INSTANCE.
I'VE BEEN IN THREE DIFFERENT MEETS WITH THE RHINO OVER THE YEARS. HIS MOVE?
HE CRUSHES A POOL BALL IN HIS HAND. GRINDS IT INTO DUST. THAT'S A WHOLE LOT OF P.S.I. RIGHT THERE.
ONE OF THOSE MEETS? THERE WASN'T EVEN A POOL TABLE AT THE PLACE.
HE BROUGHT HIS OWN POOL BALL. FROM HOME.
WHAT I'M SAYING IS, SUPER VILLAINS LIKE TO GO STRAIGHT TO THE IRON HAND. THEY SKIP THE VELVET GLOVE ENTIRELY.
NOT ME, THOUGH.
AFTER ALL, YOU GET MORE FLIES WITH HONEY, RIGHT? SOMETIMES, ALL YOU NEED...

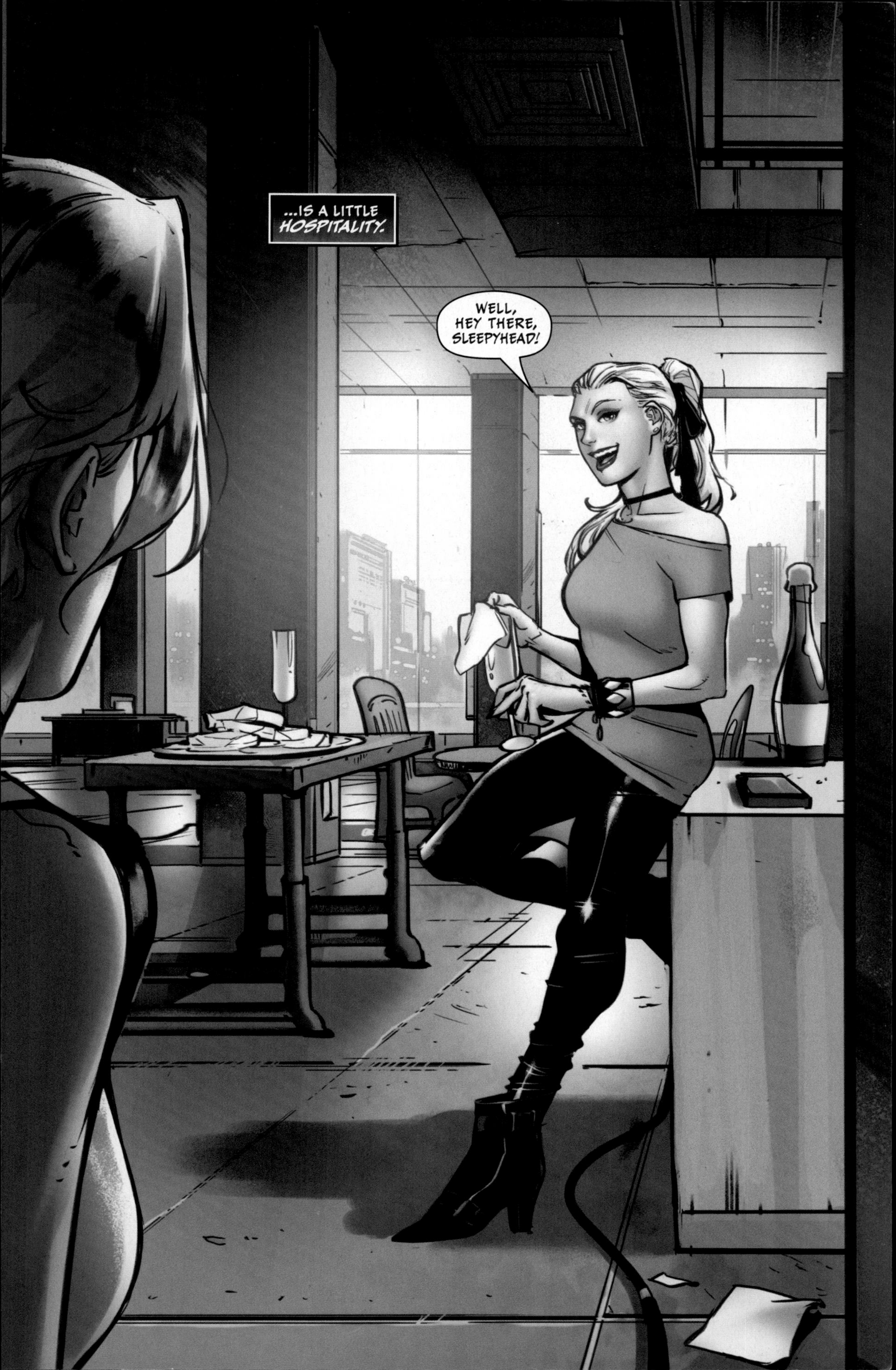
...IS A LITTLE HOSPITALITY.
WELL, HEY THERE, SLEEPYHEAD!

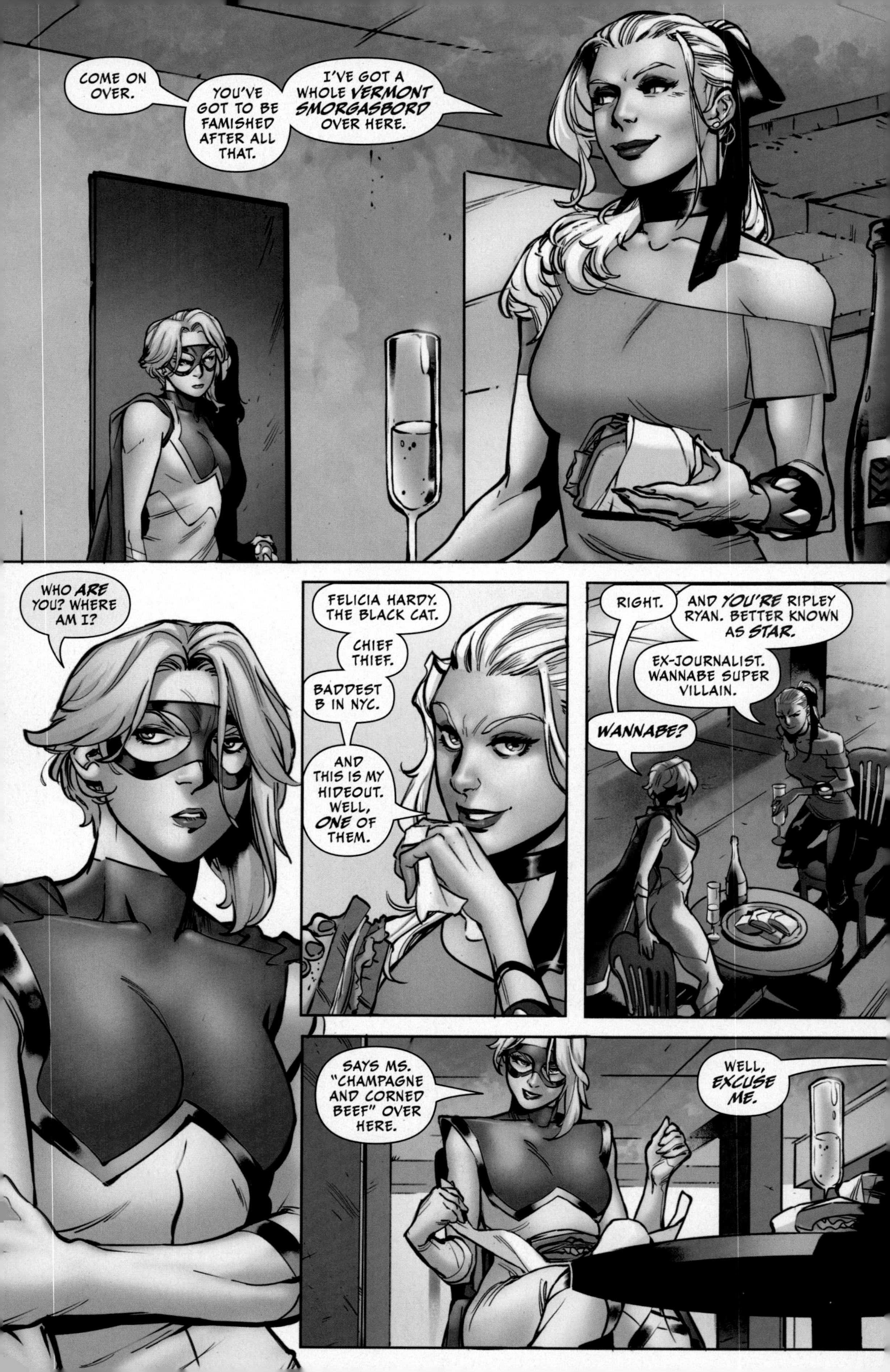
COME ON OVER.
YOU'VE GOT TO BE FAMISHED AFTER ALL THAT.
I'VE GOT A WHOLE VERMONT SMORGASBORD OVER HERE.
WHO ARE YOU? WHERE AM I?
FELICIA HARDY. THE BLACK CAT.
CHIEF THIEF.
BADDEST B IN NYC.
AND THIS IS MY HIDEOUT. WELL, ONE OF THEM.
RIGHT.
AND YOU'RE RIPLEY RYAN. BETTER KNOWN AS STAR.
EX-JOURNALIST. WANNABE SUPER VILLAIN.
WANNABE?
SAYS MS. "CHAMPAGNE AND CORNED BEEF" OVER HERE.
WELL, EXCUSE ME.

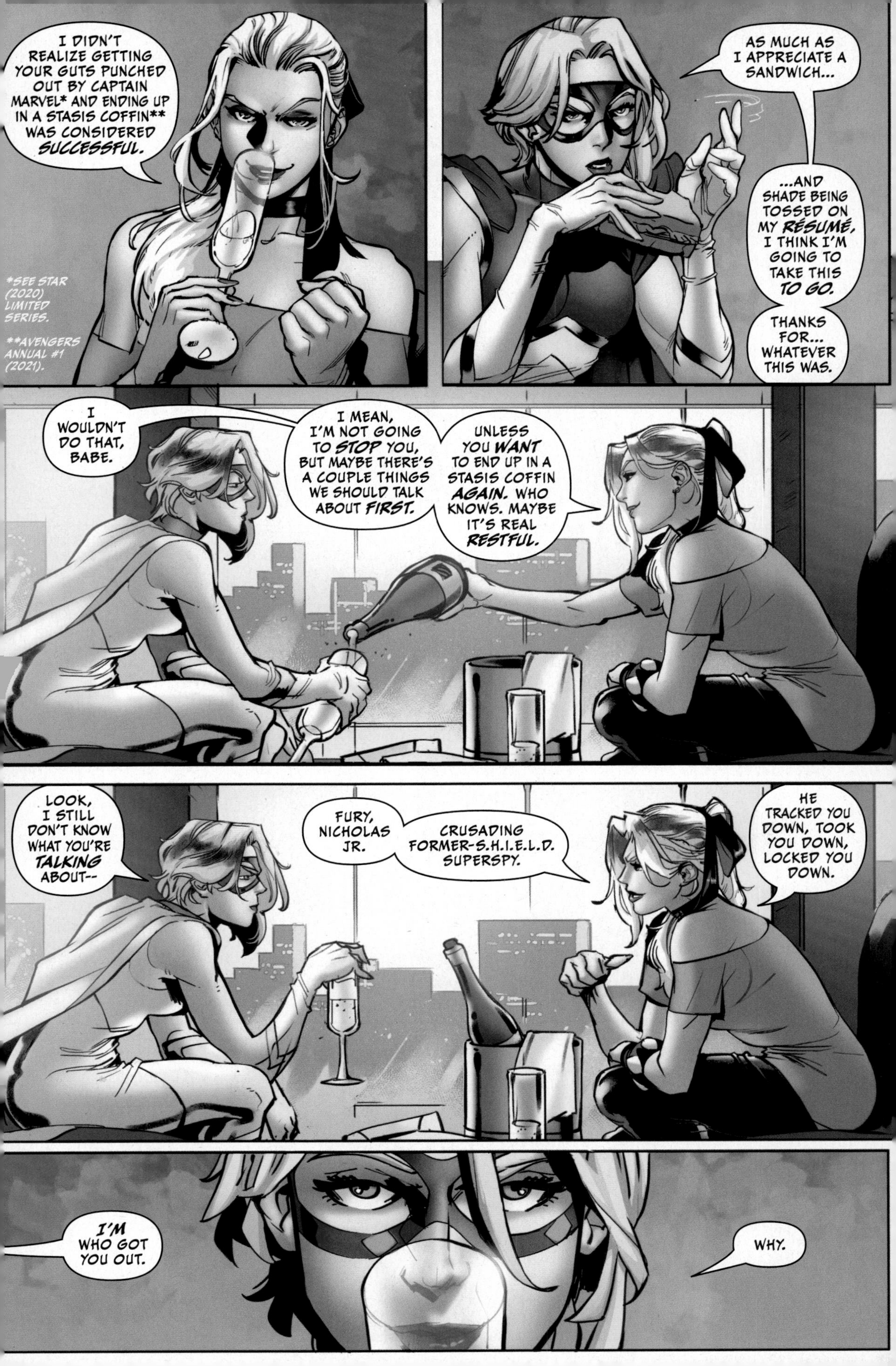
I DIDN'T REALIZE GETTING YOUR GUTS PUNCHED OUT BY CAPTAIN MARVEL* AND ENDING UP IN A STASIS COFFIN** WAS CONSIDERED SUCCESSFUL.
*SEE STAR (2020) LIMITED SERIES.
**AVENGERS ANNUAL #1 (2021).
AS MUCH AS I APPRECIATE A SANDWICH...
...AND SHADE BEING TOSSED ON MY RÉSUMÉ, I THINK I'M GOING TO TAKE THIS TO GO.
THANKS FOR... WHATEVER THIS WAS.
I WOULDN'T DO THAT, BABE.
I MEAN, I'M NOT GOING TO STOP YOU, BUT MAYBE THERE'S A COUPLE THINGS WE SHOULD TALK ABOUT FIRST.
UNLESS YOU WANT TO END UP IN A STASIS COFFIN AGAIN. WHO KNOWS. MAYBE IT'S REAL RESTFUL.
LOOK, I STILL DON'T KNOW WHAT YOU'RE TALKING ABOUT--
FURY, NICHOLAS JR.
CRUSADING FORMER-S.H.I.E.L.D. SUPERSPY.
HE TRACKED YOU DOWN, TOOK YOU DOWN, LOCKED YOU DOWN.
I'M WHO GOT YOU OUT.
WHY.

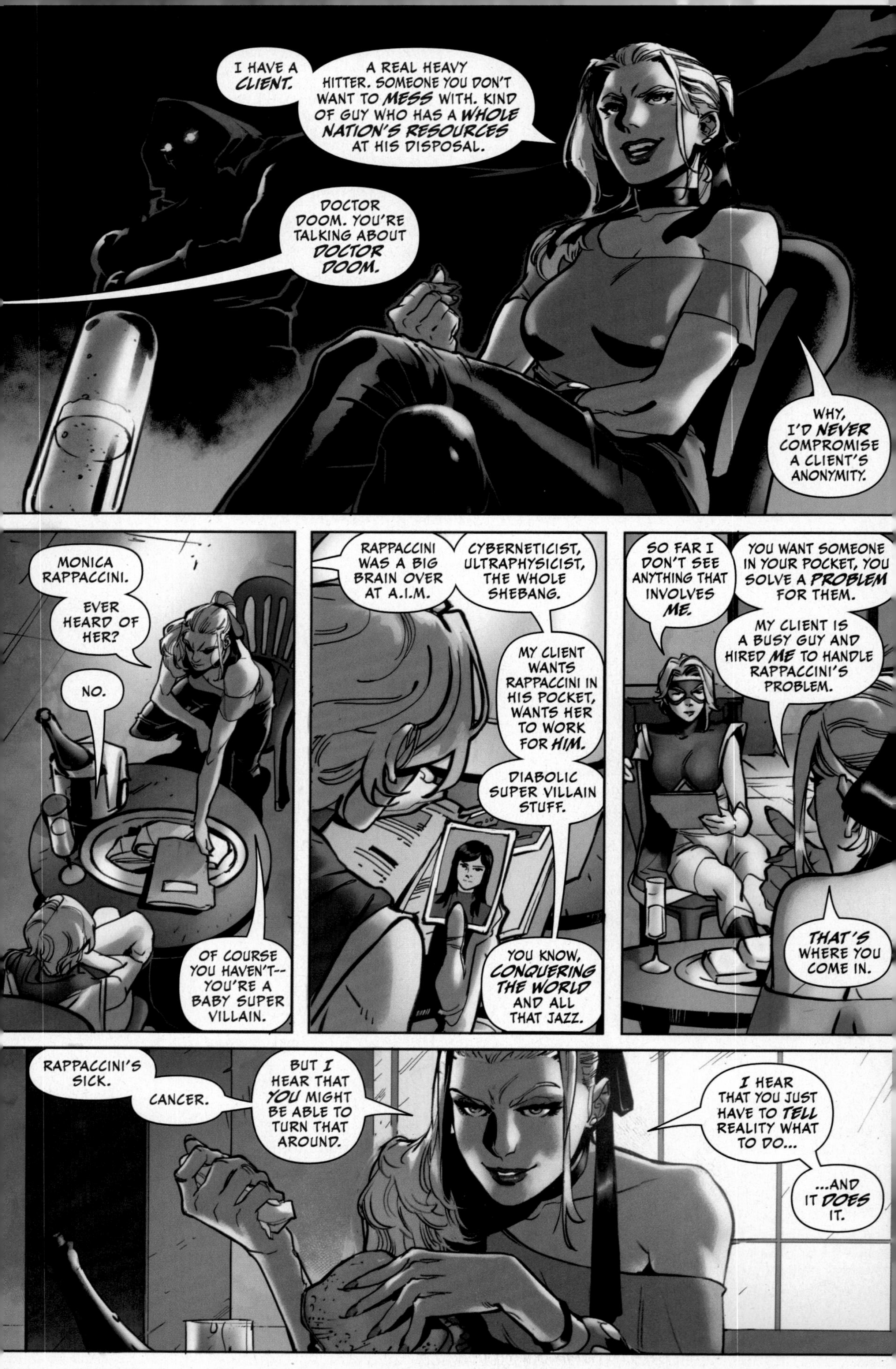
I HAVE A CLIENT.
A REAL HEAVY HITTER. SOMEONE YOU DON'T WANT TO MESS WITH. KIND OF GUY WHO HAS A WHOLE NATION'S RESOURCES AT HIS DISPOSAL.
DOCTOR DOOM. YOU'RE TALKING ABOUT DOCTOR DOOM.
WHY, I'D NEVER COMPROMISE A CLIENT'S ANONYMITY.
MONICA RAPPACCINI.
EVER HEARD OF HER?
NO.
OF COURSE YOU HAVEN'T--YOU'RE A BABY SUPER VILLAIN.
RAPPACCINI WAS A BIG BRAIN OVER AT A.I.M.
CYBERNETICIST, ULTRAPHYSICIST, THE WHOLE SHEBANG.
MY CLIENT WANTS RAPPACCINI IN HIS POCKET, WANTS HER TO WORK FOR HIM.
DIABOLIC SUPER VILLAIN STUFF.
YOU KNOW, CONQUERING THE WORLD AND ALL THAT JAZZ.
SO FAR I DON'T SEE ANYTHING THAT INVOLVES ME.
YOU WANT SOMEONE IN YOUR POCKET, YOU SOLVE A PROBLEM FOR THEM.
MY CLIENT IS A BUSY GUY AND HIRED ME TO HANDLE RAPPACCINI'S PROBLEM.
THAT'S WHERE YOU COME IN.
RAPPACCINI'S SICK.
CANCER.
BUT I HEAR THAT YOU MIGHT BE ABLE TO TURN THAT AROUND.
I HEAR THAT YOU JUST HAVE TO TELL REALITY WHAT TO DO...
...AND IT DOES IT.

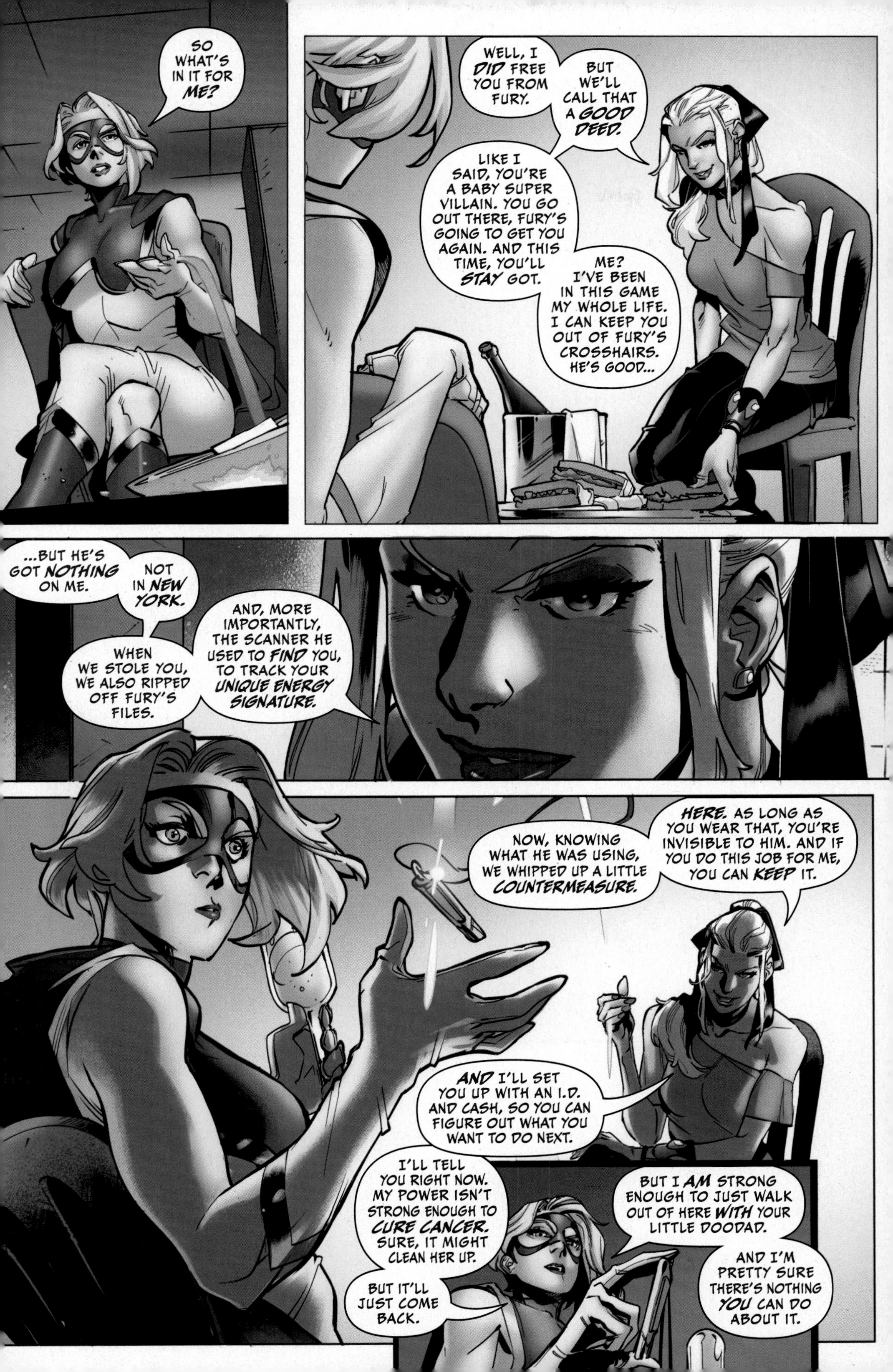
SO WHAT'S IN IT FOR ME?
WELL, I DID FREE YOU FROM FURY.
BUT WE'LL CALL THAT A GOOD DEED.
LIKE I SAID, YOU'RE A BABY SUPER VILLAIN. YOU GO OUT THERE, FURY'S GOING TO GET YOU AGAIN. AND THIS TIME, YOU'LL STAY GOT.
ME? I'VE BEEN IN THIS GAME MY WHOLE LIFE. I CAN KEEP YOU OUT OF FURY'S CROSSHAIRS. HE'S GOOD...
...BUT HE'S GOT NOTHING ON ME.
NOT IN NEW YORK.
WHEN WE STOLE YOU, WE ALSO RIPPED OFF FURY'S FILES.
AND, MORE IMPORTANTLY, THE SCANNER HE USED TO FIND YOU, TO TRACK YOUR UNIQUE ENERGY SIGNATURE.
NOW, KNOWING WHAT HE WAS USING, WE WHIPPED UP A LITTLE COUNTERMEASURE.
HERE. AS LONG AS YOU WEAR THAT, YOU'RE INVISIBLE TO HIM. AND IF YOU DO THIS JOB FOR ME, YOU CAN KEEP IT.
AND I'LL SET YOU UP WITH AN I.D. AND CASH, SO YOU CAN FIGURE OUT WHAT YOU WANT TO DO NEXT.
I'LL TELL YOU RIGHT NOW. MY POWER ISN'T STRONG ENOUGH TO CURE CANCER. SURE, IT MIGHT CLEAN HER UP.
BUT IT'LL JUST COME BACK.
BUT I AM STRONG ENOUGH TO JUST WALK OUT OF HERE WITH YOUR LITTLE DOODAD.
AND I'M PRETTY SURE THERE'S NOTHING YOU CAN DO ABOUT IT.

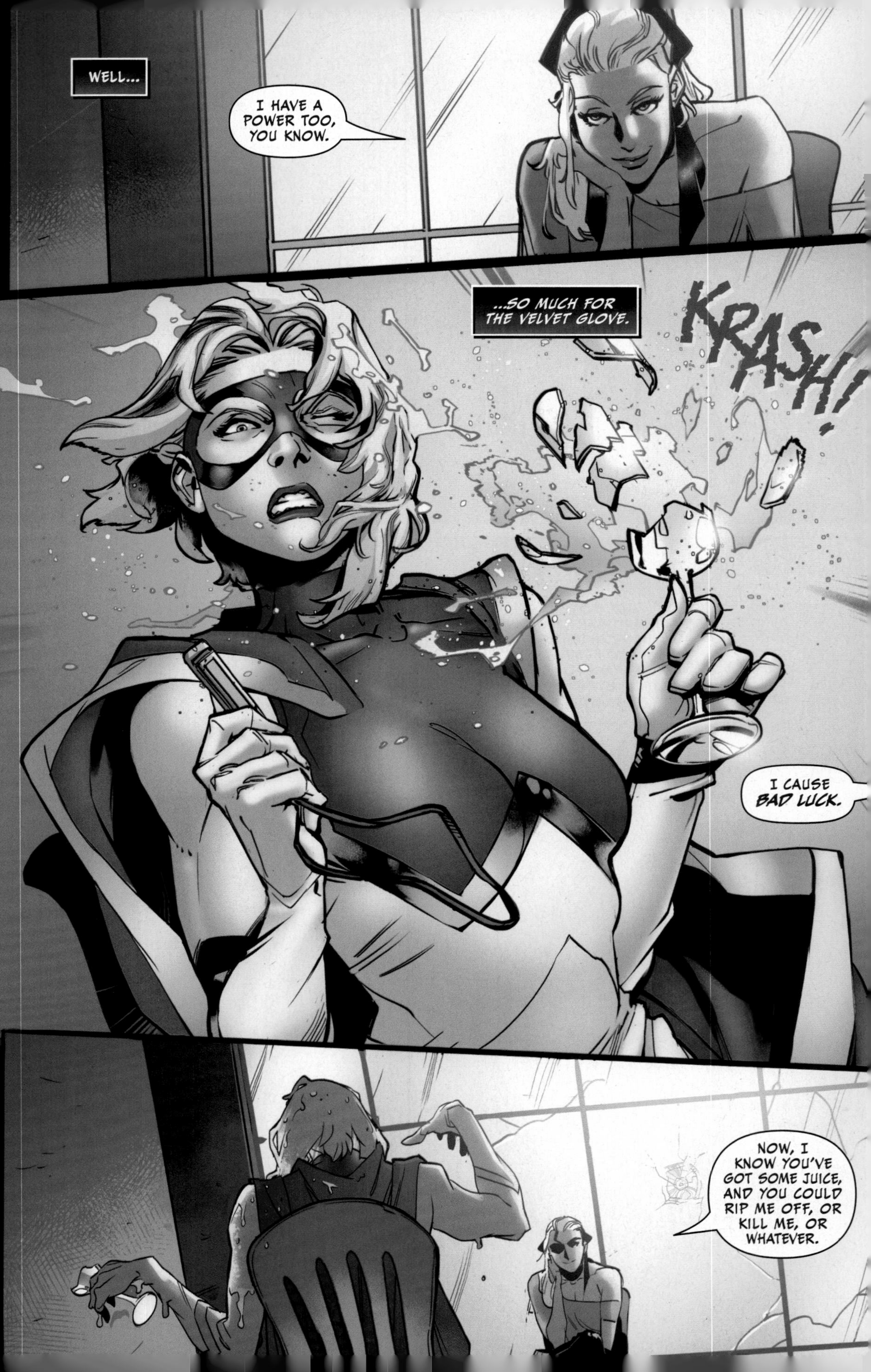
WELL...
I HAVE A POWER TOO, YOU KNOW.
...SO MUCH FOR THE VELVET GLOVE.
KRASH!
I CAUSE BAD LUCK.
NOW, I KNOW YOU'VE GOT SOME JUICE, AND YOU COULD RIP ME OFF, OR KILL ME, OR WHATEVER.

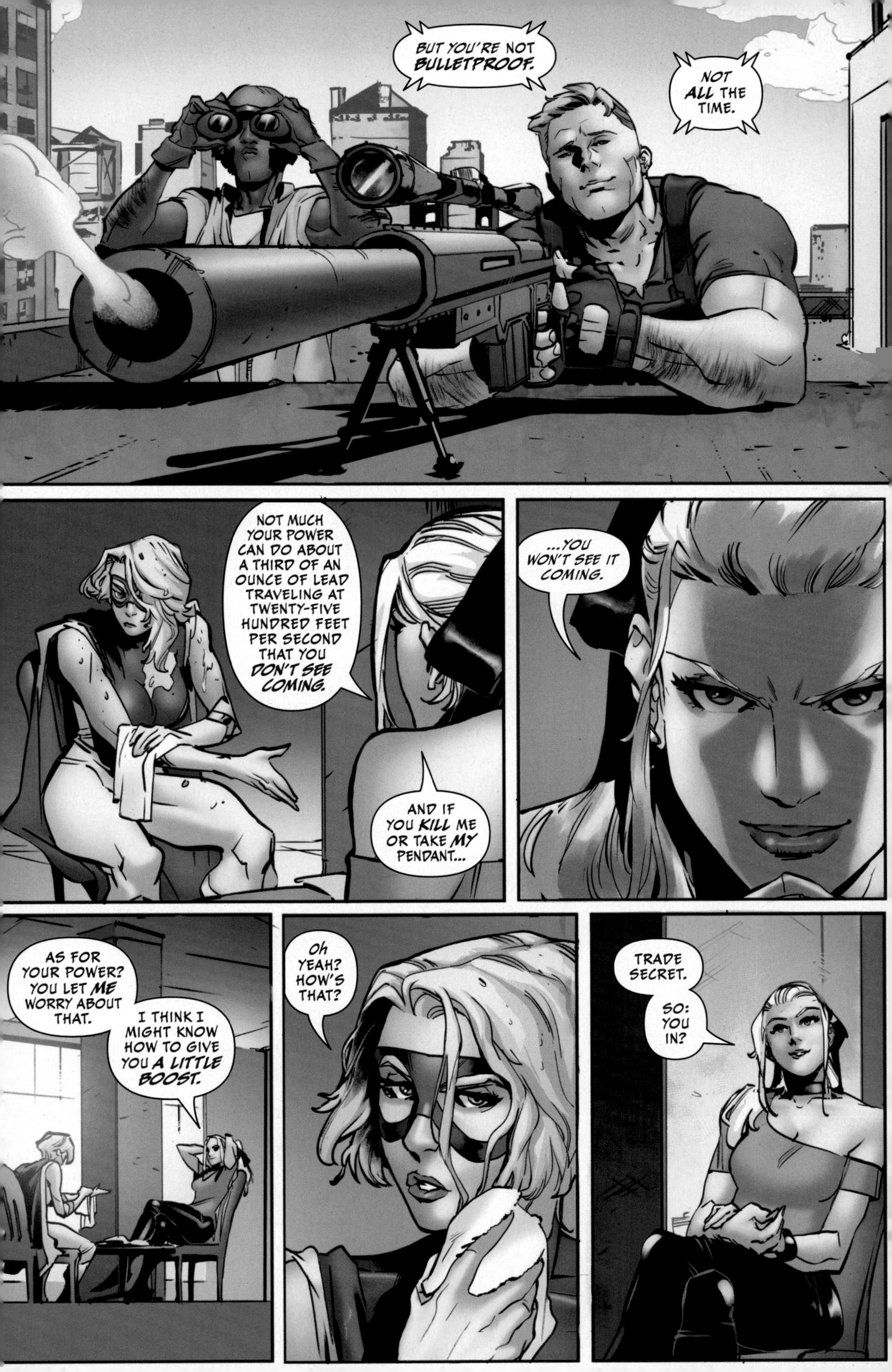
BUT YOU'RE NOT BULLETPROOF.
NOT ALL THE TIME.
NOT MUCH YOUR POWER CAN DO ABOUT A THIRD OF AN OUNCE OF LEAD TRAVELING AT TWENTY-FIVE HUNDRED FEET PER SECOND THAT YOU DON'T SEE COMING.
AND IF YOU KILL ME OR TAKE MY PENDANT...
...YOU WON'T SEE IT COMING.
AS FOR YOUR POWER? YOU LET ME WORRY ABOUT THAT.
I THINK I MIGHT KNOW HOW TO GIVE YOU A LITTLE BOOST.
Oh YEAH? HOW'S THAT?
TRADE SECRET.
SO: YOU IN?

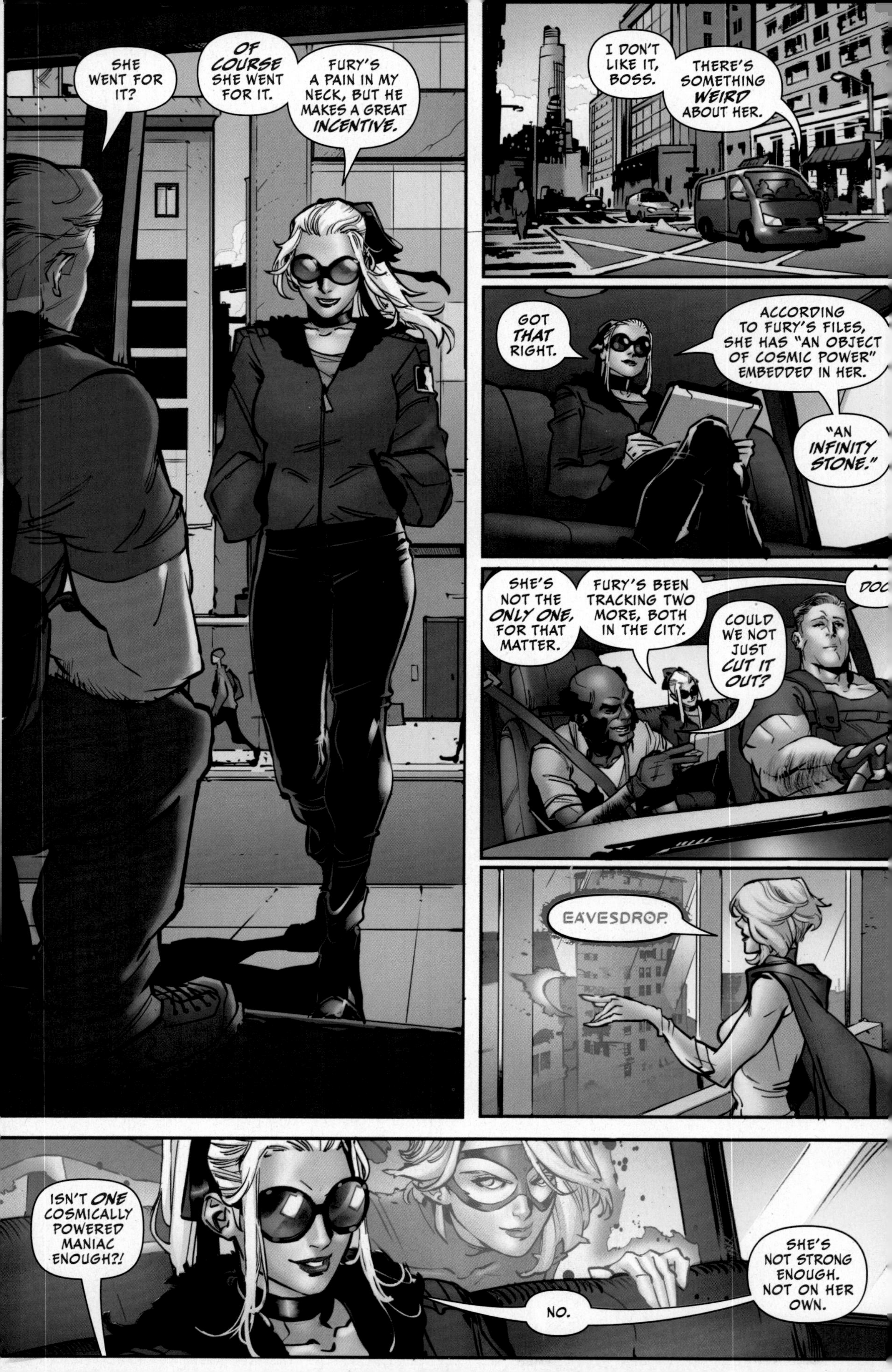

SHE WENT FOR IT?
OF COURSE SHE WENT FOR IT.
FURY'S A PAIN IN MY NECK, BUT HE MAKES A GREAT INCENTIVE.
I DON'T LIKE IT, BOSS.
THERE'S SOMETHING WEIRD ABOUT HER.
GOT THAT RIGHT.
ACCORDING TO FURY'S FILES, SHE HAS "AN OBJECT OF COSMIC POWER" EMBEDDED IN HER.
"AN INFINITY STONE."
SHE'S NOT THE ONLY ONE, FOR THAT MATTER.
FURY'S BEEN TRACKING TWO MORE, BOTH IN THE CITY.
DOC
COULD WE NOT JUST CUT IT OUT?
EAVESDROP.
ISN'T ONE COSMICALLY POWERED MANIAC ENOUGH?!
NO.
SHE'S NOT STRONG ENOUGH. NOT ON HER OWN.

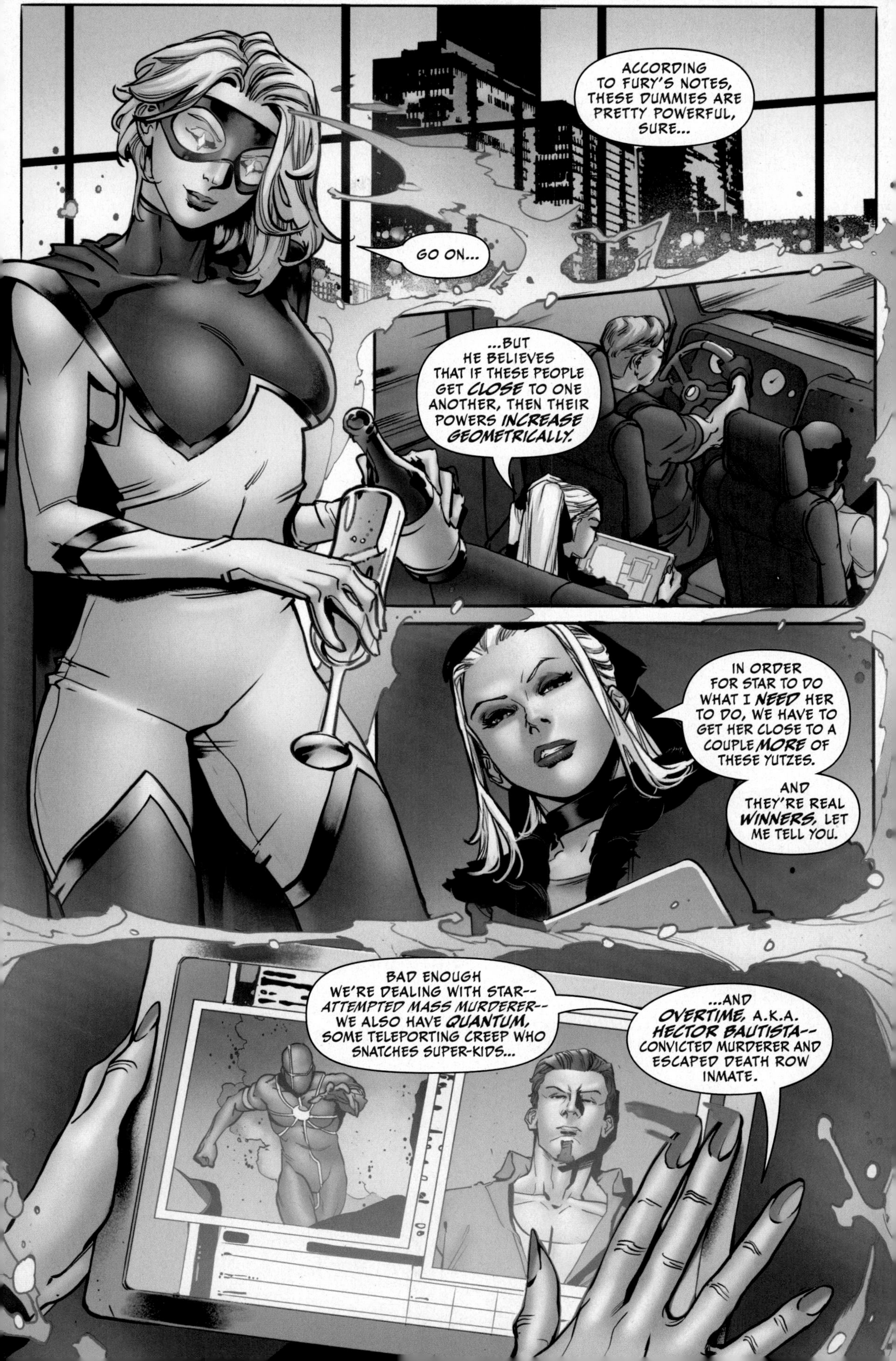
ACCORDING TO FURY'S NOTES, THESE DUMMIES ARE PRETTY POWERFUL, SURE...
GO ON...
...BUT HE BELIEVES THAT IF THESE PEOPLE GET CLOSE TO ONE ANOTHER, THEN THEIR POWERS INCREASE GEOMETRICALLY.
IN ORDER FOR STAR TO DO WHAT I NEED HER TO DO, WE HAVE TO GET HER CLOSE TO A COUPLE MORE OF THESE YUTZES.
AND THEY'RE REAL WINNERS, LET ME TELL YOU.
BAD ENOUGH WE'RE DEALING WITH STAR--ATTEMPTED MASS MURDERER--WE ALSO HAVE QUANTUM, SOME TELEPORTING CREEP WHO SNATCHES SUPER-KIDS...
...AND OVERTIME, A.K.A. HECTOR BAUTISTA--CONVICTED MURDERER AND ESCAPED DEATH ROW INMATE.

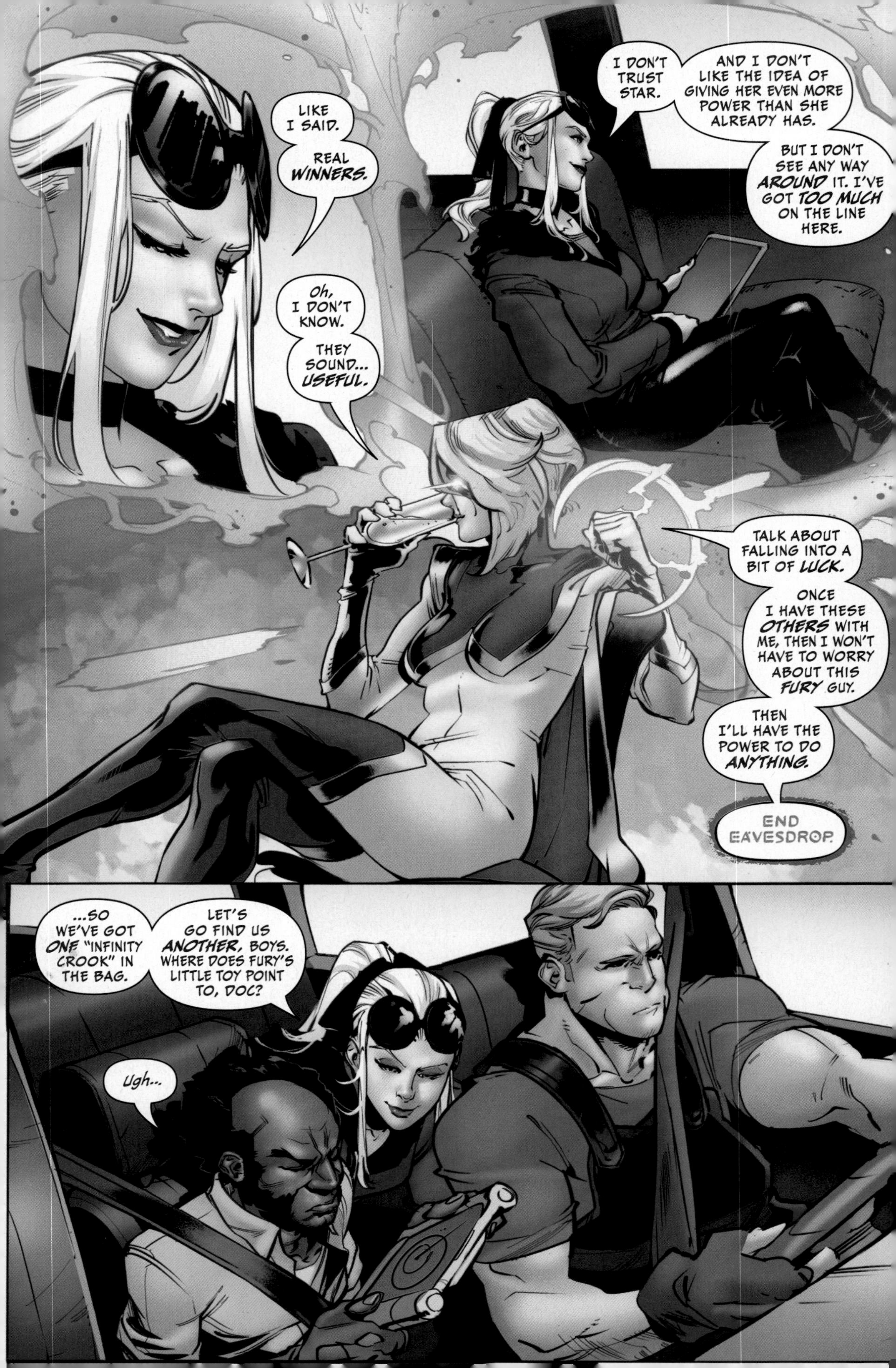
LIKE I SAID.
REAL WINNERS.
I DON'T TRUST STAR.
AND I DON'T LIKE THE IDEA OF GIVING HER EVEN MORE POWER THAN SHE ALREADY HAS.
BUT I DON'T SEE ANY WAY AROUND IT. I'VE GOT TOO MUCH ON THE LINE HERE.
Oh, I DON'T KNOW.
THEY SOUND... USEFUL.
TALK ABOUT FALLING INTO A BIT OF LUCK.
ONCE I HAVE THESE OTHERS WITH ME, THEN I WON'T HAVE TO WORRY ABOUT THIS FURY GUY.
THEN I'LL HAVE THE POWER TO DO ANYTHING.
END EAVESDROP.
...SO WE'VE GOT ONE "INFINITY CROOK" IN THE BAG.
LET'S GO FIND US ANOTHER, BOYS. WHERE DOES FURY'S LITTLE TOY POINT TO, DOC?
Ugh...

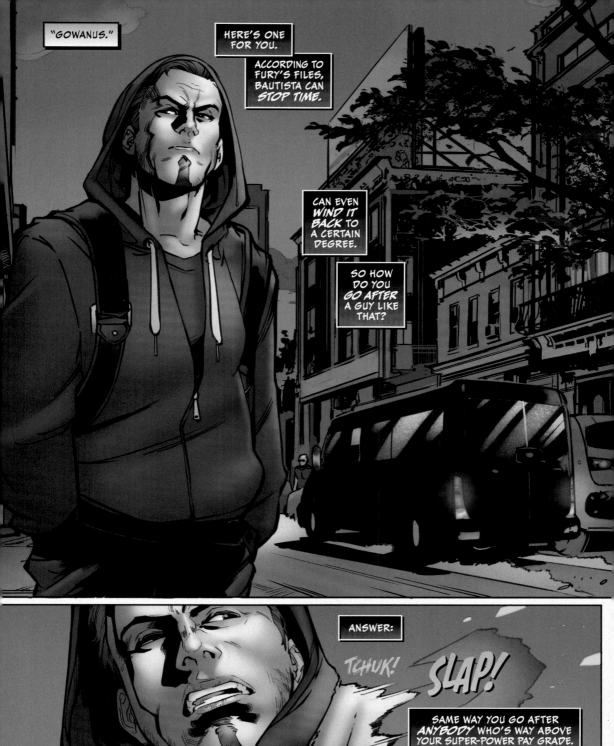

"GOWANUS."

HERE'S ONE FOR YOU.

ACCORDING TO FURY'S FILES, BAUTISTA CAN *STOP TIME.*

CAN EVEN *WIND IT BACK* TO A CERTAIN DEGREE.

SO HOW DO YOU *GO AFTER* A GUY LIKE THAT?

ANSWER:

TCHUK!

SLAP!

SAME WAY YOU GO AFTER *ANYBODY* WHO'S WAY ABOVE YOUR SUPER-POWER PAY GRADE.

WHEN THEY'RE NOT EXPECTING IT.

--WHAT THE--

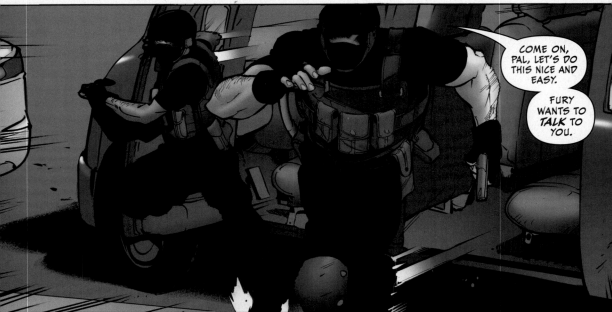

COME ON, PAL, LET'S DO THIS NICE AND EASY.

FURY WANTS TO *TALK* TO YOU.

NO--

S-S-STOP-P-P

SORRY, KID.

THAT DART HAD ENOUGH JUICE IN IT TO SCRAMBLE AN *ELEPHANT*. YOU AIN'T DOING *NOTHING* WITH THOSE POWERS.

WH-P!!

LET--

--ME--

--GO!

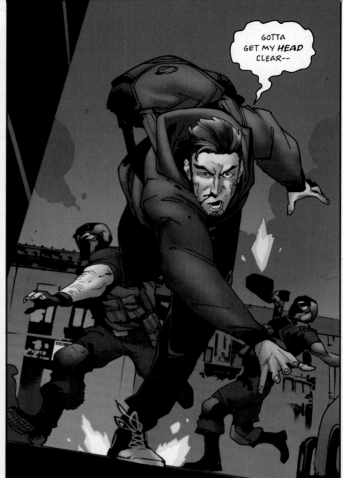

GOTTA GET MY *HEAD* CLEAR--

JUST NEED A LITTLE--

--MORE--

--TIME!

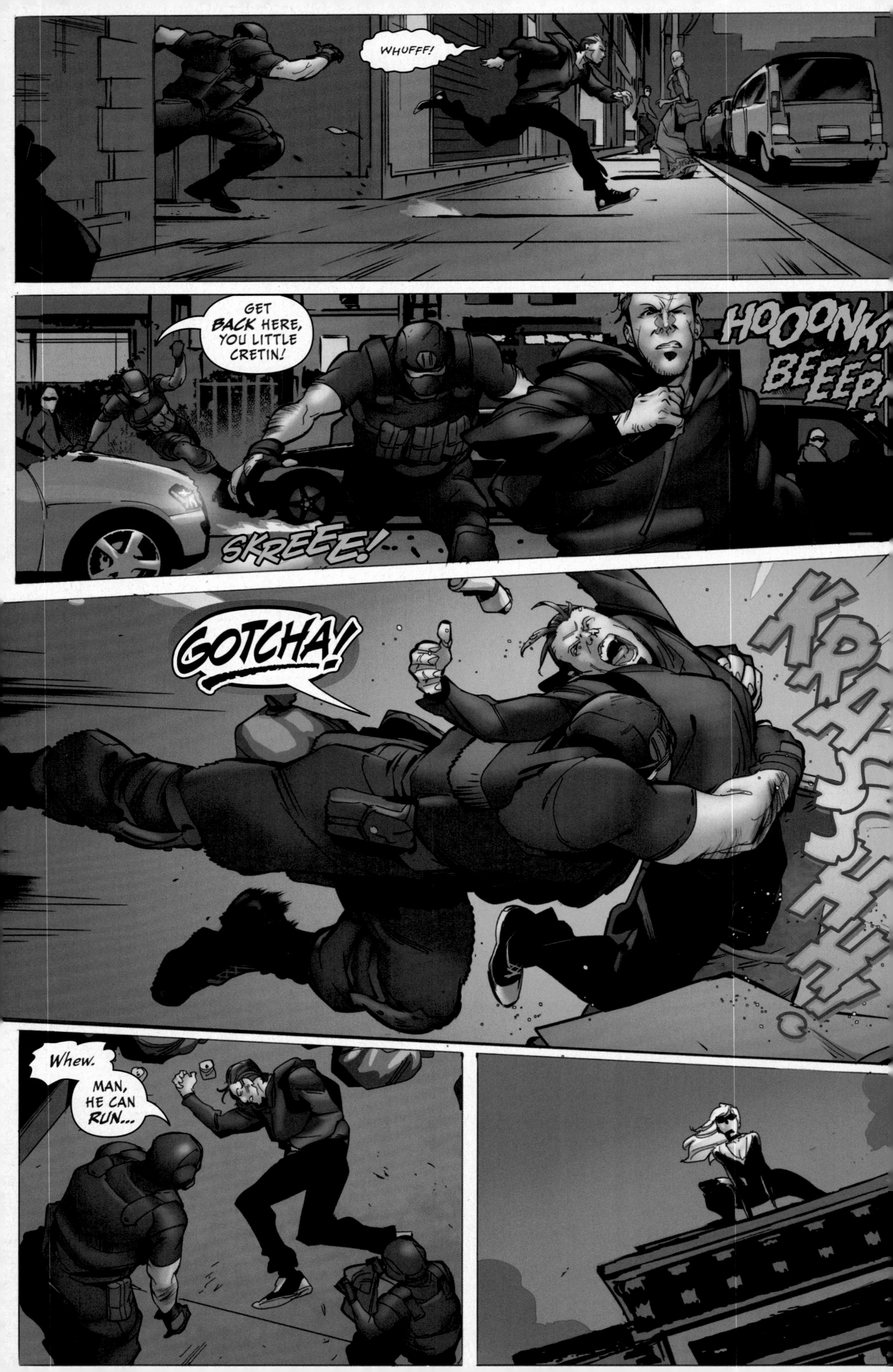
WHUFFF!
GET BACK HERE, YOU LITTLE CRETIN!
HOOONK! BEEEP!
SKREEEE!
GOTCHA!
KRASSHHH!
Whew.
MAN, HE CAN RUN...

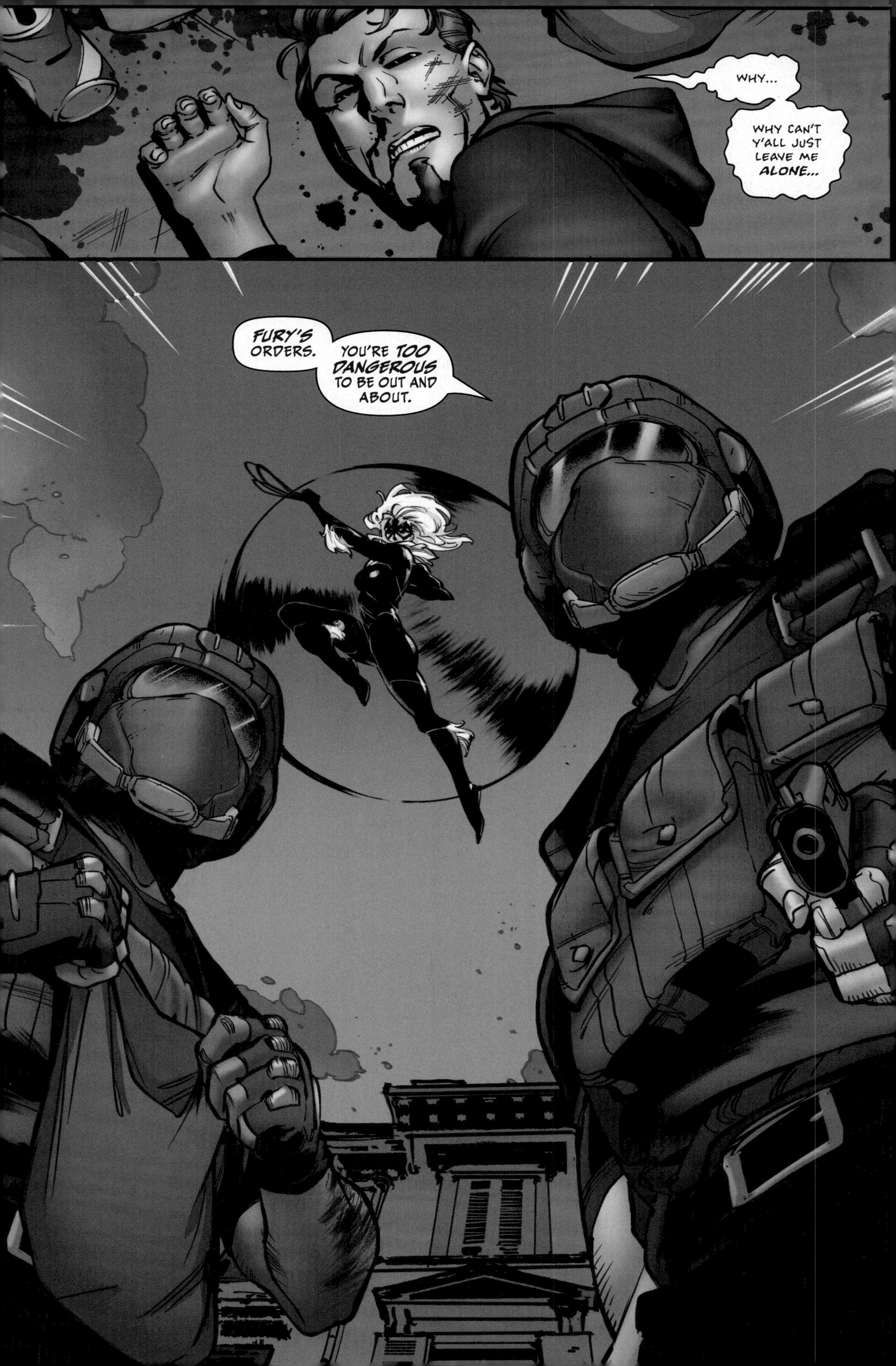
WHY...
WHY CAN'T Y'ALL JUST LEAVE ME ALONE...
FURY'S ORDERS.
YOU'RE TOO DANGEROUS TO BE OUT AND ABOUT.

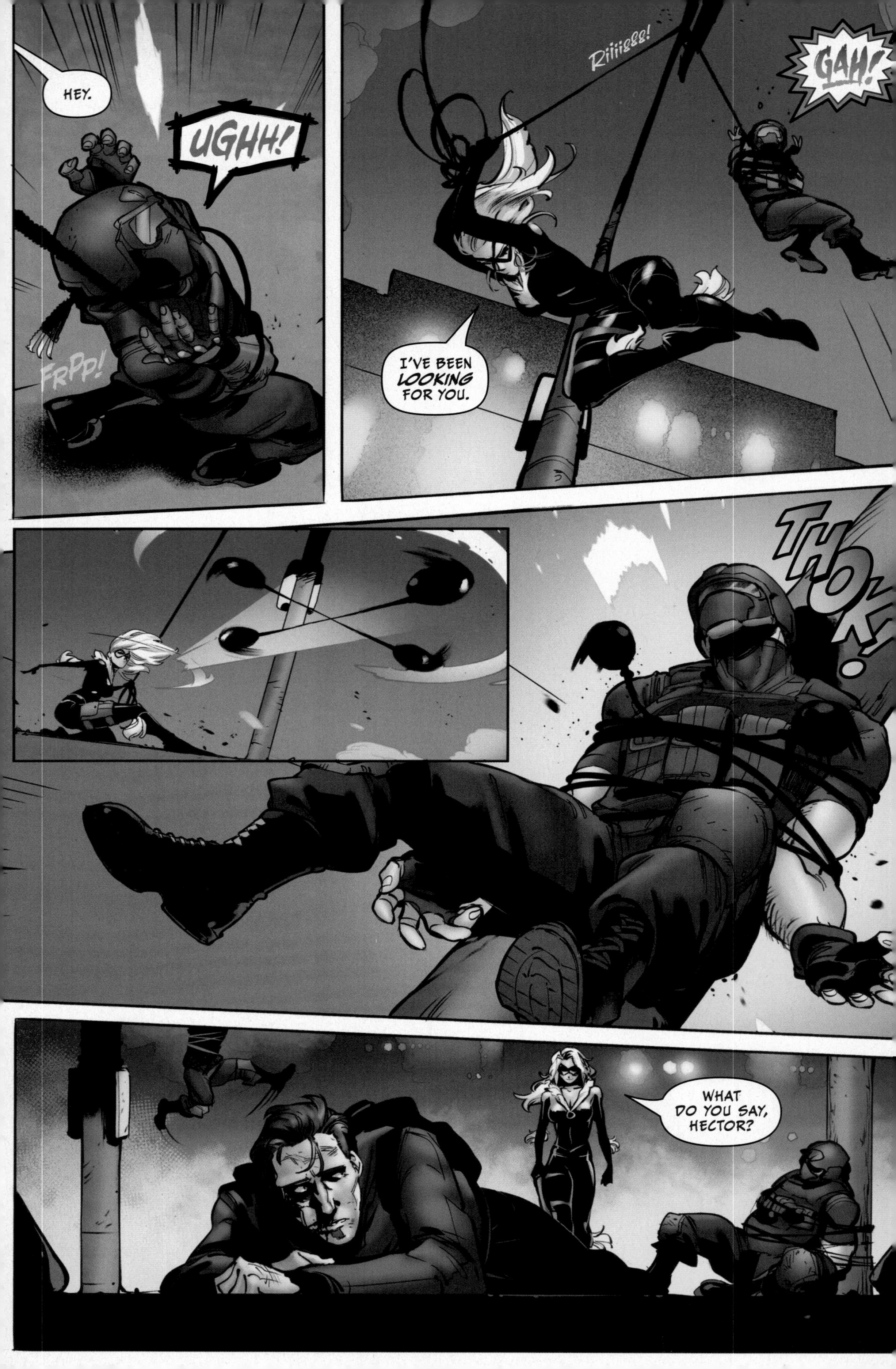
HEY.
UGHH!
FRPP!
Riiiiggg!
GAH!
I'VE BEEN LOOKING FOR YOU.
THOK!
WHAT DO YOU SAY, HECTOR?

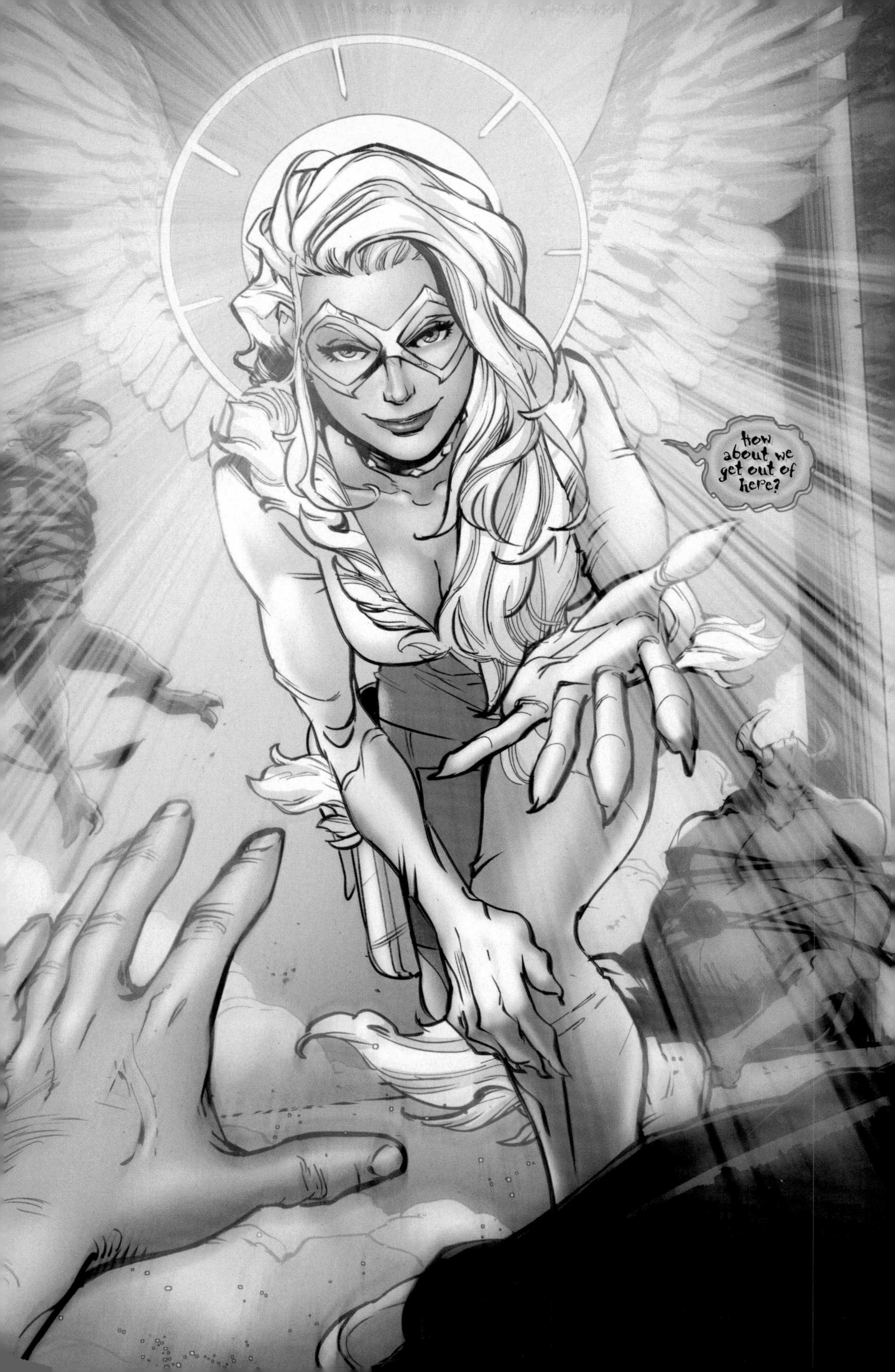
How about we get out of here?

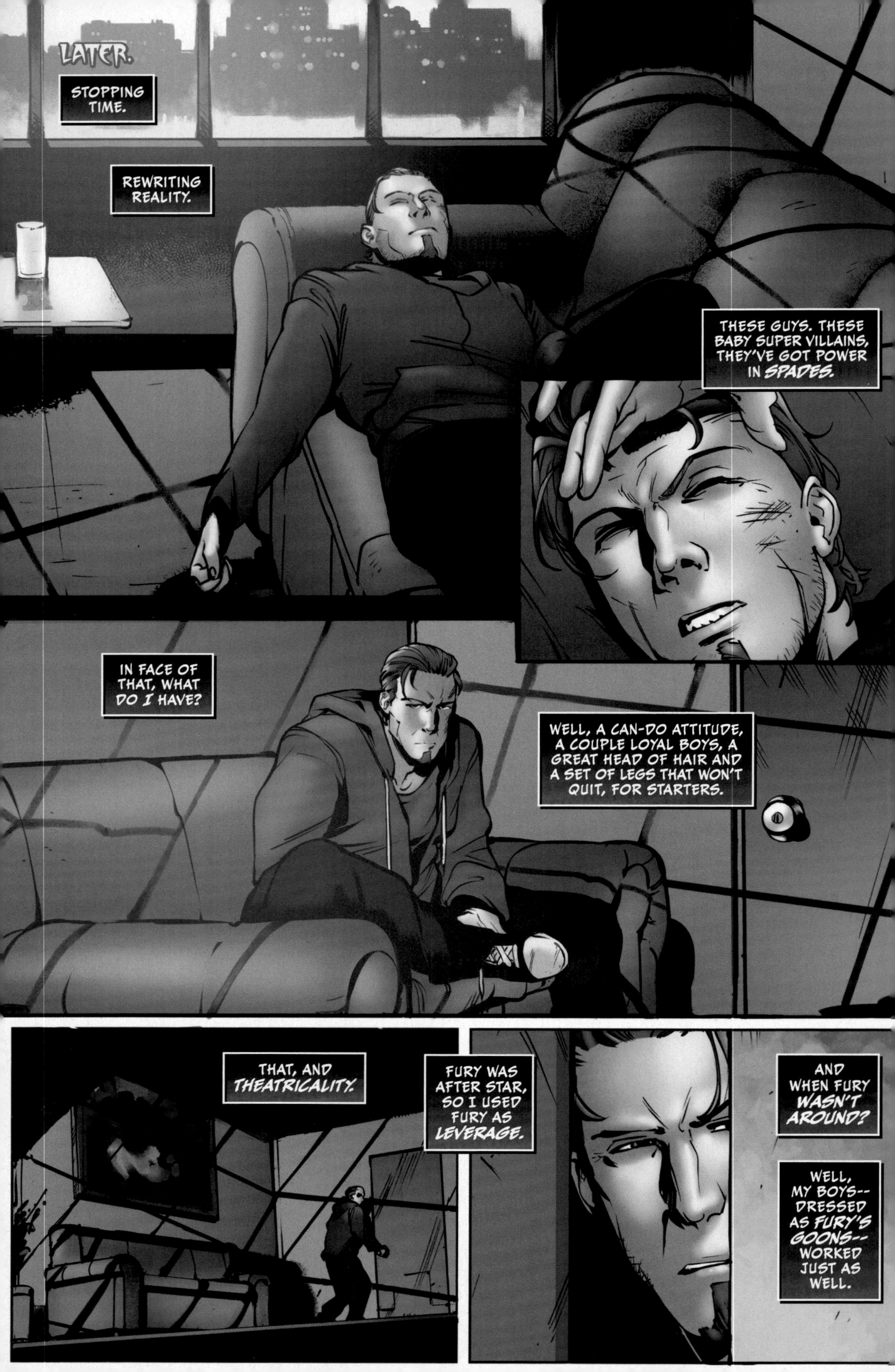
LATER.
STOPPING TIME.
REWRITING REALITY.
THESE GUYS. THESE BABY SUPER VILLAINS, THEY'VE GOT POWER IN SPADES.
IN FACE OF THAT, WHAT DO I HAVE?
WELL, A CAN-DO ATTITUDE, A COUPLE LOYAL BOYS, A GREAT HEAD OF HAIR AND A SET OF LEGS THAT WON'T QUIT, FOR STARTERS.
THAT, AND THEATRICALITY.
FURY WAS AFTER STAR, SO I USED FURY AS LEVERAGE.
AND WHEN FURY WASN'T AROUND?
WELL, MY BOYS--DRESSED AS FURY'S GOONS--WORKED JUST AS WELL.

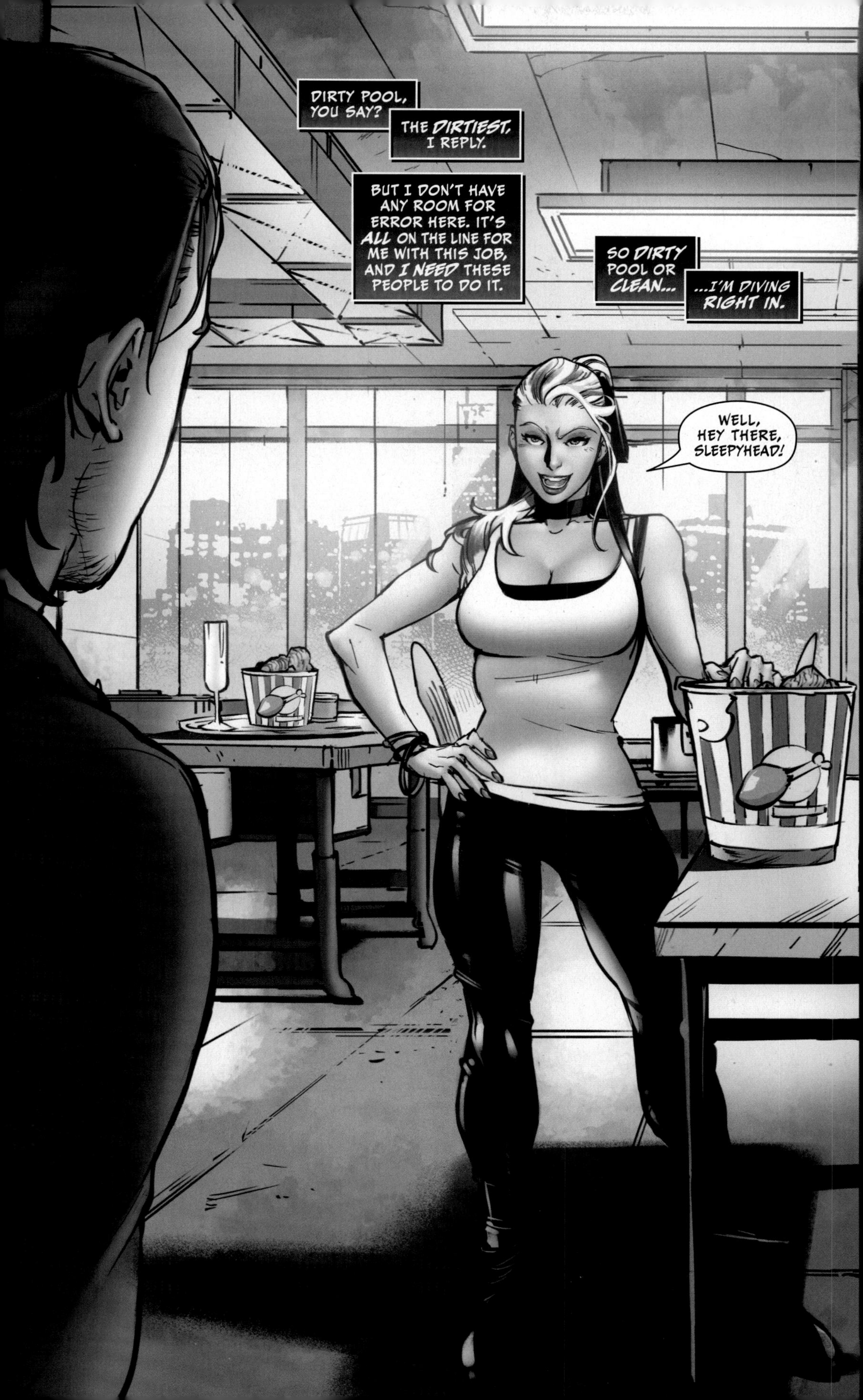
DIRTY POOL, YOU SAY?
THE DIRTIEST, I REPLY.
BUT I DON'T HAVE ANY ROOM FOR ERROR HERE. IT'S ALL ON THE LINE FOR ME WITH THIS JOB, AND I NEED THESE PEOPLE TO DO IT.
SO DIRTY POOL OR CLEAN...
...I'M DIVING RIGHT IN.
WELL, HEY THERE, SLEEPYHEAD!

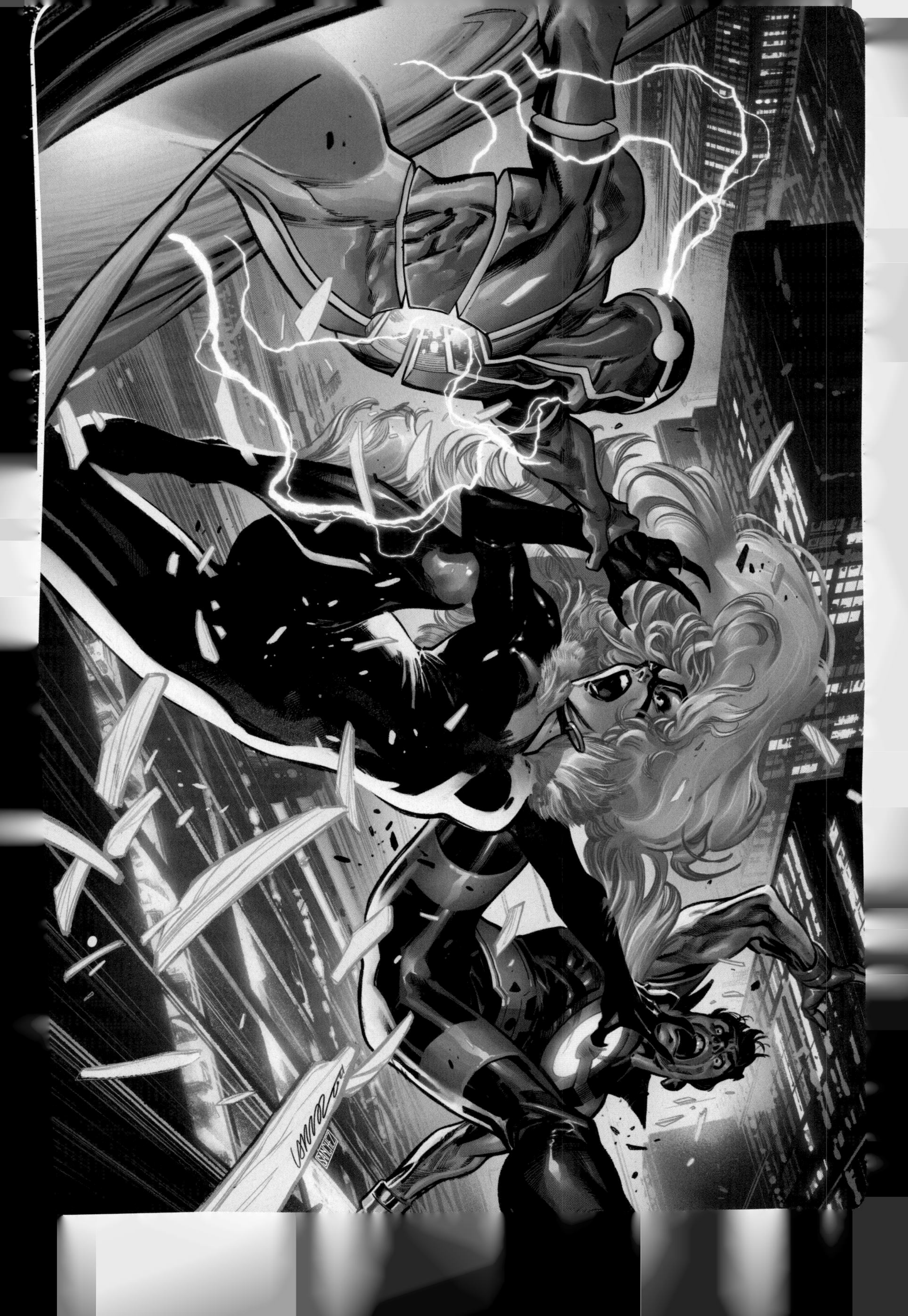

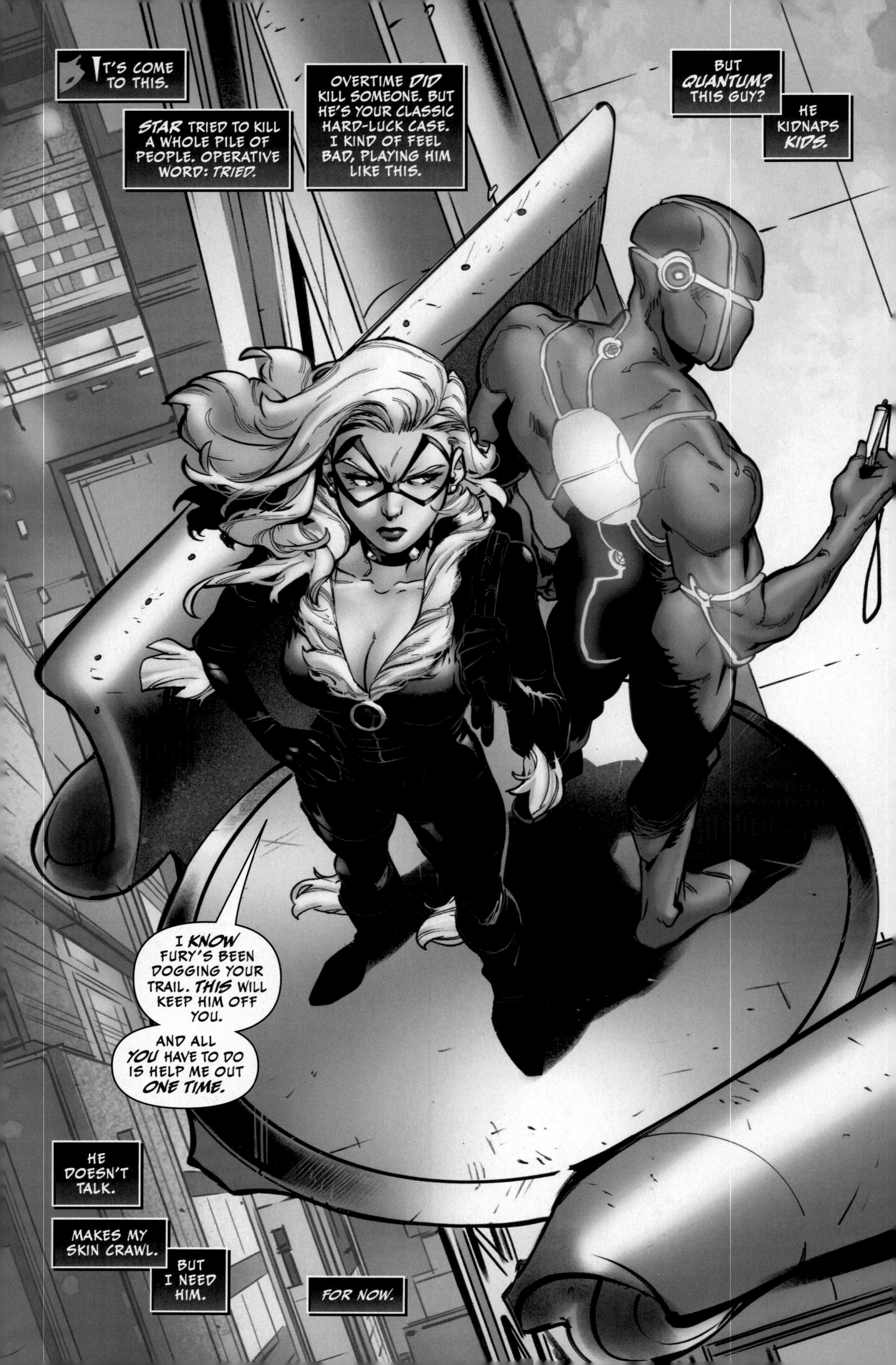
IT'S COME TO THIS.
STAR TRIED TO KILL A WHOLE PILE OF PEOPLE. OPERATIVE WORD: TRIED.
OVERTIME DID KILL SOMEONE. BUT HE'S YOUR CLASSIC HARD-LUCK CASE. I KIND OF FEEL BAD, PLAYING HIM LIKE THIS.
BUT QUANTUM? THIS GUY?
HE KIDNAPS KIDS.
I KNOW FURY'S BEEN DOGGING YOUR TRAIL. THIS WILL KEEP HIM OFF YOU.
AND ALL YOU HAVE TO DO IS HELP ME OUT ONE TIME.
HE DOESN'T TALK.
MAKES MY SKIN CRAWL.
BUT I NEED HIM.
FOR NOW.

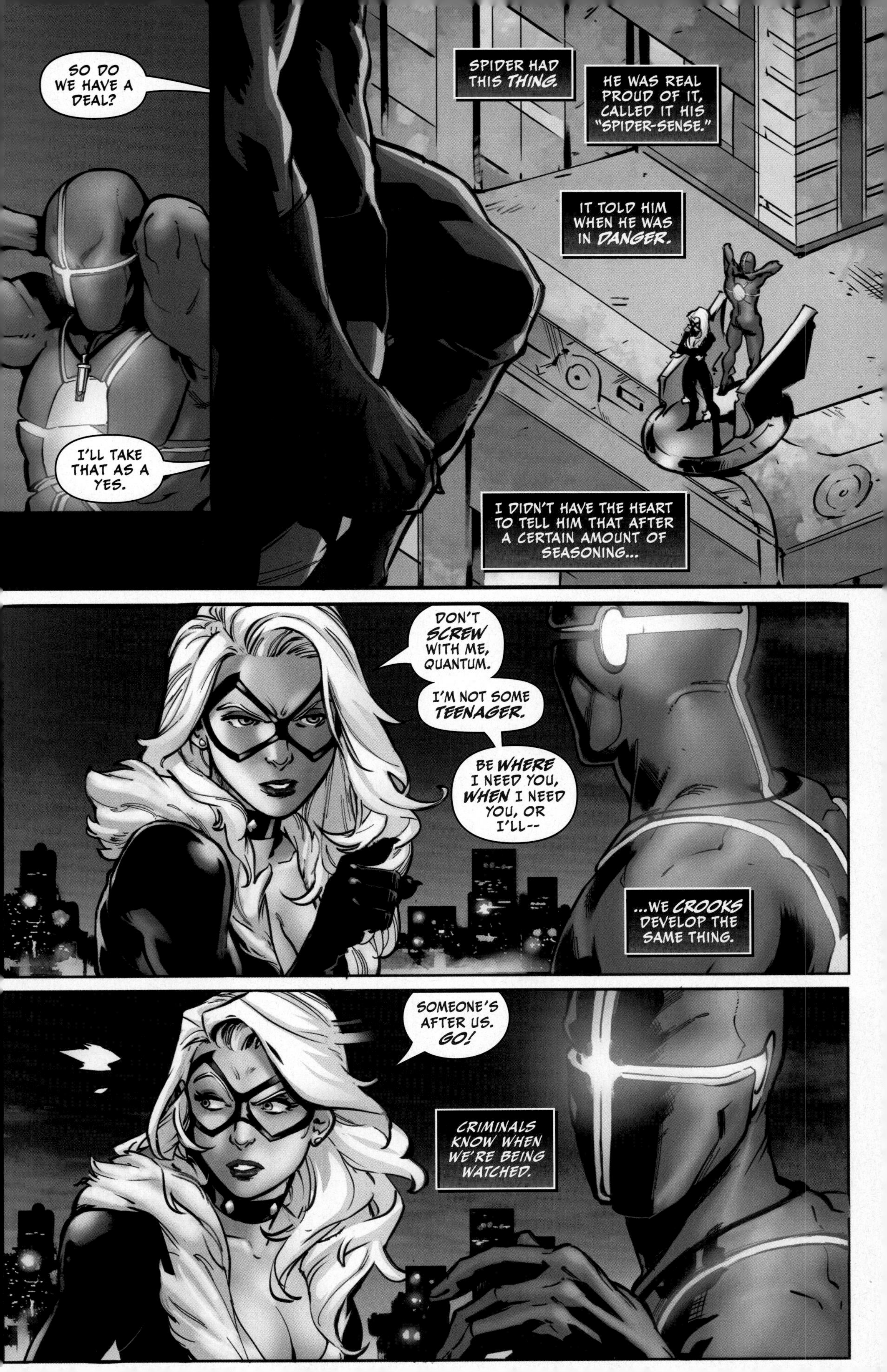

SO DO WE HAVE A DEAL?
I'LL TAKE THAT AS A YES.
SPIDER HAD THIS *THING.*
HE WAS REAL PROUD OF IT, CALLED IT HIS "SPIDER-SENSE."
IT TOLD HIM WHEN HE WAS IN *DANGER.*
I DIDN'T HAVE THE HEART TO TELL HIM THAT AFTER A CERTAIN AMOUNT OF SEASONING...
DON'T *SCREW* WITH ME, QUANTUM.
I'M NOT SOME *TEENAGER.*
BE *WHERE* I NEED YOU, *WHEN* I NEED YOU, OR I'LL--
...WE *CROOKS* DEVELOP THE SAME THING.
SOMEONE'S AFTER US. *GO!*
CRIMINALS KNOW WHEN WE'RE BEING WATCHED.

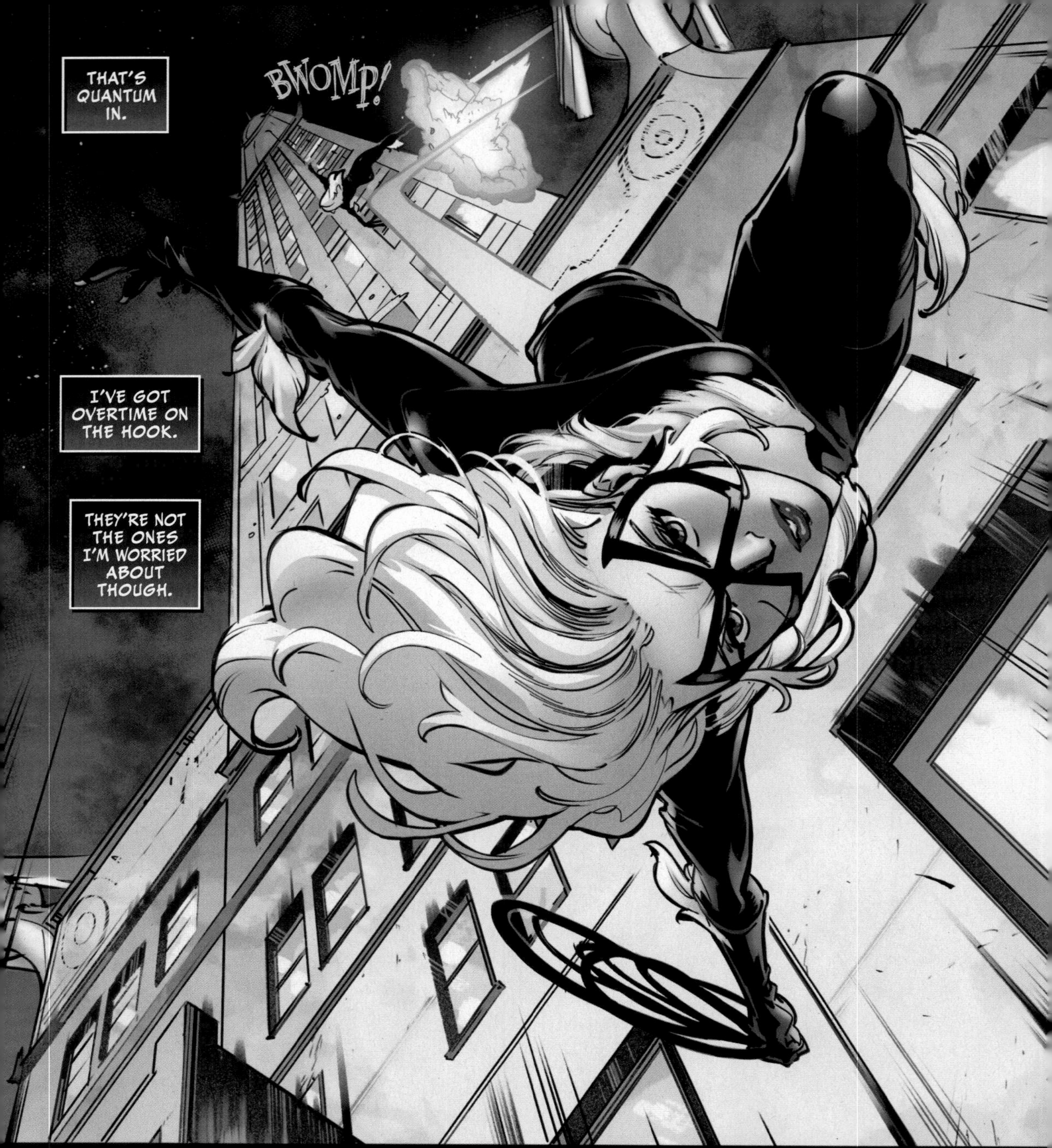
THAT'S QUANTUM IN.
BWOMP!
I'VE GOT OVERTIME ON THE HOOK.
THEY'RE NOT THE ONES I'M WORRIED ABOUT THOUGH.
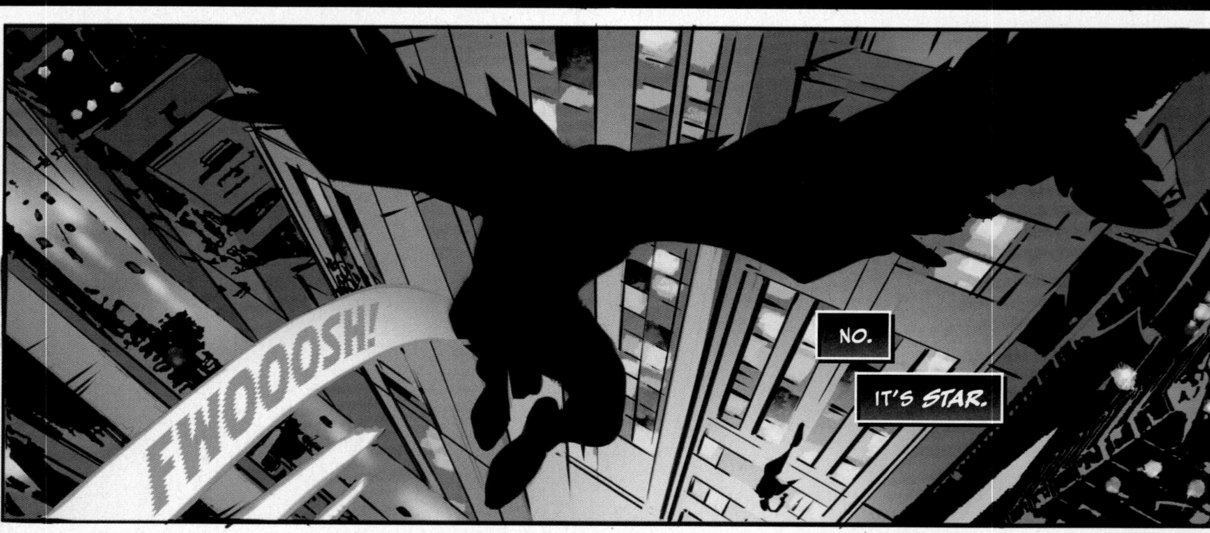
FWOOOSH!
NO.
IT'S STAR.

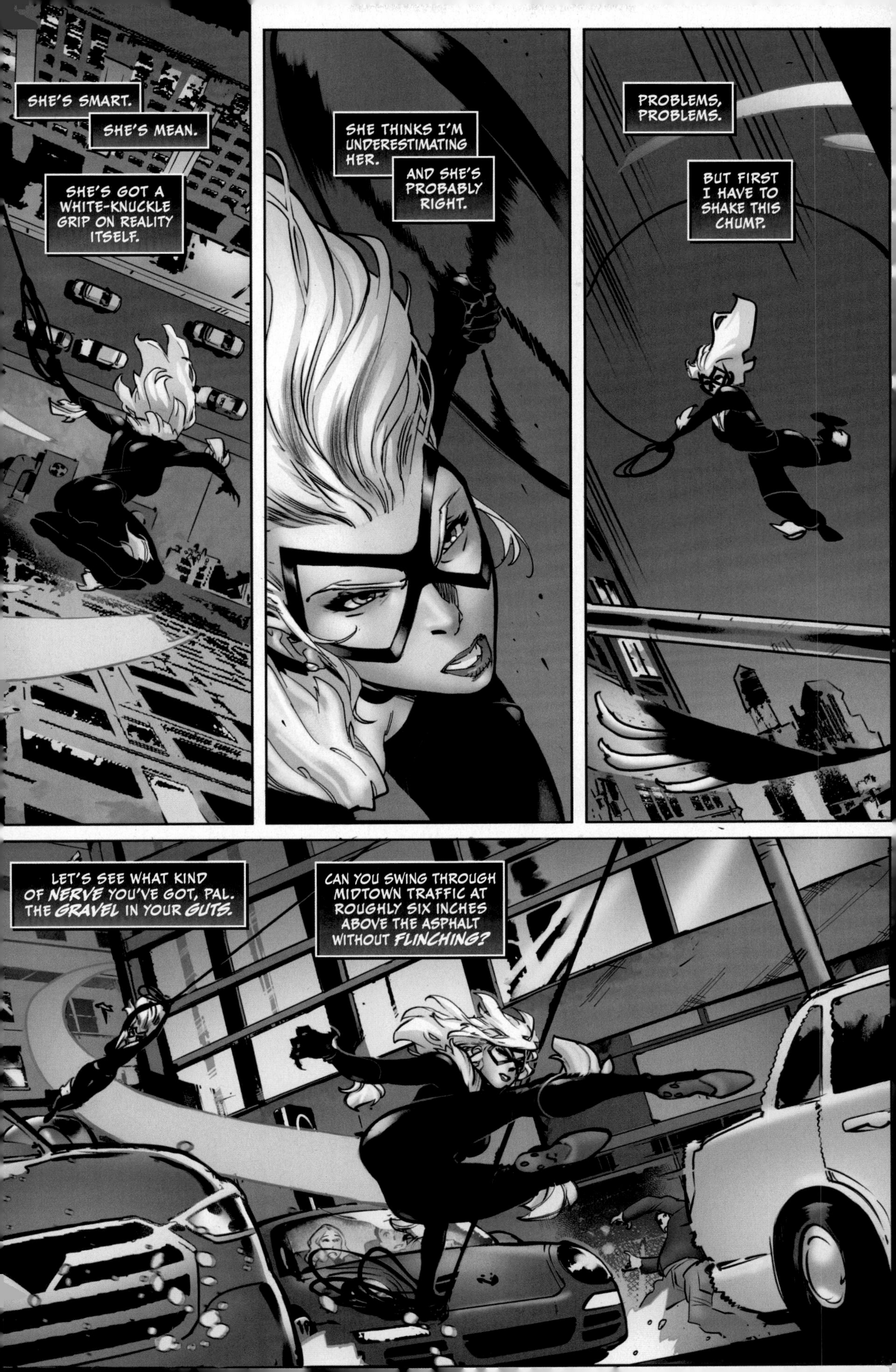

SHE'S SMART.
SHE'S MEAN.
SHE'S GOT A WHITE-KNUCKLE GRIP ON REALITY ITSELF.
SHE THINKS I'M UNDERESTIMATING HER.
AND SHE'S PROBABLY RIGHT.
PROBLEMS, PROBLEMS.
BUT FIRST I HAVE TO SHAKE THIS CHUMP.
LET'S SEE WHAT KIND OF NERVE YOU'VE GOT, PAL. THE GRAVEL IN YOUR GUTS.
CAN YOU SWING THROUGH MIDTOWN TRAFFIC AT ROUGHLY SIX INCHES ABOVE THE ASPHALT WITHOUT FLINCHING?

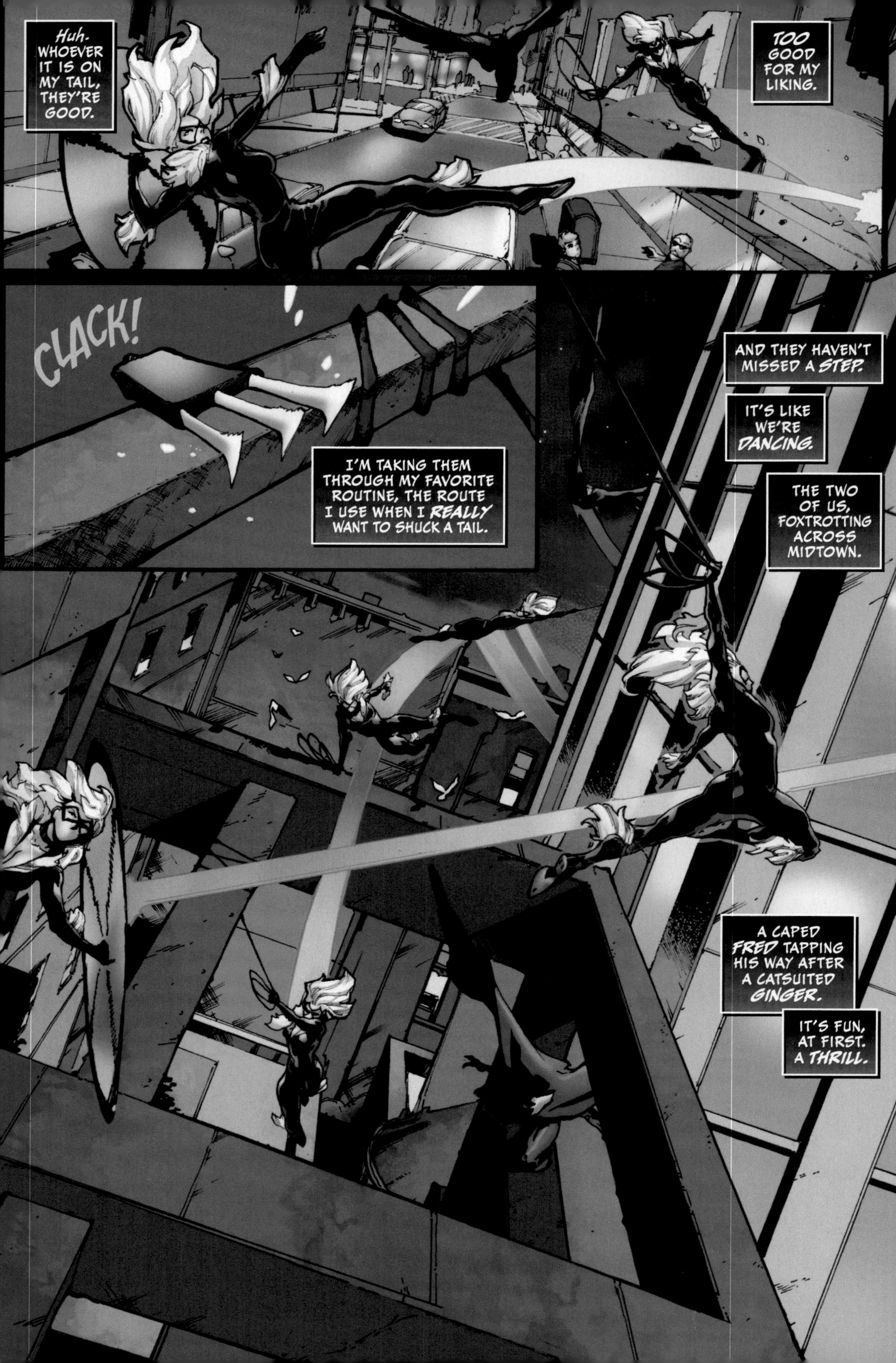
Huh. WHOEVER IT IS ON MY TAIL, THEY'RE GOOD.
TOO GOOD FOR MY LIKING.
CLACK!
I'M TAKING THEM THROUGH MY FAVORITE ROUTINE, THE ROUTE I USE WHEN I REALLY WANT TO SHUCK A TAIL.
AND THEY HAVEN'T MISSED A STEP.
IT'S LIKE WE'RE DANCING.
THE TWO OF US, FOXTROTTING ACROSS MIDTOWN.
A CAPED FRED TAPPING HIS WAY AFTER A CATSUITED GINGER.
IT'S FUN, AT FIRST. A THRILL.

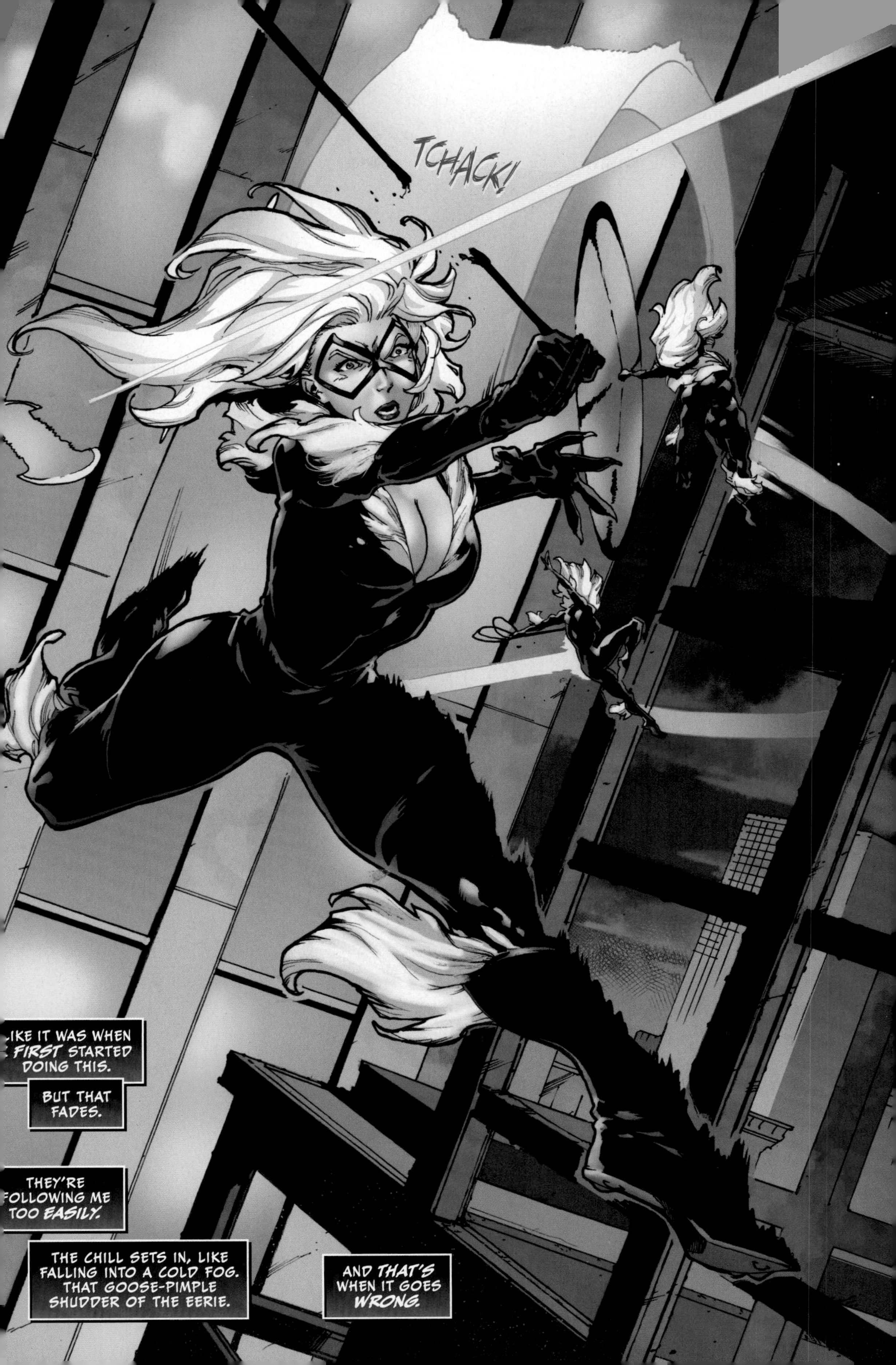
TCHACK!
IKE IT WAS WHEN
FIRST STARTED
DOING THIS.
BUT THAT
FADES.
THEY'RE
FOLLOWING ME
TOO EASILY.
THE CHILL SETS IN, LIKE
FALLING INTO A COLD FOG.
THAT GOOSE-PIMPLE
SHUDDER OF THE EERIE.
AND THAT'S
WHEN IT GOES
WRONG.

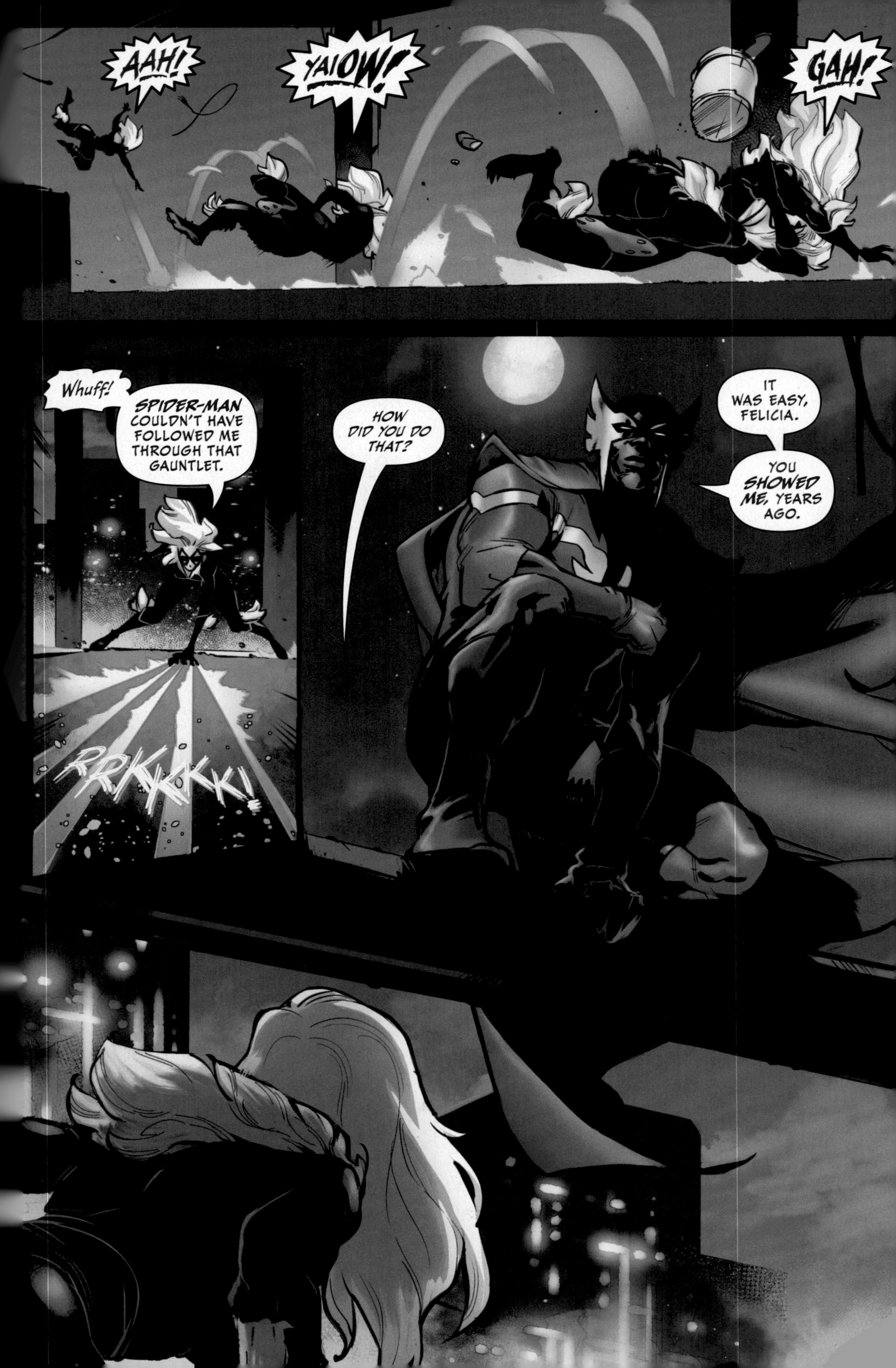
AAH!
YAIOW!
GAH!
Whuff!
SPIDER-MAN COULDN'T HAVE FOLLOWED ME THROUGH THAT GAUNTLET.
RRKKKK!
HOW DID YOU DO THAT?
IT WAS EASY, FELICIA.
YOU SHOWED ME, YEARS AGO.

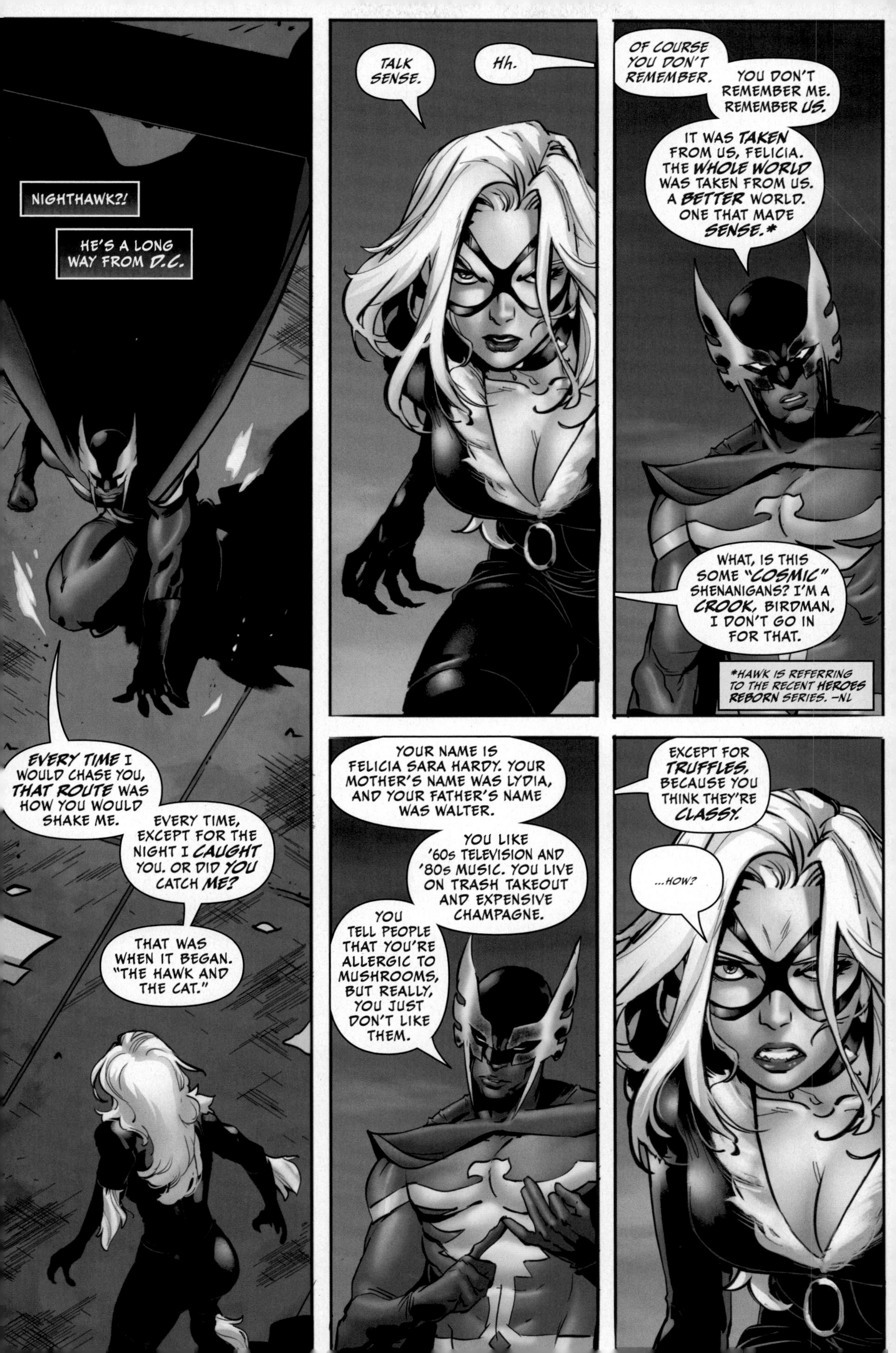
NIGHTHAWK?!
HE'S A LONG WAY FROM D.C.
TALK SENSE.
Hh.
OF COURSE YOU DON'T REMEMBER.
YOU DON'T REMEMBER ME. REMEMBER US.
IT WAS TAKEN FROM US, FELICIA. THE WHOLE WORLD WAS TAKEN FROM US. A BETTER WORLD. ONE THAT MADE SENSE.*
WHAT, IS THIS SOME "COSMIC" SHENANIGANS? I'M A CROOK, BIRDMAN, I DON'T GO IN FOR THAT.
*HAWK IS REFERRING TO THE RECENT HEROES REBORN SERIES. –NL
EVERY TIME I WOULD CHASE YOU, THAT ROUTE WAS HOW YOU WOULD SHAKE ME.
EVERY TIME, EXCEPT FOR THE NIGHT I CAUGHT YOU. OR DID YOU CATCH ME?
THAT WAS WHEN IT BEGAN. "THE HAWK AND THE CAT."
YOUR NAME IS FELICIA SARA HARDY. YOUR MOTHER'S NAME WAS LYDIA, AND YOUR FATHER'S NAME WAS WALTER.
YOU LIKE '60s TELEVISION AND '80s MUSIC. YOU LIVE ON TRASH TAKEOUT AND EXPENSIVE CHAMPAGNE.
YOU TELL PEOPLE THAT YOU'RE ALLERGIC TO MUSHROOMS, BUT REALLY, YOU JUST DON'T LIKE THEM.
EXCEPT FOR TRUFFLES, BECAUSE YOU THINK THEY'RE CLASSY.
...HOW?

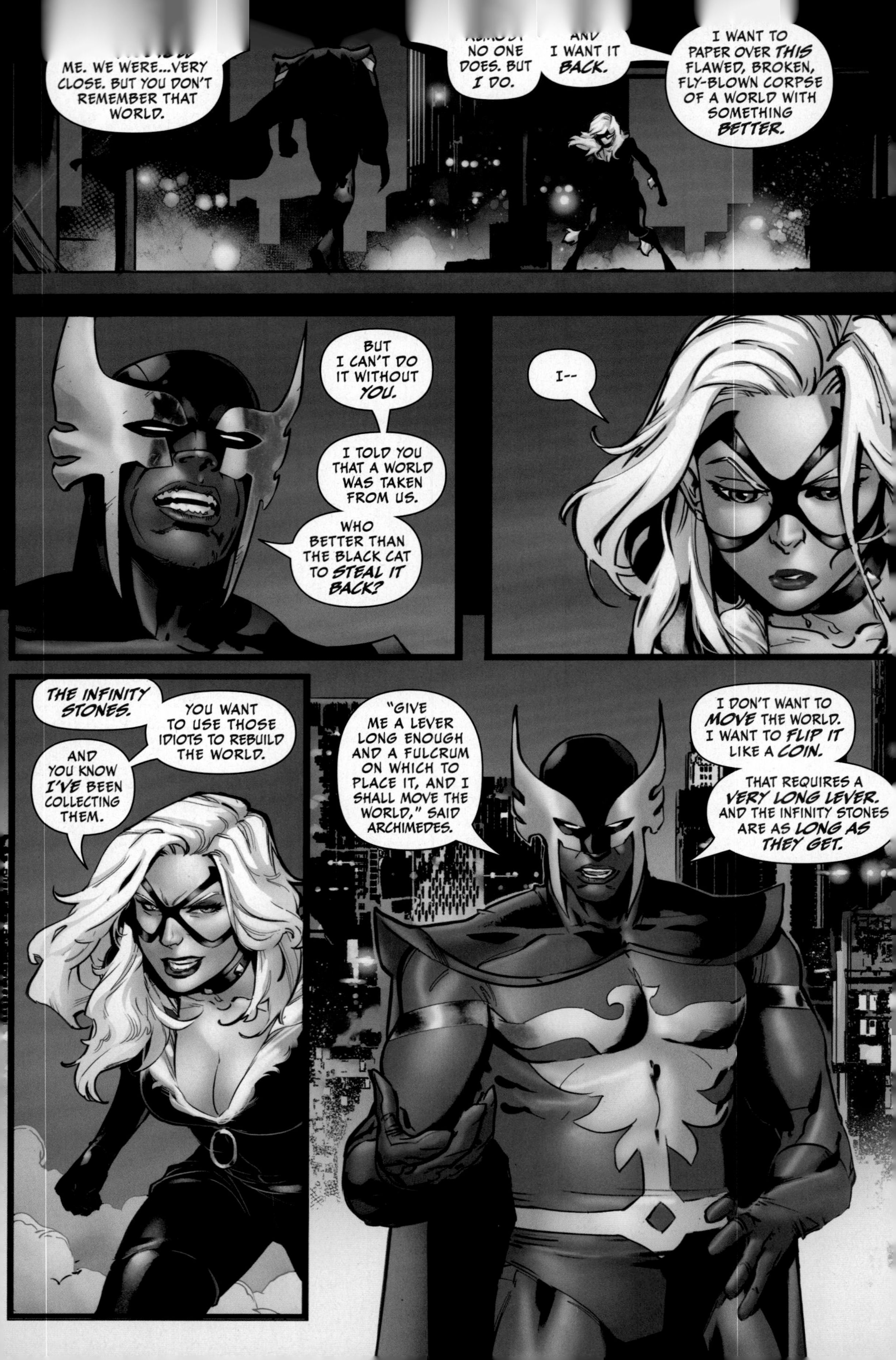
ME. WE WERE...VERY CLOSE. BUT YOU DON'T REMEMBER THAT WORLD.
NO ONE DOES. BUT I DO.
AND I WANT IT BACK.
I WANT TO PAPER OVER THIS FLAWED, BROKEN, FLY-BLOWN CORPSE OF A WORLD WITH SOMETHING BETTER.
BUT I CAN'T DO IT WITHOUT YOU.
I TOLD YOU THAT A WORLD WAS TAKEN FROM US.
WHO BETTER THAN THE BLACK CAT TO STEAL IT BACK?
I--
THE INFINITY STONES.
YOU WANT TO USE THOSE IDIOTS TO REBUILD THE WORLD.
AND YOU KNOW I'VE BEEN COLLECTING THEM.
"GIVE ME A LEVER LONG ENOUGH AND A FULCRUM ON WHICH TO PLACE IT, AND I SHALL MOVE THE WORLD," SAID ARCHIMEDES.
I DON'T WANT TO MOVE THE WORLD. I WANT TO FLIP IT LIKE A COIN.
THAT REQUIRES A VERY LONG LEVER. AND THE INFINITY STONES ARE AS LONG AS THEY GET.

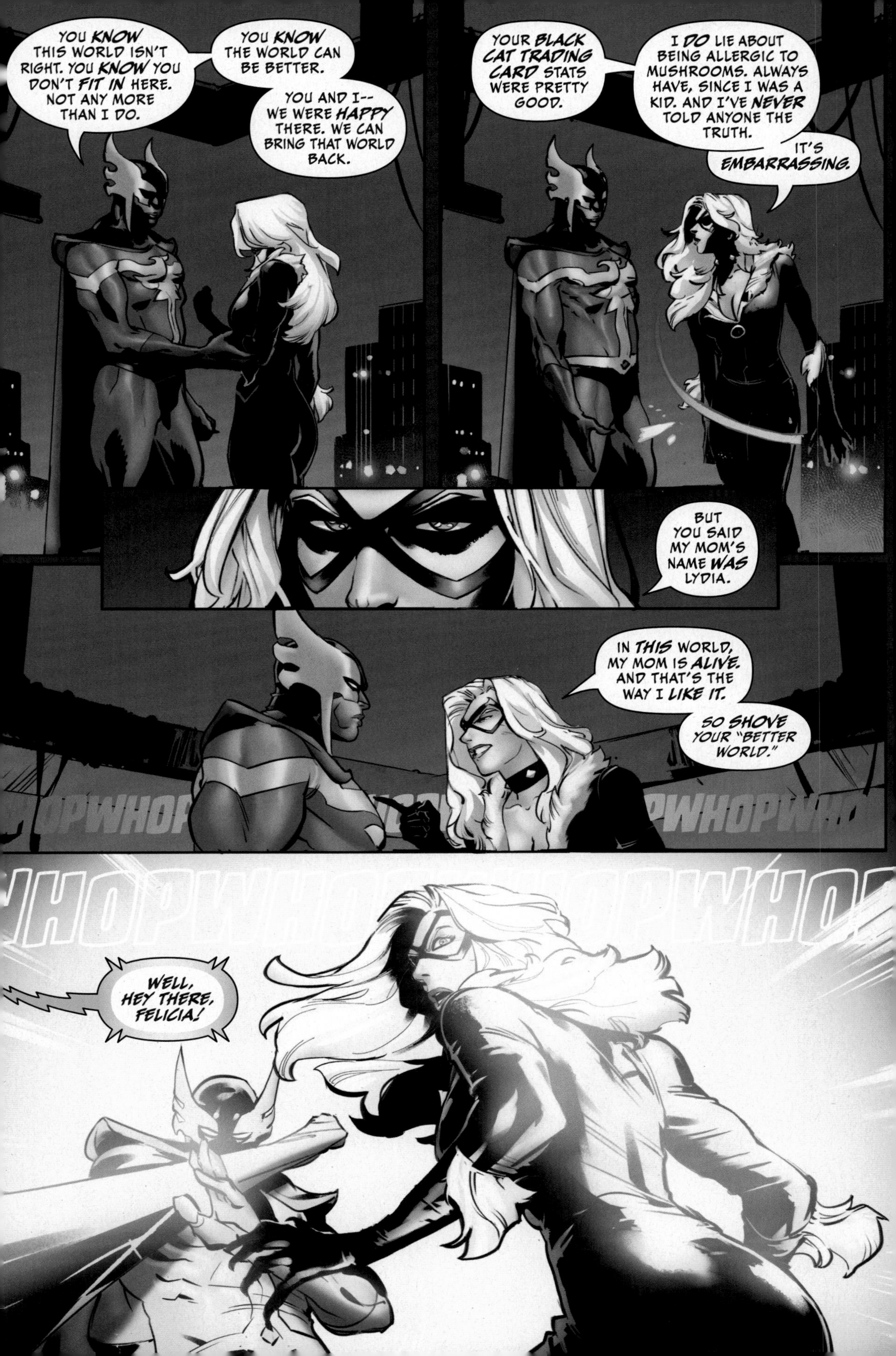

YOU KNOW THIS WORLD ISN'T RIGHT. YOU KNOW YOU DON'T FIT IN HERE. NOT ANY MORE THAN I DO.
YOU KNOW THE WORLD CAN BE BETTER.
YOU AND I-- WE WERE HAPPY THERE. WE CAN BRING THAT WORLD BACK.
YOUR BLACK CAT TRADING CARD STATS WERE PRETTY GOOD.
I DO LIE ABOUT BEING ALLERGIC TO MUSHROOMS. ALWAYS HAVE, SINCE I WAS A KID. AND I'VE NEVER TOLD ANYONE THE TRUTH.
IT'S EMBARRASSING.
BUT YOU SAID MY MOM'S NAME WAS LYDIA.
IN THIS WORLD, MY MOM IS ALIVE. AND THAT'S THE WAY I LIKE IT.
SO SHOVE YOUR "BETTER WORLD."
WELL, HEY THERE, FELICIA!

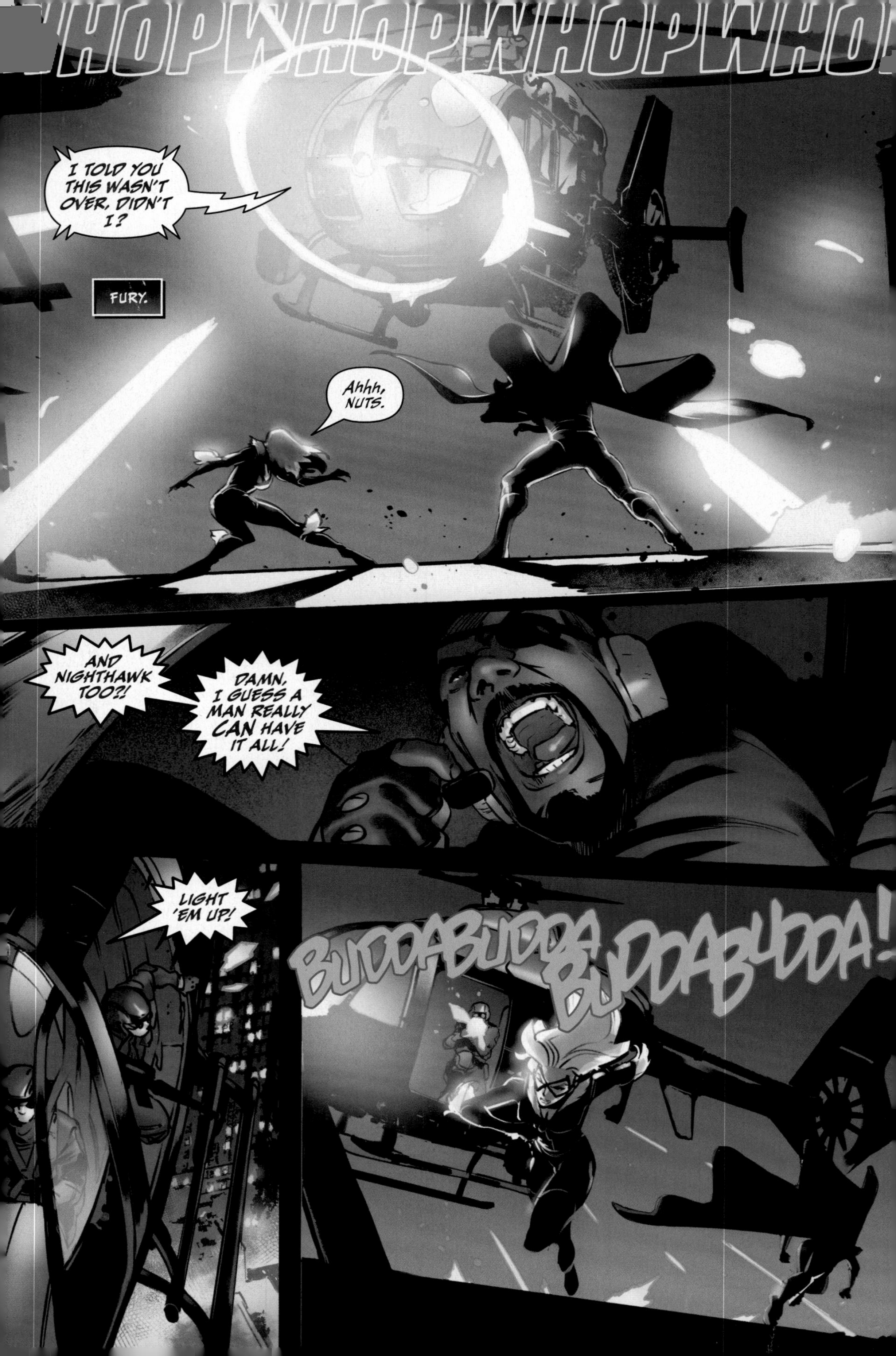
WHOPWHOPWHOPWHOP
I TOLD YOU THIS WASN'T OVER, DIDN'T I?
FURY.
Ahhh, NUTS.
AND NIGHTHAWK TOO?!
DAMN, I GUESS A MAN REALLY CAN HAVE IT ALL!
LIGHT 'EM UP!
BUDDABUDDA BUDDABUDDA!

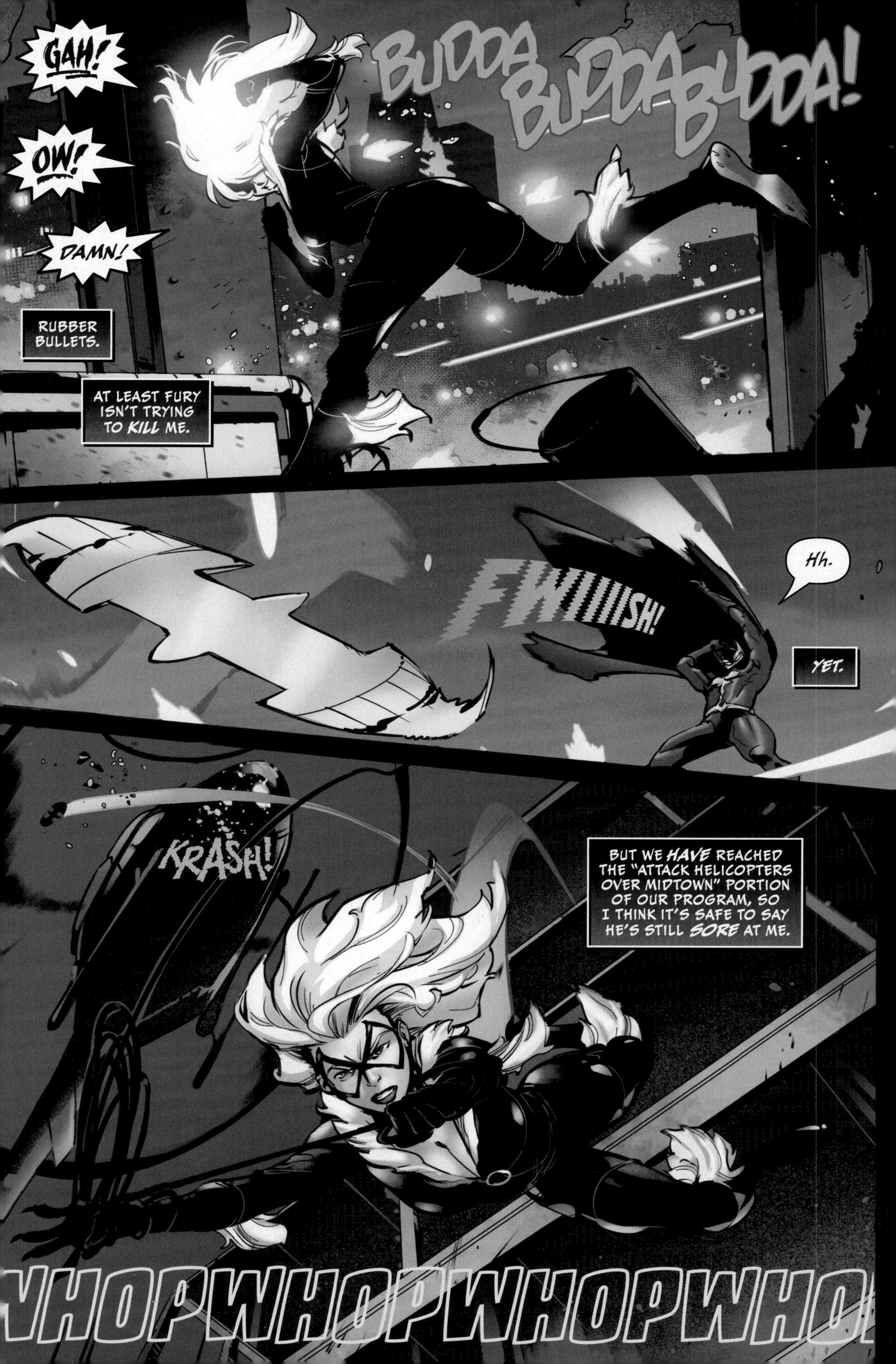
GAH!
OW!
DAMN!
BUDDA BUDDA BUDDA!
RUBBER BULLETS.
AT LEAST FURY ISN'T TRYING TO KILL ME.
FWUUUSH!
Hh.
YET.
KRASH!
BUT WE HAVE REACHED THE "ATTACK HELICOPTERS OVER MIDTOWN" PORTION OF OUR PROGRAM, SO I THINK IT'S SAFE TO SAY HE'S STILL SORE AT ME.
WHOPWHOPWHOPWHO

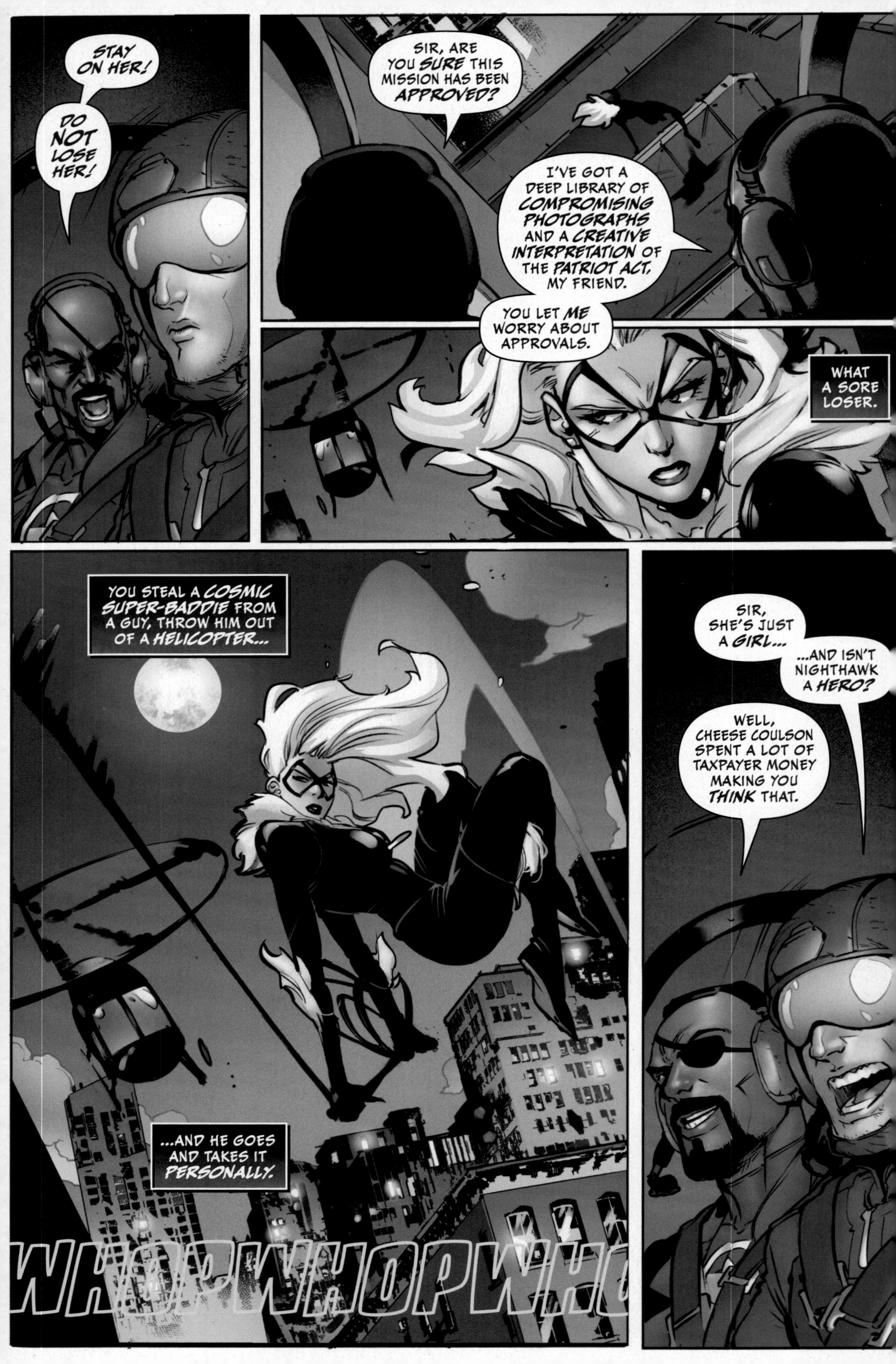
STAY ON HER!
DO NOT LOSE HER!
SIR, ARE YOU SURE THIS MISSION HAS BEEN APPROVED?
I'VE GOT A DEEP LIBRARY OF COMPROMISING PHOTOGRAPHS AND A CREATIVE INTERPRETATION OF THE PATRIOT ACT, MY FRIEND.
YOU LET ME WORRY ABOUT APPROVALS.
WHAT A SORE LOSER.
YOU STEAL A COSMIC SUPER-BADDIE FROM A GUY, THROW HIM OUT OF A HELICOPTER...
...AND HE GOES AND TAKES IT PERSONALLY.
WHOPWHOPWHO
SIR, SHE'S JUST A GIRL...
...AND ISN'T NIGHTHAWK A HERO?
WELL, CHEESE COULSON SPENT A LOT OF TAXPAYER MONEY MAKING YOU THINK THAT.

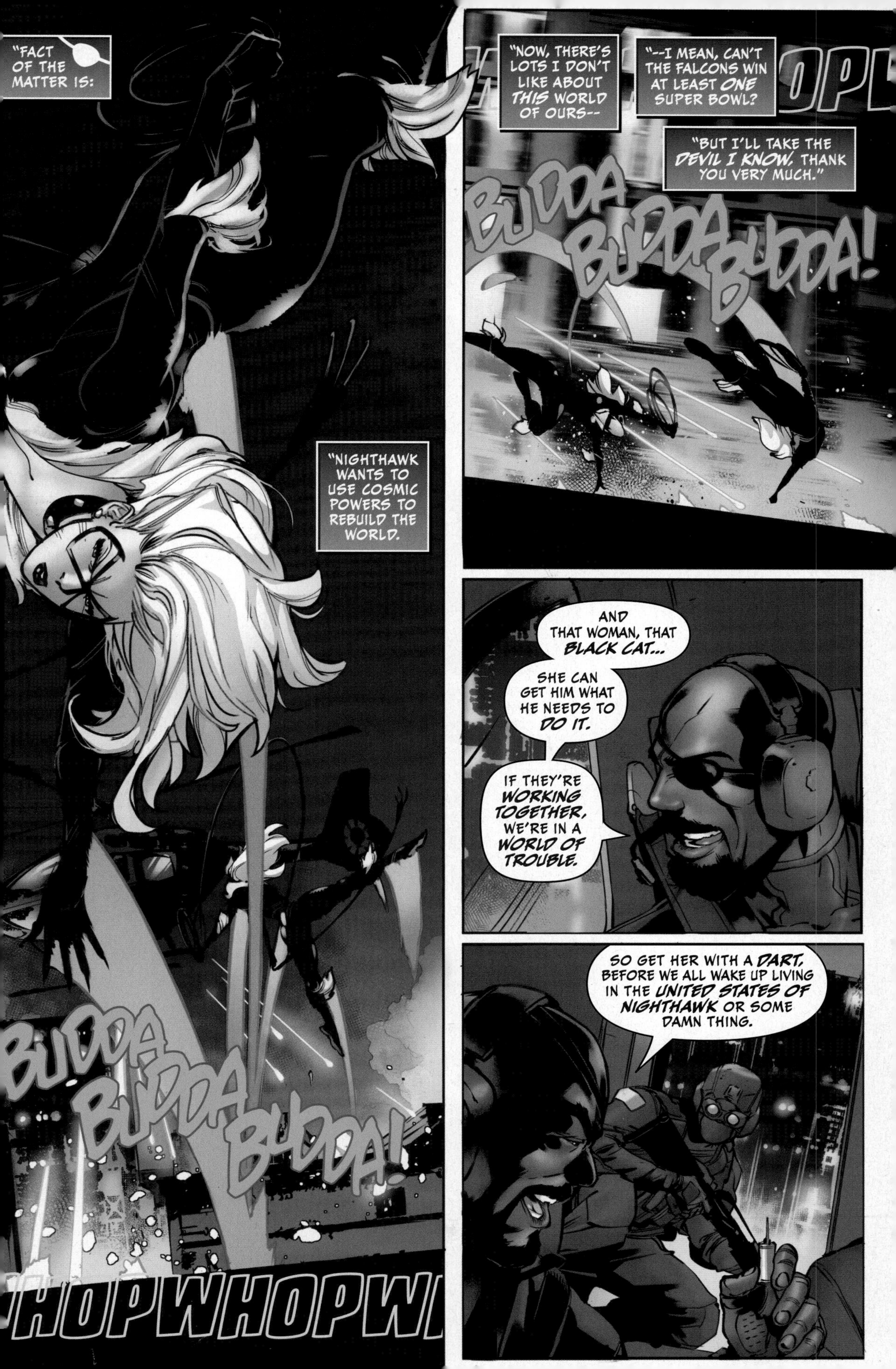
"FACT OF THE MATTER IS:
"NIGHTHAWK WANTS TO USE COSMIC POWERS TO REBUILD THE WORLD.
BUDDA BUDDA BUDDA!
WHOPWHOPWH
"NOW, THERE'S LOTS I DON'T LIKE ABOUT THIS WORLD OF OURS--
"--I MEAN, CAN'T THE FALCONS WIN AT LEAST ONE SUPER BOWL?
"BUT I'LL TAKE THE DEVIL I KNOW, THANK YOU VERY MUCH."
BUDDA BUDDA BUDDA!
AND THAT WOMAN, THAT BLACK CAT...
SHE CAN GET HIM WHAT HE NEEDS TO DO IT.
IF THEY'RE WORKING TOGETHER, WE'RE IN A WORLD OF TROUBLE.
SO GET HER WITH A DART, BEFORE WE ALL WAKE UP LIVING IN THE UNITED STATES OF NIGHTHAWK OR SOME DAMN THING.

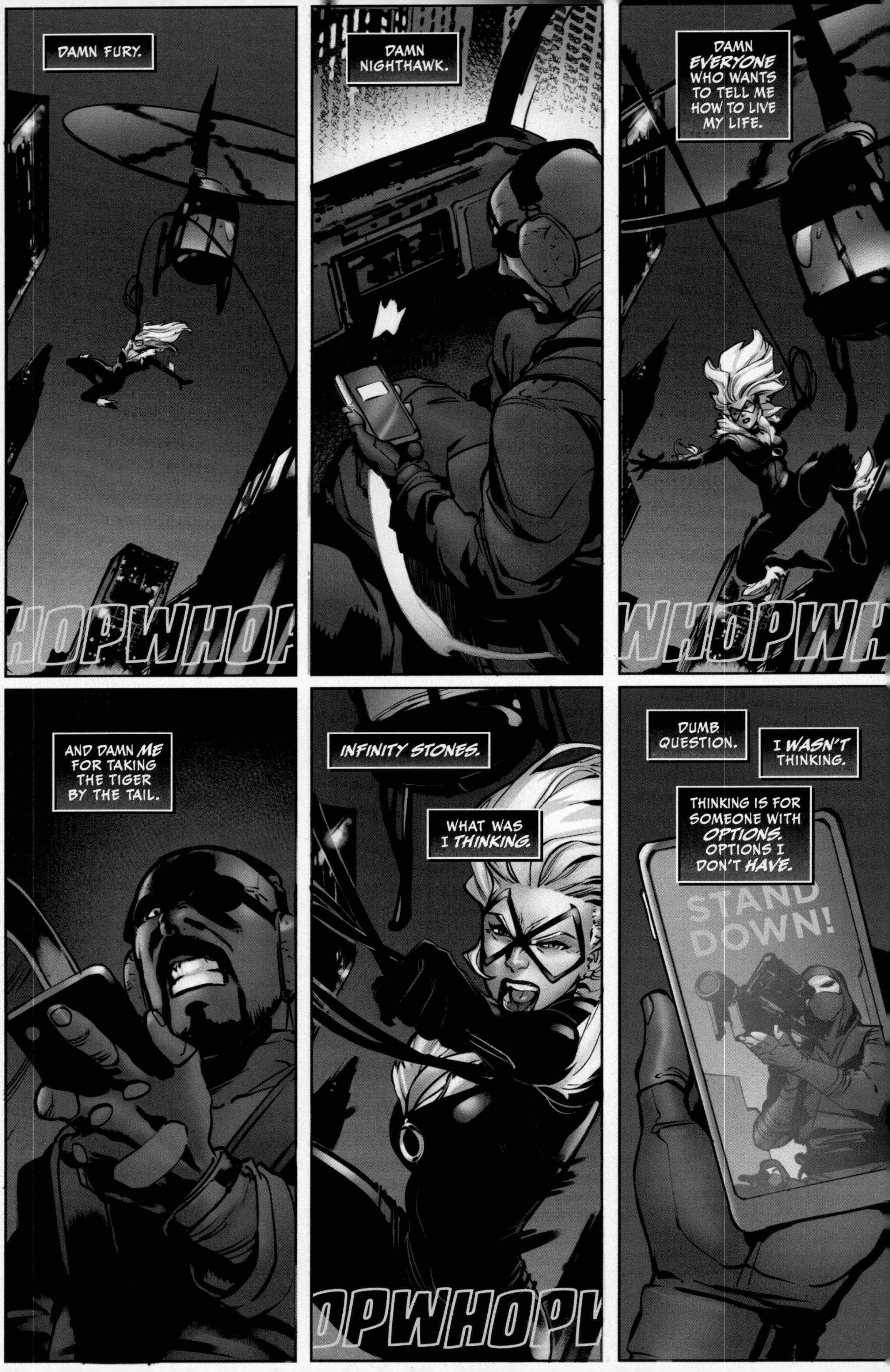
DAMN FURY.
HOPWHOP
DAMN NIGHTHAWK.
DAMN EVERYONE WHO WANTS TO TELL ME HOW TO LIVE MY LIFE.
WHOPWH
AND DAMN ME FOR TAKING THE TIGER BY THE TAIL.
INFINITY STONES.
WHAT WAS I THINKING.
OPWHOPW
DUMB QUESTION.
I WASN'T THINKING.
THINKING IS FOR SOMEONE WITH OPTIONS. OPTIONS I DON'T HAVE.
STAND DOWN!

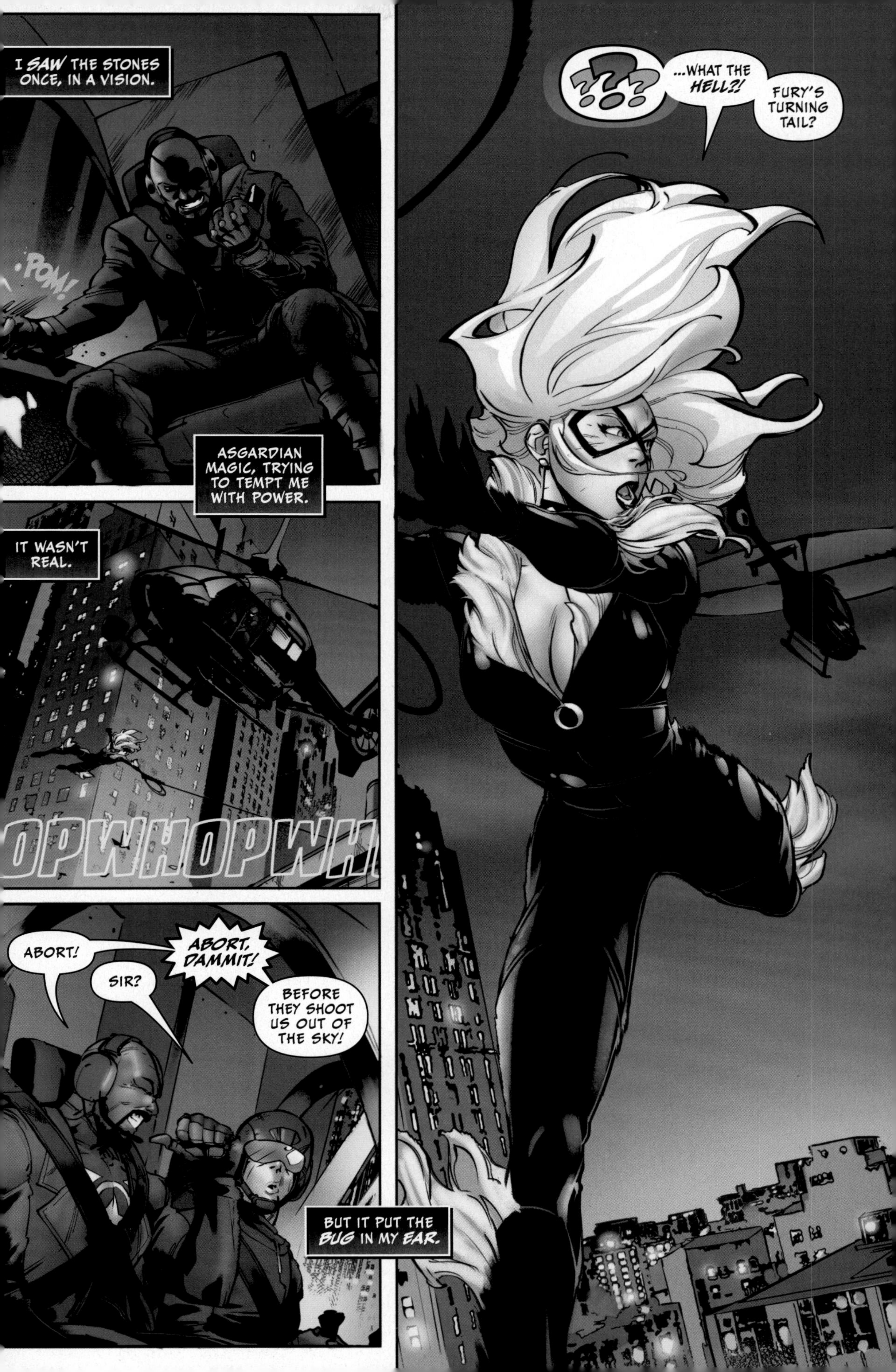

I SAW THE STONES ONCE, IN A VISION.
POM!
ASGARDIAN MAGIC, TRYING TO TEMPT ME WITH POWER.
IT WASN'T REAL.
OPWHOPWHOPWH
ABORT!
SIR?
ABORT, DAMMIT!
BEFORE THEY SHOOT US OUT OF THE SKY!
BUT IT PUT THE BUG IN MY EAR.
???
...WHAT THE HELL?!
FURY'S TURNING TAIL?

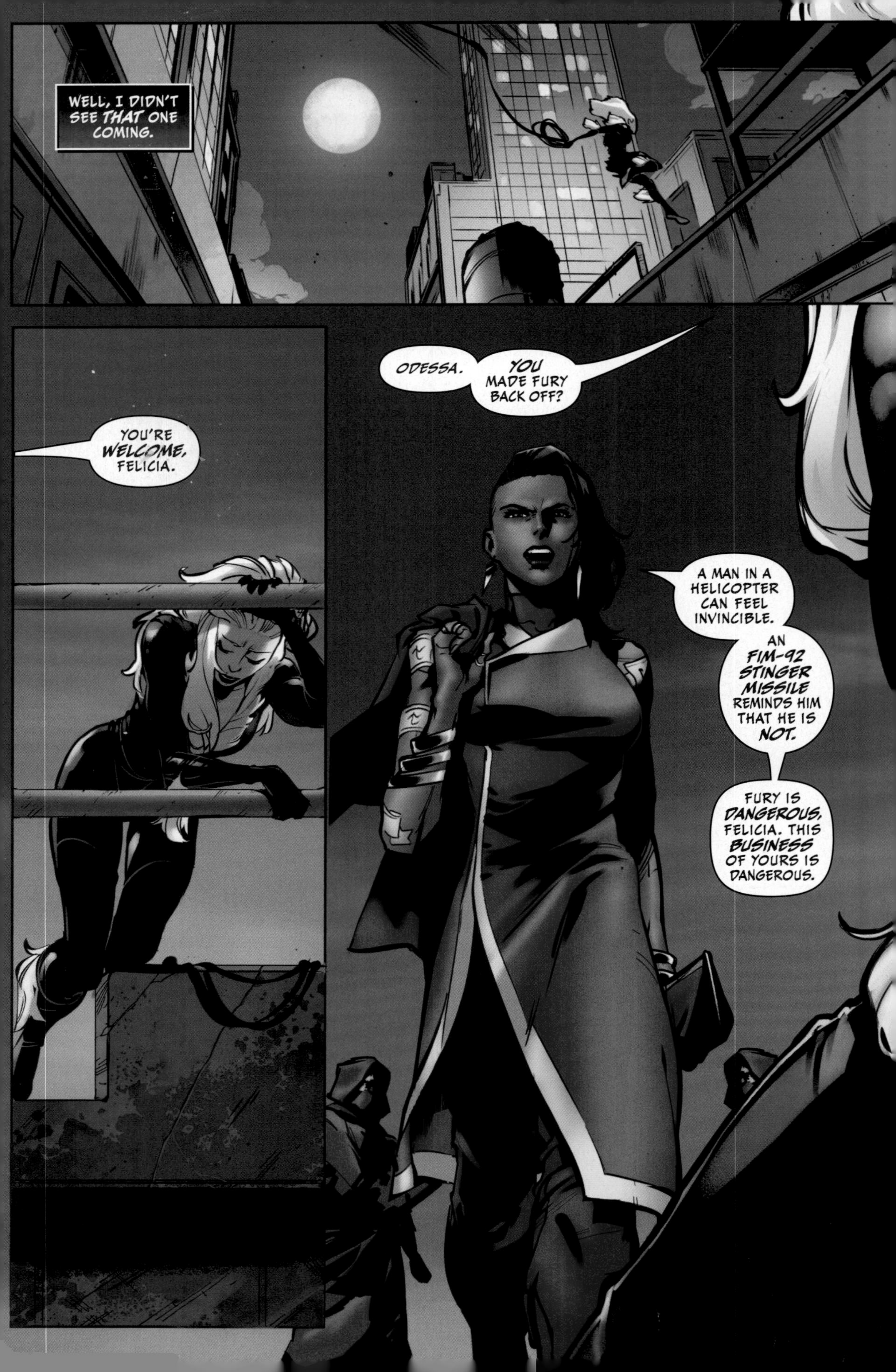
WELL, I DIDN'T SEE THAT ONE COMING.
ODESSA.
YOU MADE FURY BACK OFF?
YOU'RE WELCOME, FELICIA.
A MAN IN A HELICOPTER CAN FEEL INVINCIBLE.
AN FIM-92 STINGER MISSILE REMINDS HIM THAT HE IS NOT.
FURY IS DANGEROUS, FELICIA. THIS BUSINESS OF YOURS IS DANGEROUS.

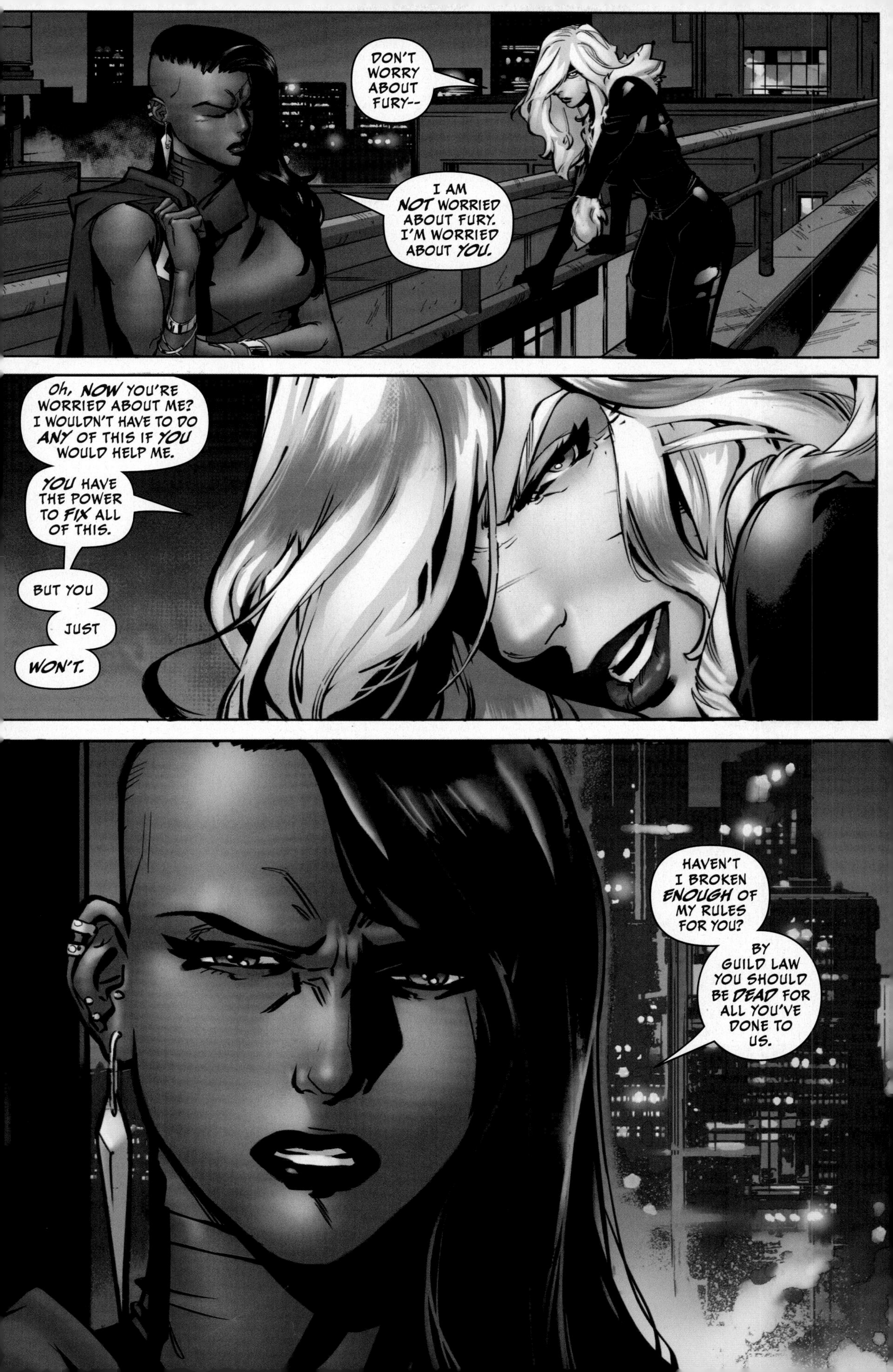

DON'T WORRY ABOUT FURY--
I AM *NOT* WORRIED ABOUT FURY. I'M WORRIED ABOUT *YOU.*
Oh, *NOW* YOU'RE WORRIED ABOUT ME? I WOULDN'T HAVE TO DO *ANY* OF THIS IF *YOU* WOULD HELP ME.
YOU HAVE THE POWER TO *FIX* ALL OF THIS.
BUT YOU
JUST
WON'T.
HAVEN'T I BROKEN *ENOUGH* OF MY RULES FOR YOU?
BY GUILD LAW YOU SHOULD BE *DEAD* FOR ALL YOU'VE DONE TO US.

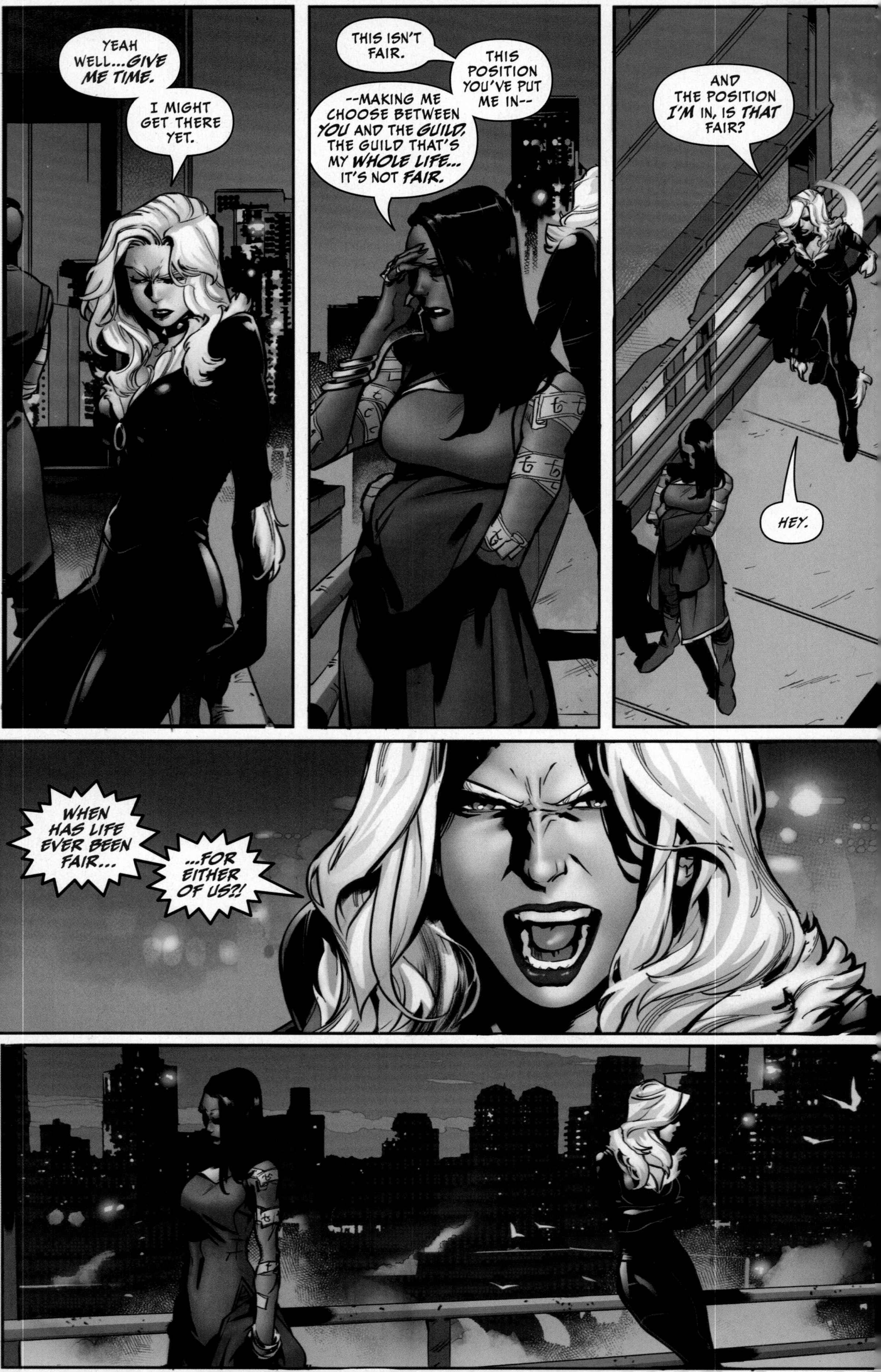
YEAH WELL...GIVE ME TIME.
I MIGHT GET THERE YET.
THIS ISN'T FAIR.
THIS POSITION YOU'VE PUT ME IN--
--MAKING ME CHOOSE BETWEEN YOU AND THE GUILD, THE GUILD THAT'S MY WHOLE LIFE... IT'S NOT FAIR.
AND THE POSITION I'M IN, IS THAT FAIR?
HEY.
WHEN HAS LIFE EVER BEEN FAIR...
...FOR EITHER OF US?!

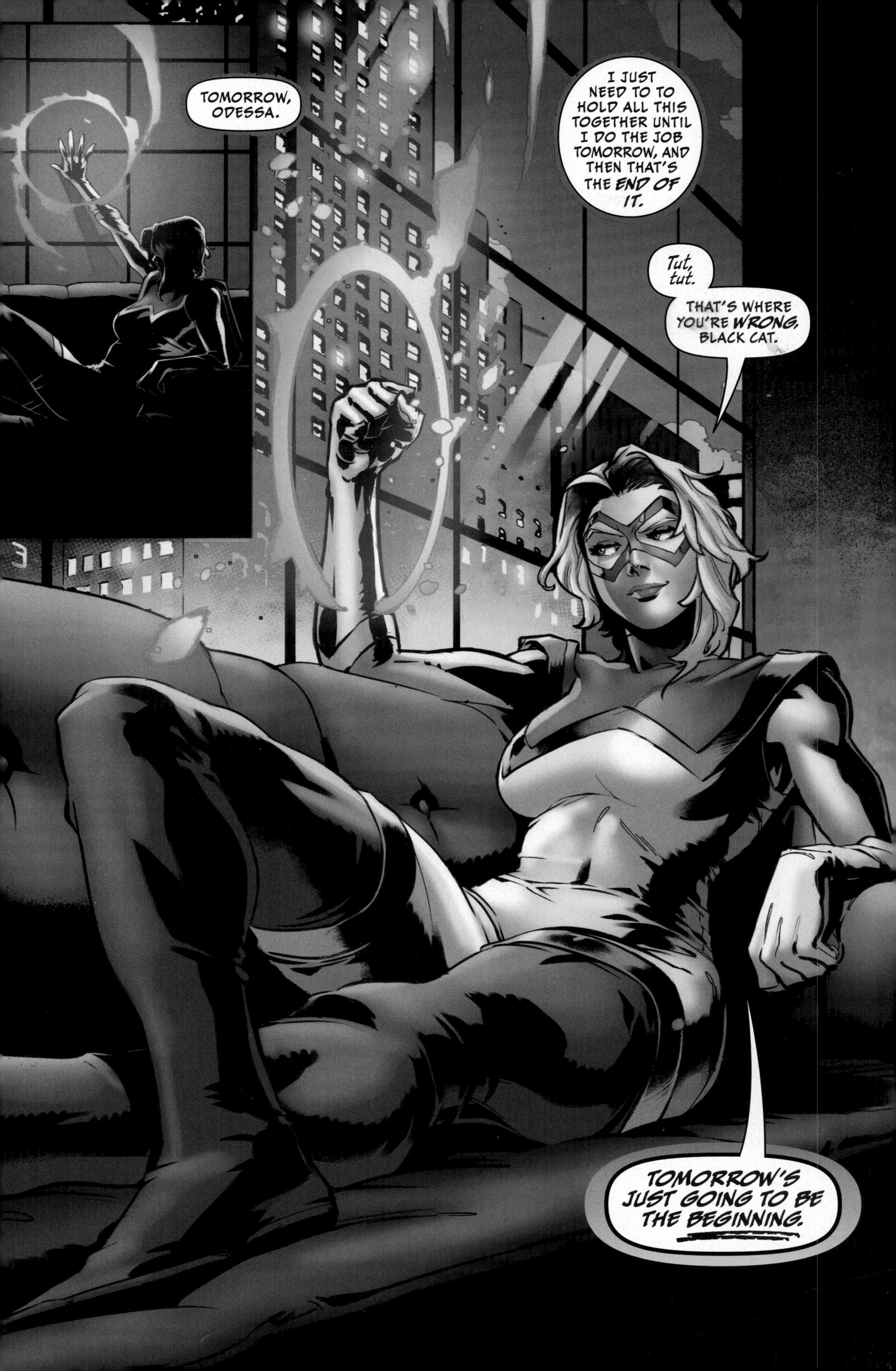

TOMORROW, ODESSA.
I JUST NEED TO TO HOLD ALL THIS TOGETHER UNTIL I DO THE JOB TOMORROW, AND THEN THAT'S THE END OF IT.
Tut, tut.
THAT'S WHERE YOU'RE WRONG, BLACK CAT.
TOMORROW'S JUST GOING TO BE THE BEGINNING.

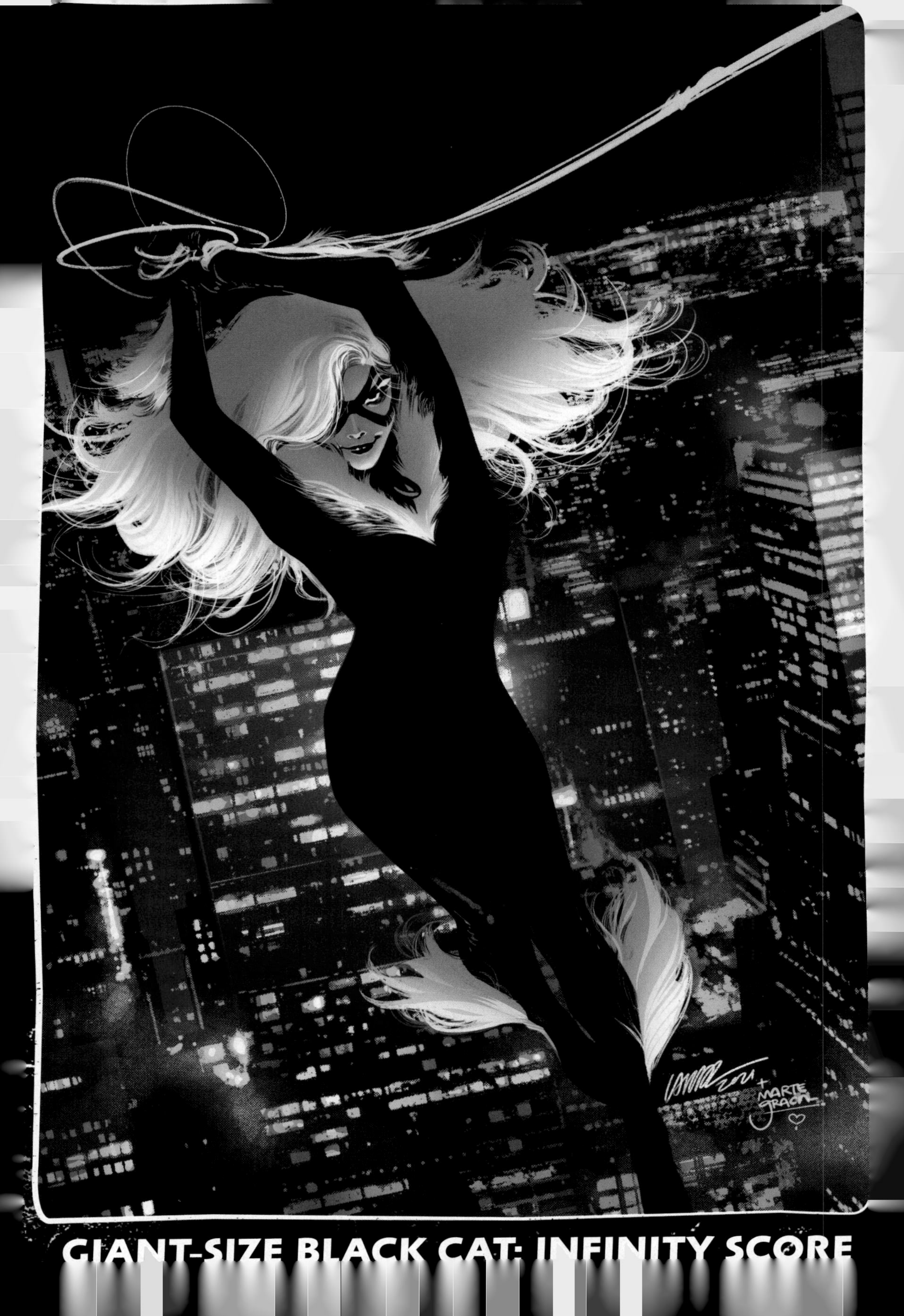

GIANT-SIZE BLACK CAT: INFINITY SCORE

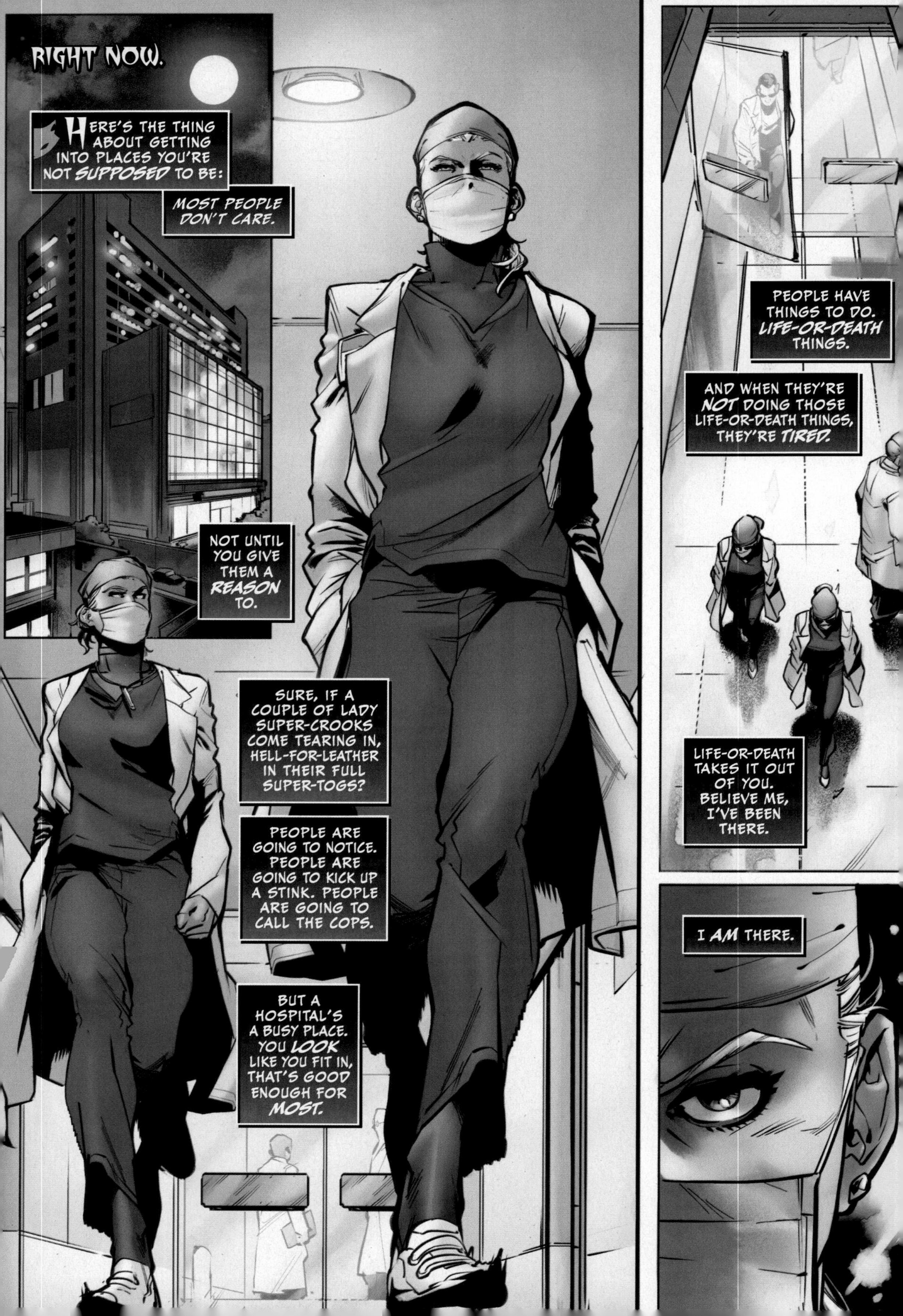
RIGHT NOW.
HERE'S THE THING ABOUT GETTING INTO PLACES YOU'RE NOT SUPPOSED TO BE:
MOST PEOPLE DON'T CARE.
NOT UNTIL YOU GIVE THEM A REASON TO.
SURE, IF A COUPLE OF LADY SUPER-CROOKS COME TEARING IN, HELL-FOR-LEATHER IN THEIR FULL SUPER-TOGS?
PEOPLE ARE GOING TO NOTICE. PEOPLE ARE GOING TO KICK UP A STINK. PEOPLE ARE GOING TO CALL THE COPS.
BUT A HOSPITAL'S A BUSY PLACE. YOU LOOK LIKE YOU FIT IN, THAT'S GOOD ENOUGH FOR MOST.
PEOPLE HAVE THINGS TO DO. LIFE-OR-DEATH THINGS.
AND WHEN THEY'RE NOT DOING THOSE LIFE-OR-DEATH THINGS, THEY'RE TIRED.
LIFE-OR-DEATH TAKES IT OUT OF YOU. BELIEVE ME, I'VE BEEN THERE.
I AM THERE.

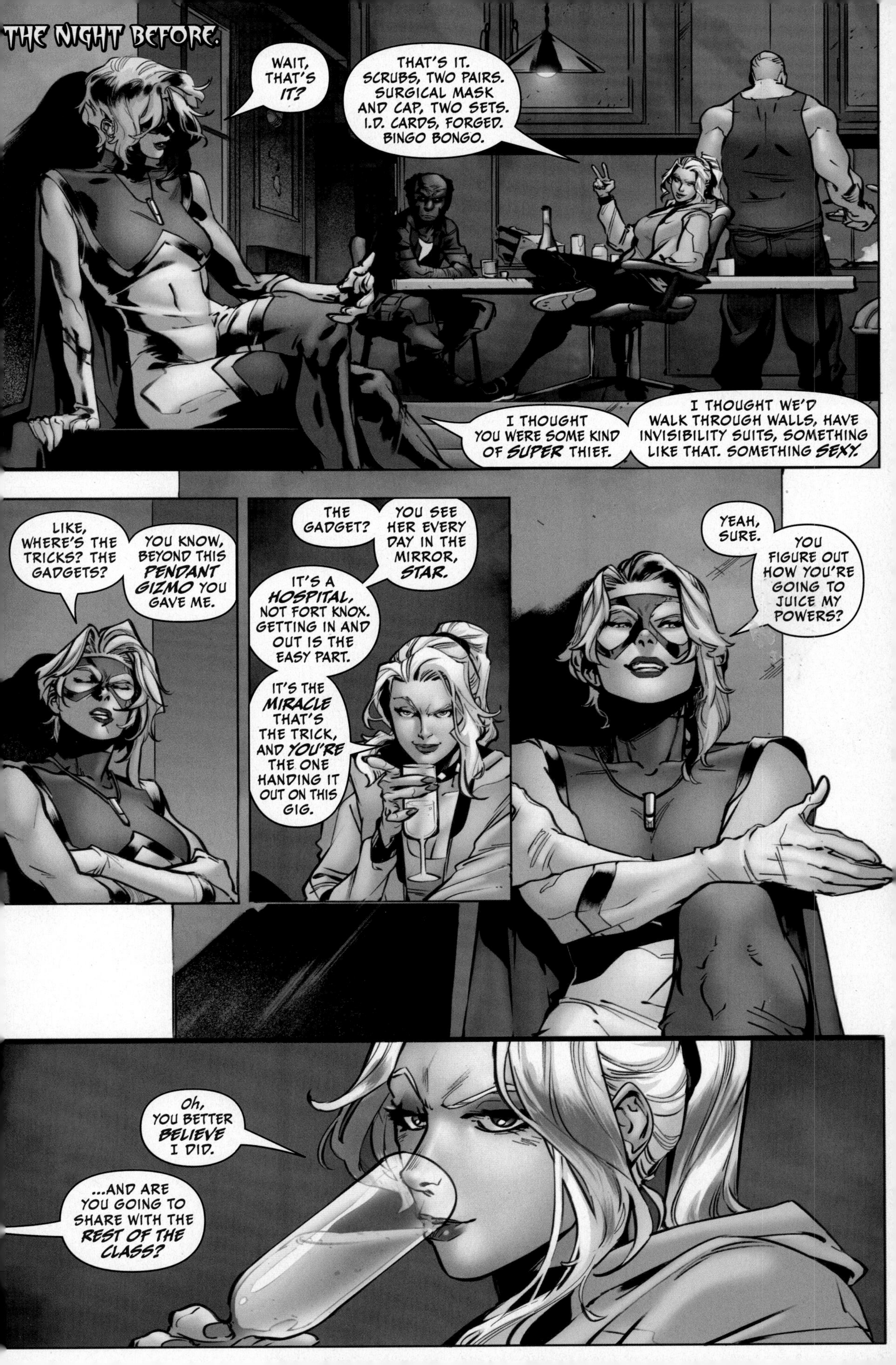
THE NIGHT BEFORE.
WAIT, THAT'S IT?
THAT'S IT. SCRUBS, TWO PAIRS. SURGICAL MASK AND CAP, TWO SETS. I.D. CARDS, FORGED. BINGO BONGO.
I THOUGHT YOU WERE SOME KIND OF SUPER THIEF.
I THOUGHT WE'D WALK THROUGH WALLS, HAVE INVISIBILITY SUITS, SOMETHING LIKE THAT. SOMETHING SEXY.
LIKE, WHERE'S THE TRICKS? THE GADGETS?
YOU KNOW, BEYOND THIS PENDANT GIZMO YOU GAVE ME.
THE GADGET?
YOU SEE HER EVERY DAY IN THE MIRROR, STAR.
IT'S A HOSPITAL, NOT FORT KNOX. GETTING IN AND OUT IS THE EASY PART.
IT'S THE MIRACLE THAT'S THE TRICK, AND YOU'RE THE ONE HANDING IT OUT ON THIS GIG.
YEAH, SURE.
YOU FIGURE OUT HOW YOU'RE GOING TO JUICE MY POWERS?
Oh, YOU BETTER BELIEVE I DID.
...AND ARE YOU GOING TO SHARE WITH THE REST OF THE CLASS?

SHE *KNOWS.*

I DON'T KNOW *HOW* SHE KNOWS, BUT SHE KNOWS.

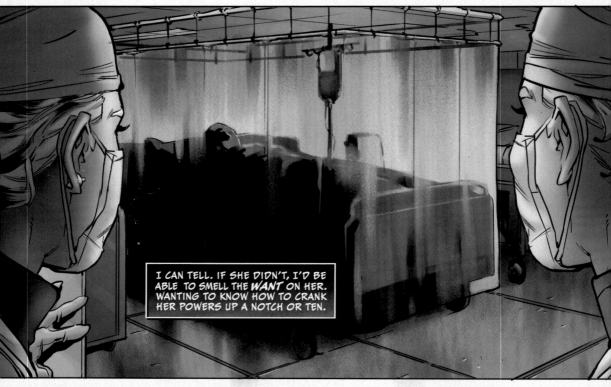

I CAN TELL. IF SHE DIDN'T, I'D BE ABLE TO SMELL THE *WANT* ON HER. WANTING TO KNOW HOW TO CRANK HER POWERS UP A NOTCH OR TEN.

I'M GOOD AT THAT. KNOWING WHAT PEOPLE WANT.

THERE WAS *NOTHING* OF WANTING IN HER QUESTION.

IT WAS JUST FOR *SHOW.*

WHICH MEANS I'M IN *TROUBLE.*

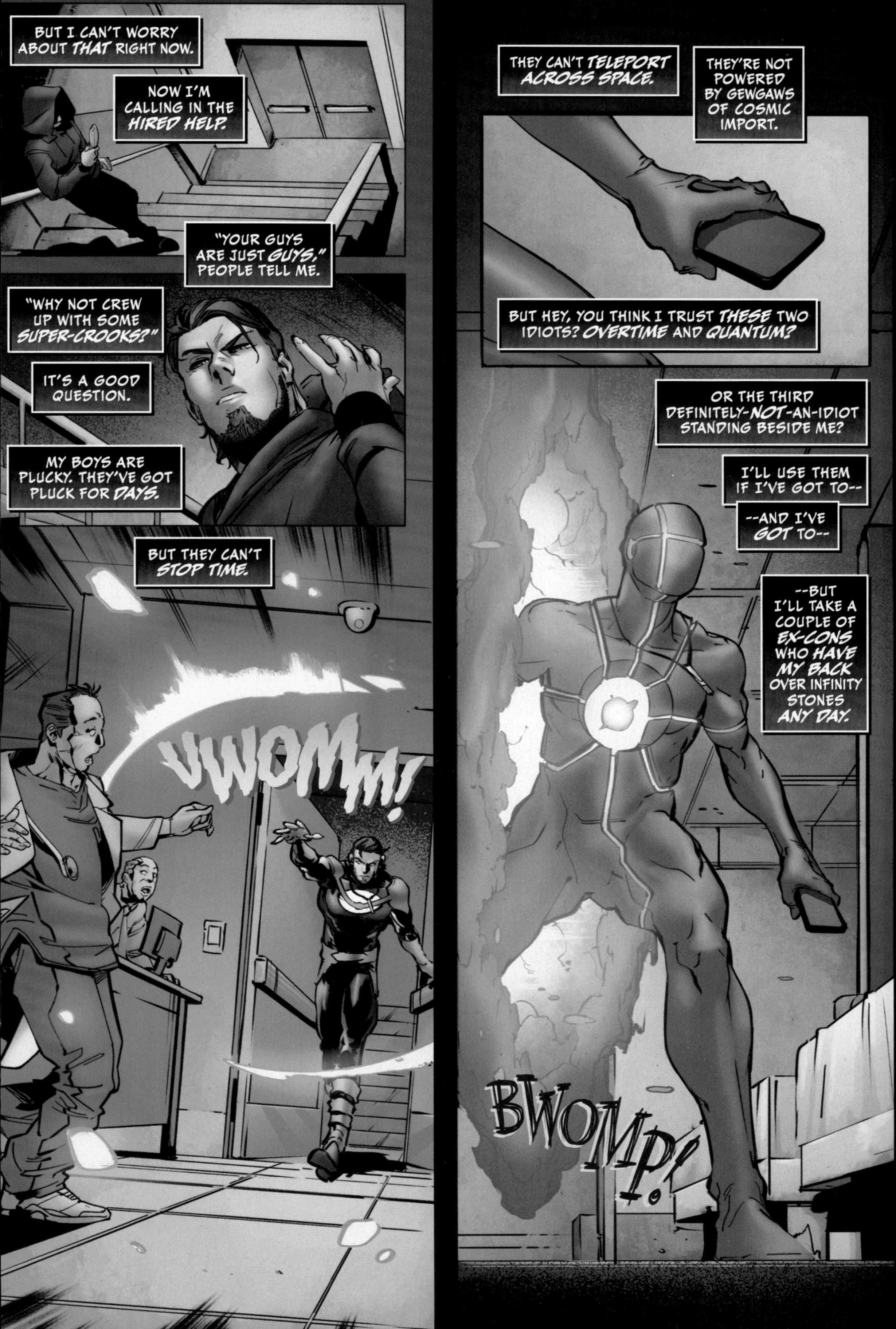
BUT I CAN'T WORRY ABOUT THAT RIGHT NOW.
NOW I'M CALLING IN THE HIRED HELP.
"YOUR GUYS ARE JUST GUYS," PEOPLE TELL ME.
"WHY NOT CREW UP WITH SOME SUPER-CROOKS?"
IT'S A GOOD QUESTION.
MY BOYS ARE PLUCKY. THEY'VE GOT PLUCK FOR DAYS.
BUT THEY CAN'T STOP TIME.
VWOMM!
THEY CAN'T TELEPORT ACROSS SPACE.
THEY'RE NOT POWERED BY GEWGAWS OF COSMIC IMPORT.
BUT HEY, YOU THINK I TRUST THESE TWO IDIOTS? OVERTIME AND QUANTUM?
OR THE THIRD DEFINITELY-NOT-AN-IDIOT STANDING BESIDE ME?
I'LL USE THEM IF I'VE GOT TO--
--AND I'VE GOT TO--
--BUT I'LL TAKE A COUPLE OF EX-CONS WHO HAVE MY BACK OVER INFINITY STONES ANY DAY.
BWOMP!

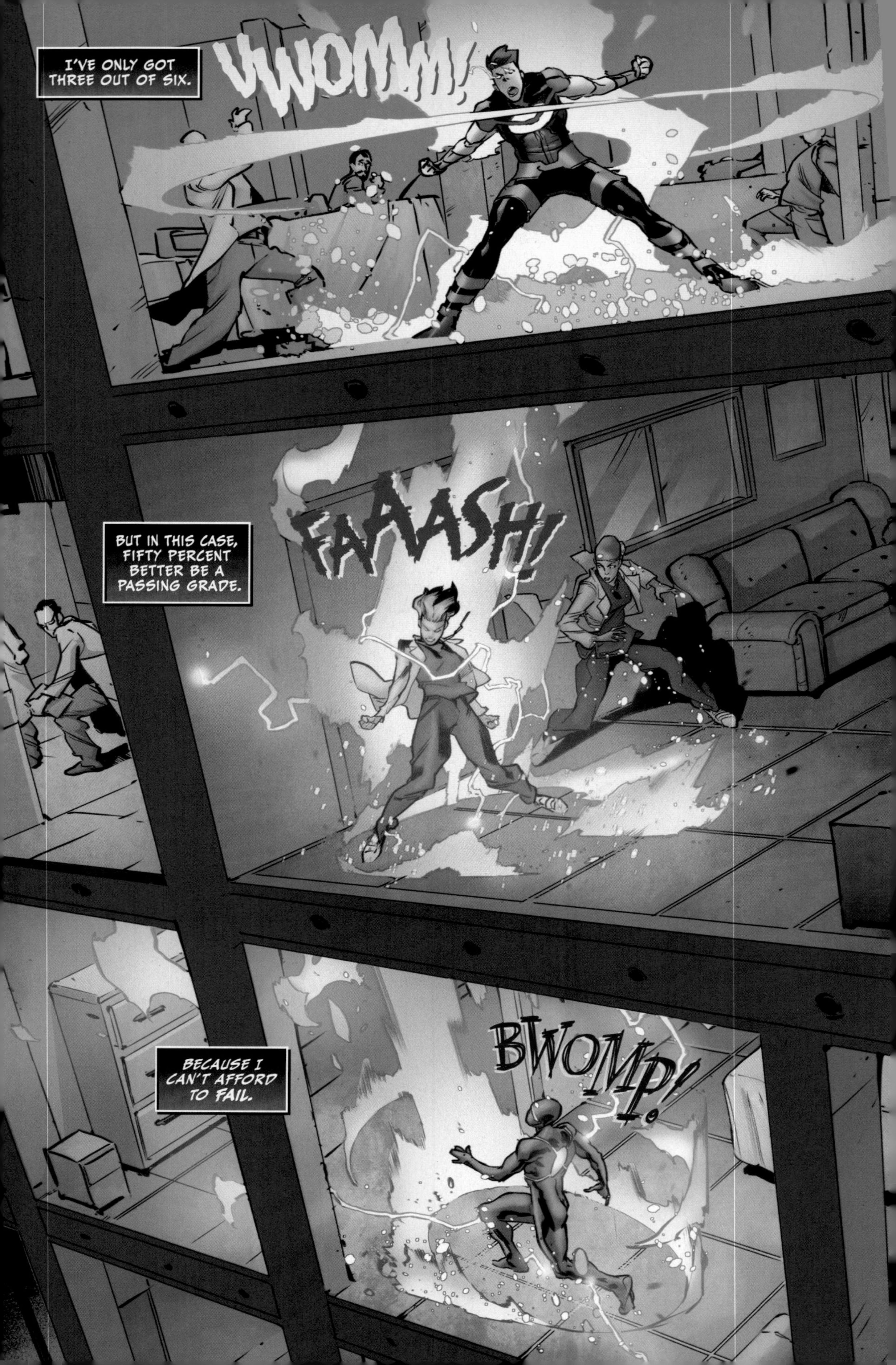

I'VE ONLY GOT THREE OUT OF SIX.
VWOMM!
FAAASH!
BUT IN THIS CASE, FIFTY PERCENT BETTER BE A PASSING GRADE.
BWOMP!
BECAUSE I CAN'T AFFORD TO FAIL.

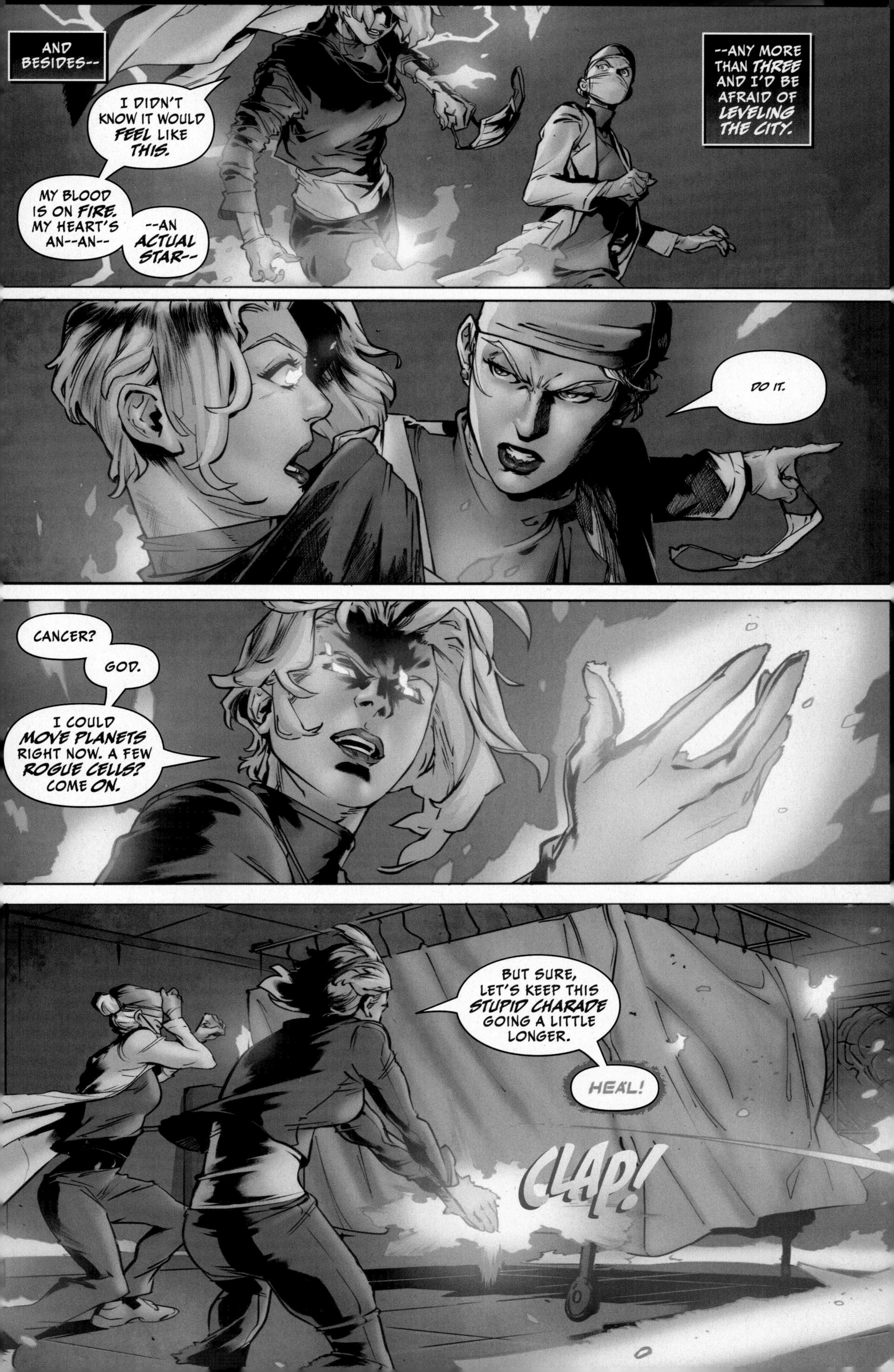
AND BESIDES--
I DIDN'T KNOW IT WOULD FEEL LIKE THIS.
MY BLOOD IS ON FIRE. MY HEART'S AN--AN--
--AN ACTUAL STAR--
--ANY MORE THAN THREE AND I'D BE AFRAID OF LEVELING THE CITY.
DO IT.
CANCER?
GOD.
I COULD MOVE PLANETS RIGHT NOW. A FEW ROGUE CELLS? COME ON.
BUT SURE, LET'S KEEP THIS STUPID CHARADE GOING A LITTLE LONGER.
HEAL!
CLAP!

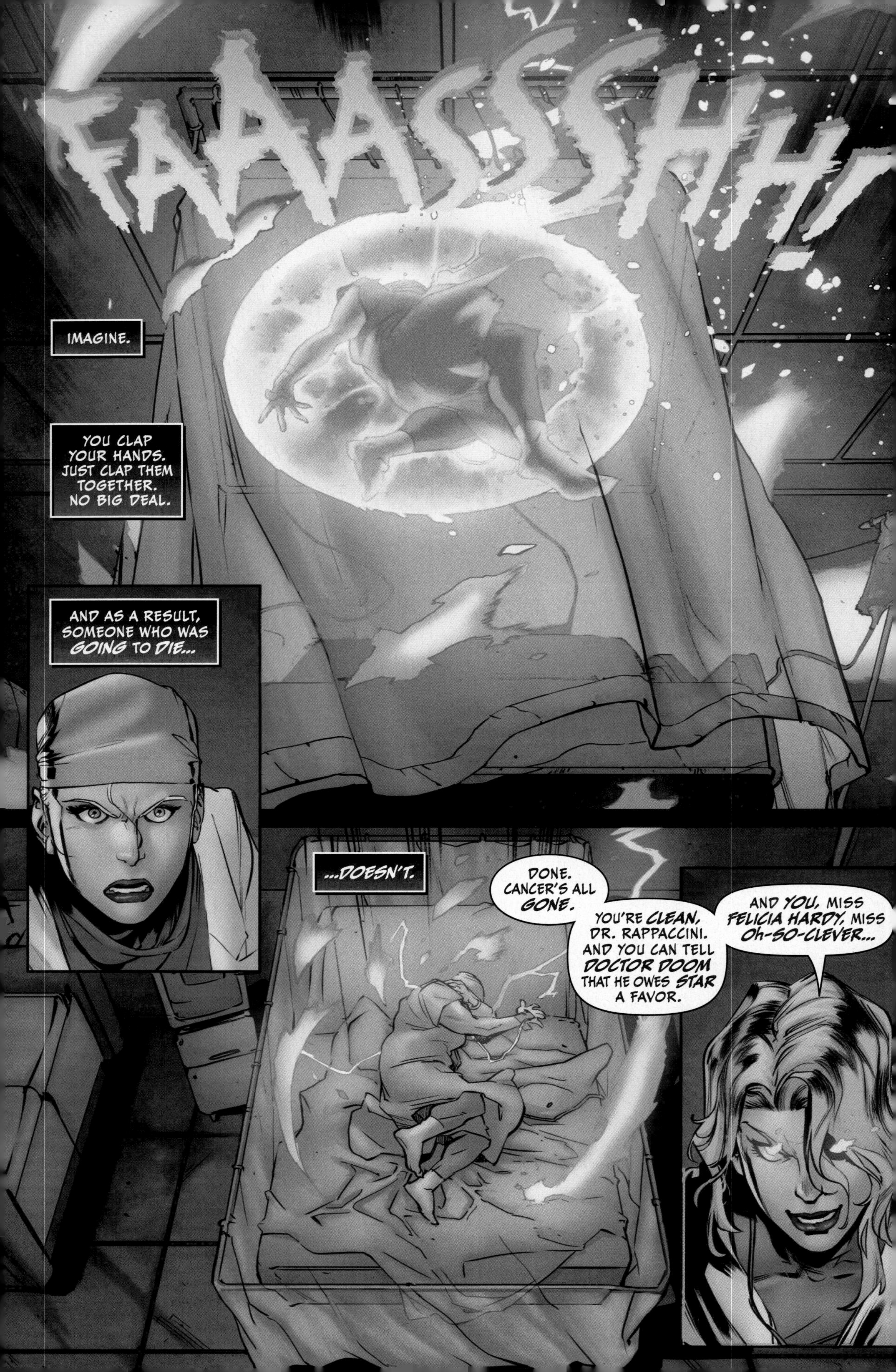
FAAASSSHH!
IMAGINE.
YOU CLAP YOUR HANDS. JUST CLAP THEM TOGETHER. NO BIG DEAL.
AND AS A RESULT, SOMEONE WHO WAS GOING TO DIE...
...DOESN'T.
DONE. CANCER'S ALL GONE.
YOU'RE CLEAN, DR. RAPPACCINI. AND YOU CAN TELL DOCTOR DOOM THAT HE OWES STAR A FAVOR.
AND YOU, MISS FELICIA HARDY, MISS Oh-SO-CLEVER...

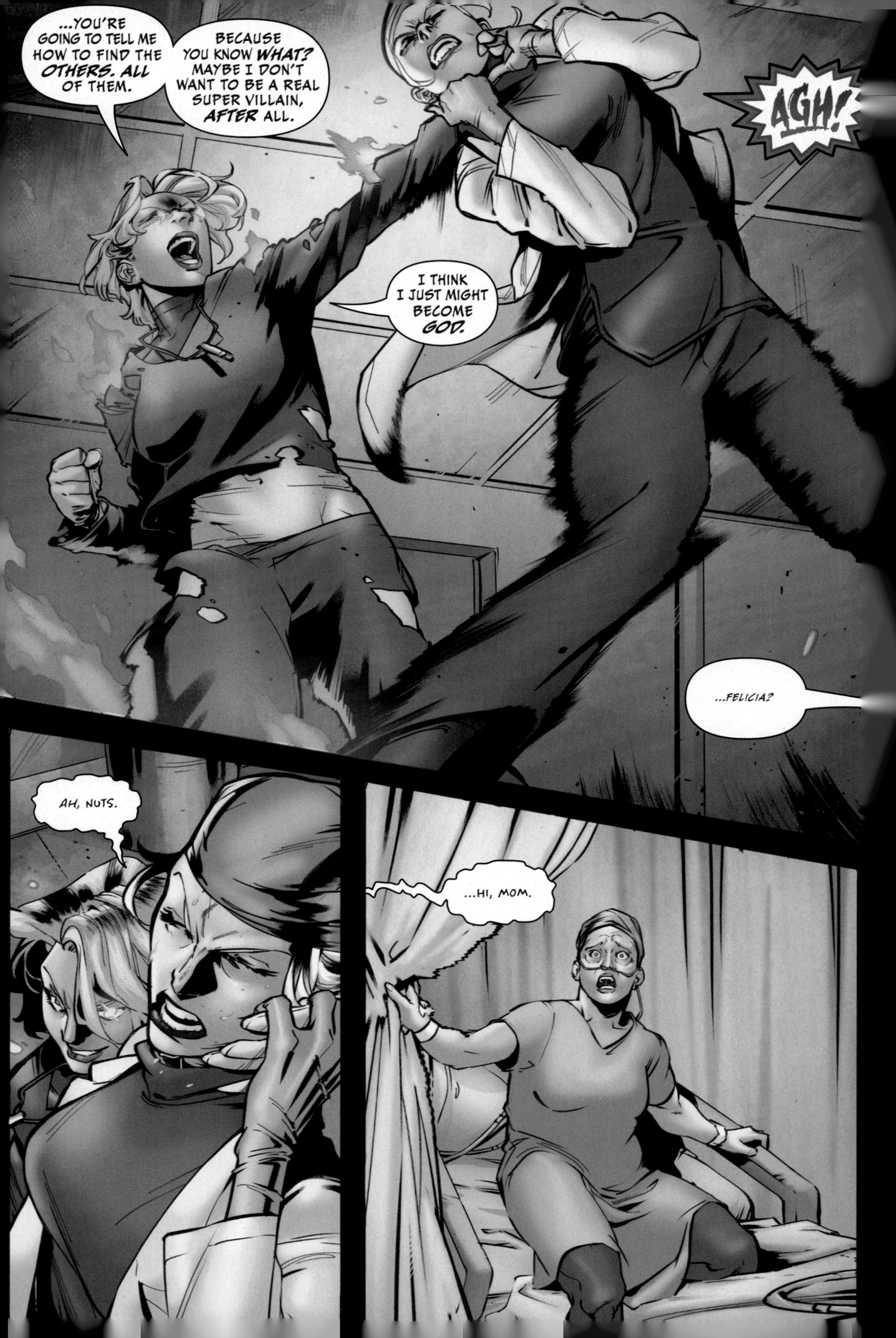
...YOU'RE GOING TO TELL ME HOW TO FIND THE OTHERS. ALL OF THEM.
BECAUSE YOU KNOW WHAT? MAYBE I DON'T WANT TO BE A REAL SUPER VILLAIN, AFTER ALL.
AGH!
I THINK I JUST MIGHT BECOME GOD.
...FELICIA?
AH, NUTS.
...HI, MOM.

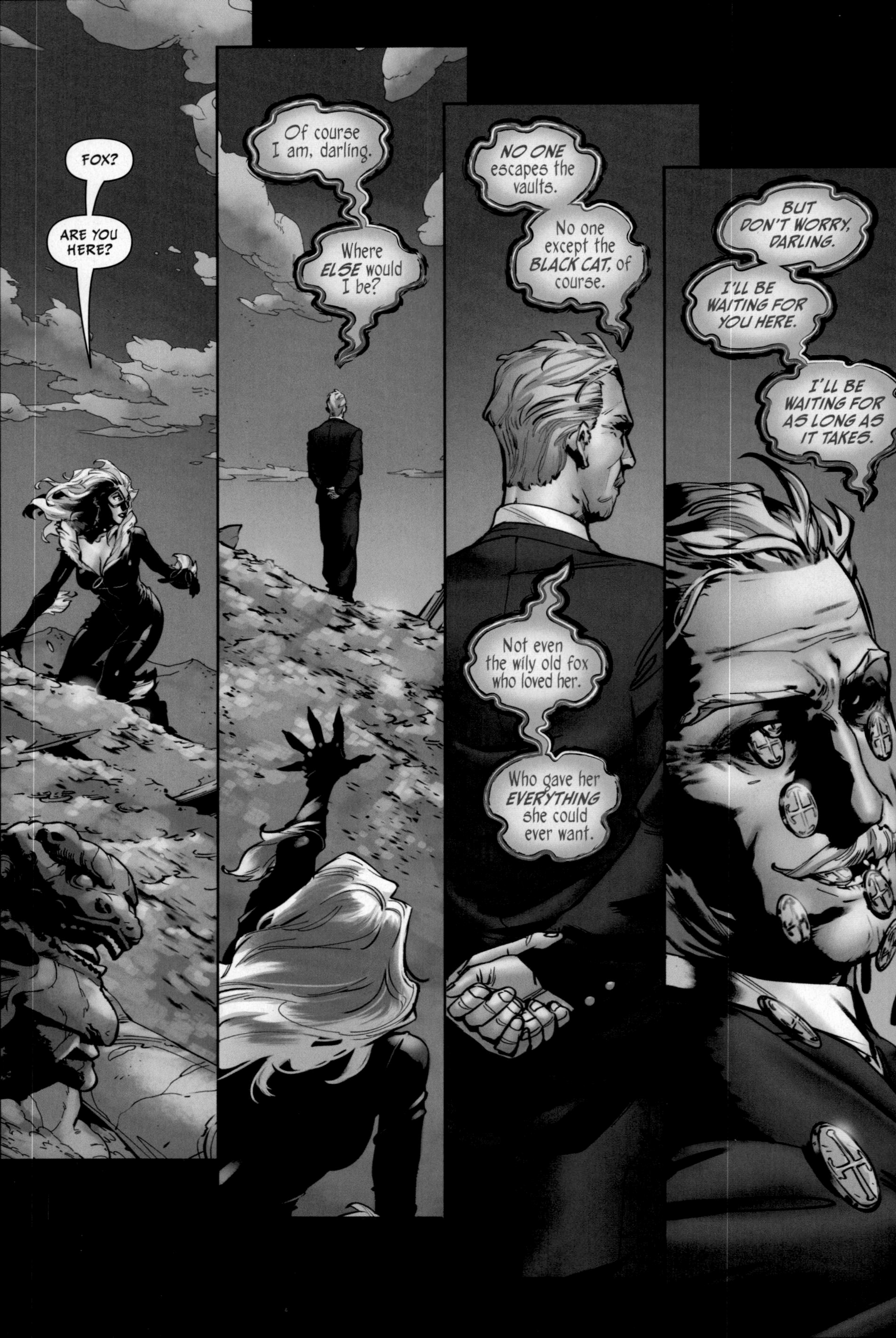

FOX?
ARE YOU HERE?
Of course I am, darling.
Where ELSE would I be?
NO ONE escapes the vaults.
No one except the BLACK CAT, of course.
Not even the wily old fox who loved her.
Who gave her EVERYTHING she could ever want.
BUT DON'T WORRY, DARLING.
I'LL BE WAITING FOR YOU HERE.
I'LL BE WAITING FOR AS LONG AS IT TAKES.

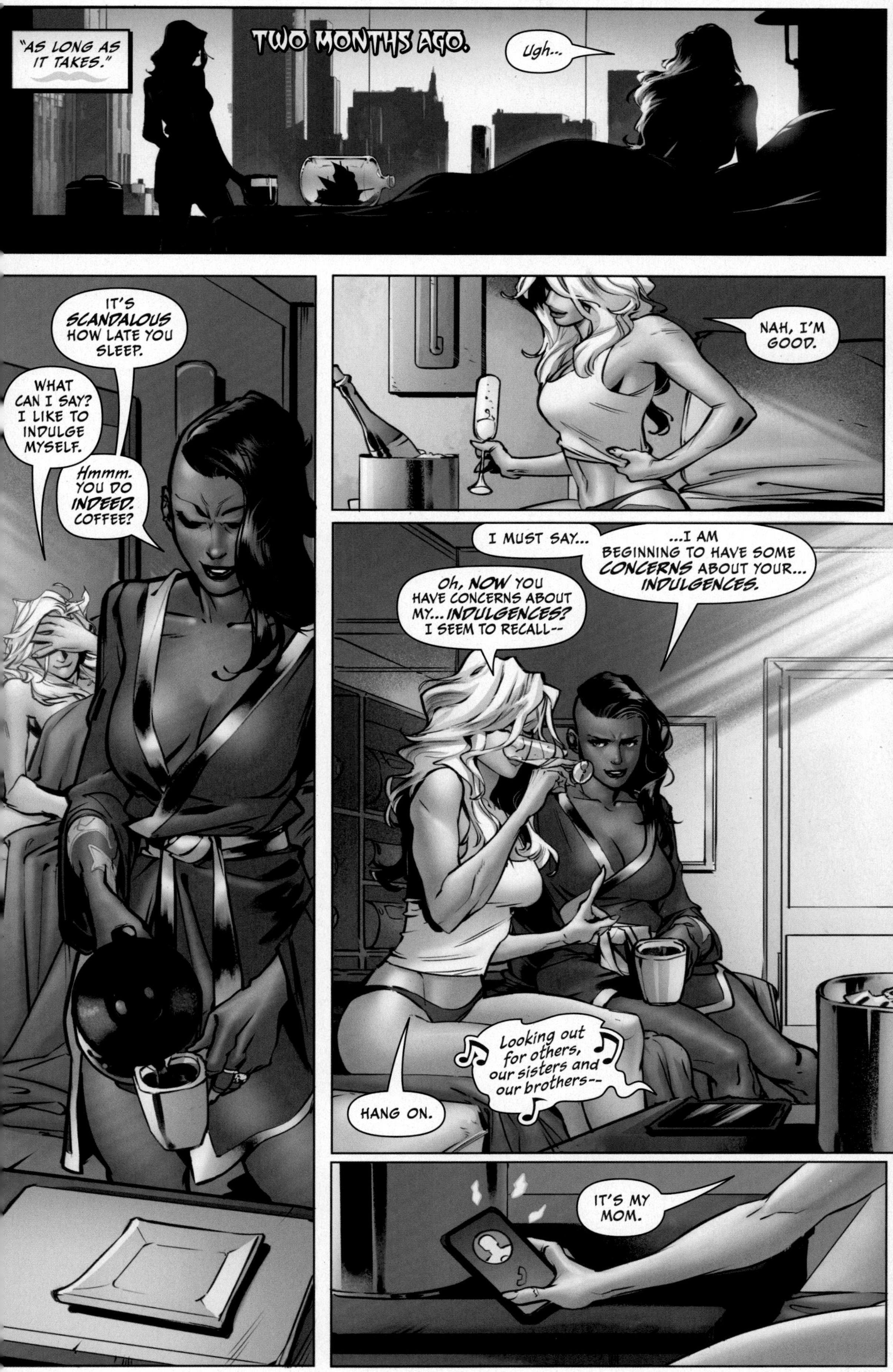
"AS LONG AS IT TAKES."
TWO MONTHS AGO.
Ugh...
IT'S SCANDALOUS HOW LATE YOU SLEEP.
WHAT CAN I SAY? I LIKE TO INDULGE MYSELF.
Hmmm. YOU DO INDEED. COFFEE?
NAH, I'M GOOD.
I MUST SAY...
...I AM BEGINNING TO HAVE SOME CONCERNS ABOUT YOUR... INDULGENCES.
Oh, NOW YOU HAVE CONCERNS ABOUT MY... INDULGENCES? I SEEM TO RECALL--
Looking out for others, our sisters and our brothers--
HANG ON.
IT'S MY MOM.

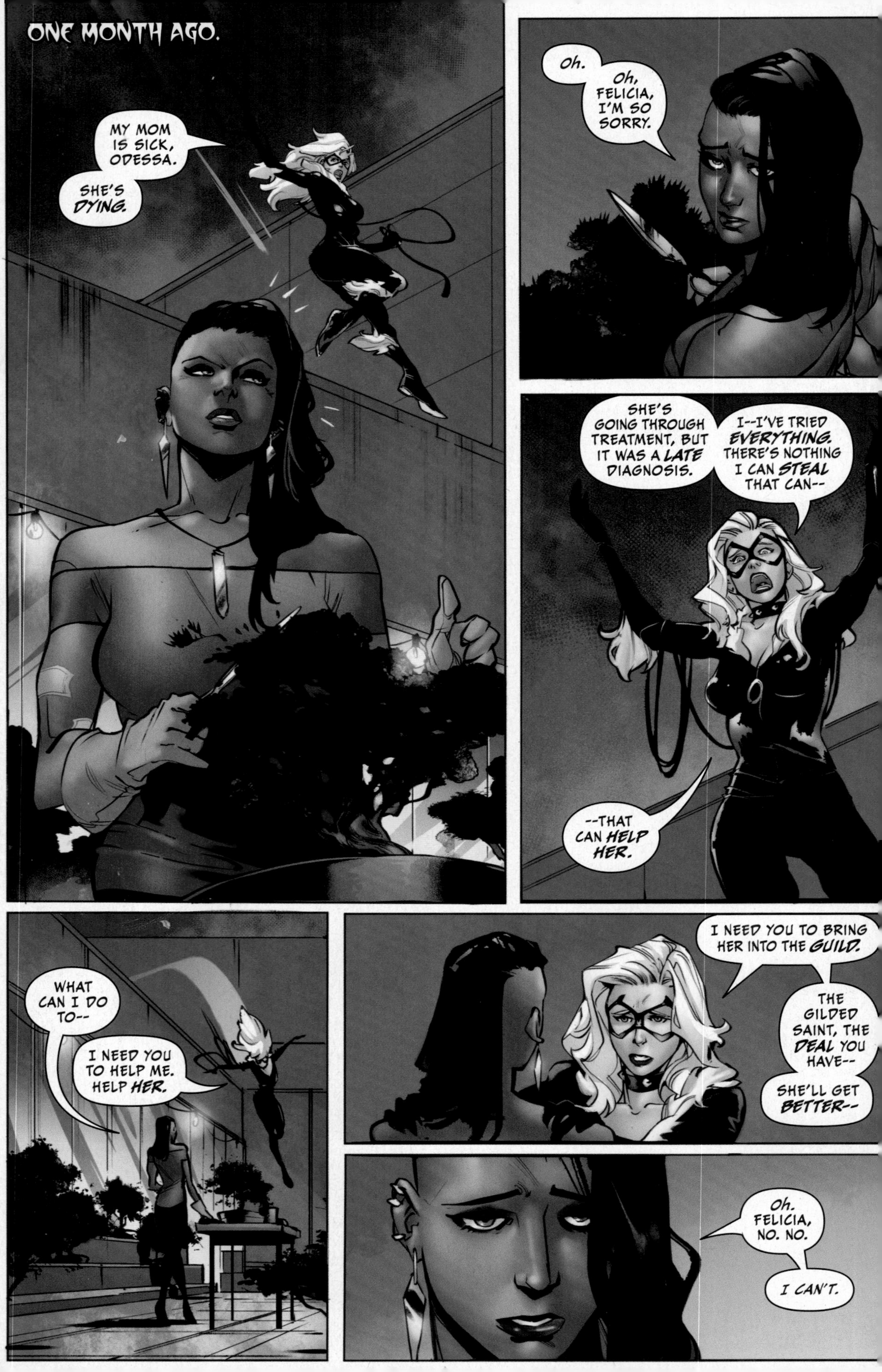
ONE MONTH AGO.
MY MOM IS SICK, ODESSA.
SHE'S DYING.
Oh.
Oh, FELICIA, I'M SO SORRY.
SHE'S GOING THROUGH TREATMENT, BUT IT WAS A LATE DIAGNOSIS.
I--I'VE TRIED EVERYTHING. THERE'S NOTHING I CAN STEAL THAT CAN--
--THAT CAN HELP HER.
WHAT CAN I DO TO--
I NEED YOU TO HELP ME. HELP HER.
I NEED YOU TO BRING HER INTO THE GUILD.
THE GILDED SAINT, THE DEAL YOU HAVE--
SHE'LL GET BETTER--
Oh. FELICIA, NO. NO.
I CAN'T.

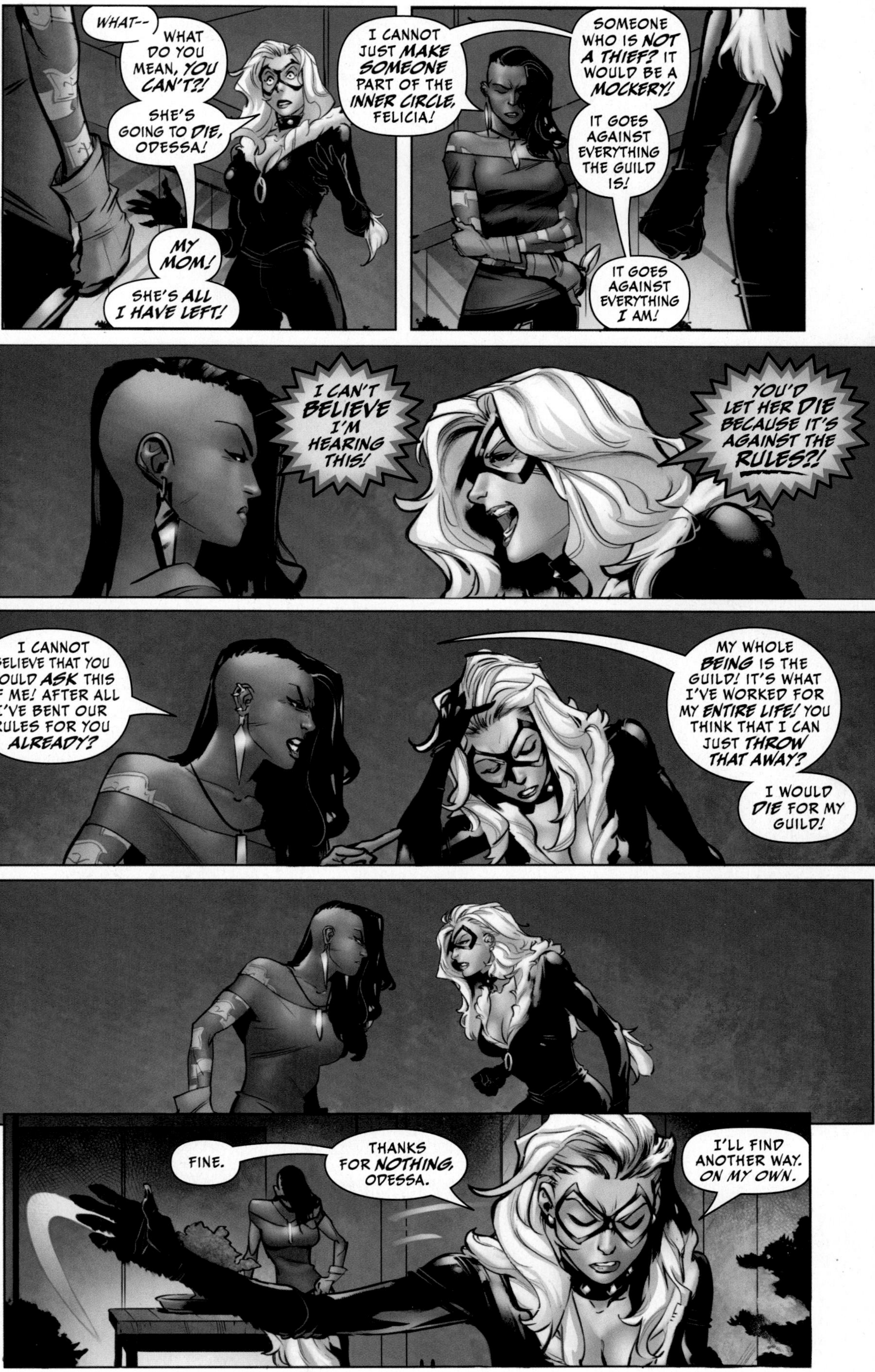
WHAT--
WHAT DO YOU MEAN, YOU CAN'T?!
SHE'S GOING TO DIE, ODESSA!
MY MOM!
SHE'S ALL I HAVE LEFT!
I CANNOT JUST MAKE SOMEONE PART OF THE INNER CIRCLE, FELICIA!
SOMEONE WHO IS NOT A THIEF? IT WOULD BE A MOCKERY!
IT GOES AGAINST EVERYTHING THE GUILD IS!
IT GOES AGAINST EVERYTHING I AM!
I CAN'T BELIEVE I'M HEARING THIS!
YOU'D LET HER DIE BECAUSE IT'S AGAINST THE RULES?!
I CANNOT BELIEVE THAT YOU WOULD ASK THIS OF ME! AFTER ALL I'VE BENT OUR RULES FOR YOU ALREADY?
MY WHOLE BEING IS THE GUILD! IT'S WHAT I'VE WORKED FOR MY ENTIRE LIFE! YOU THINK THAT I CAN JUST THROW THAT AWAY?
I WOULD DIE FOR MY GUILD!
FINE.
THANKS FOR NOTHING, ODESSA.
I'LL FIND ANOTHER WAY. ON MY OWN.

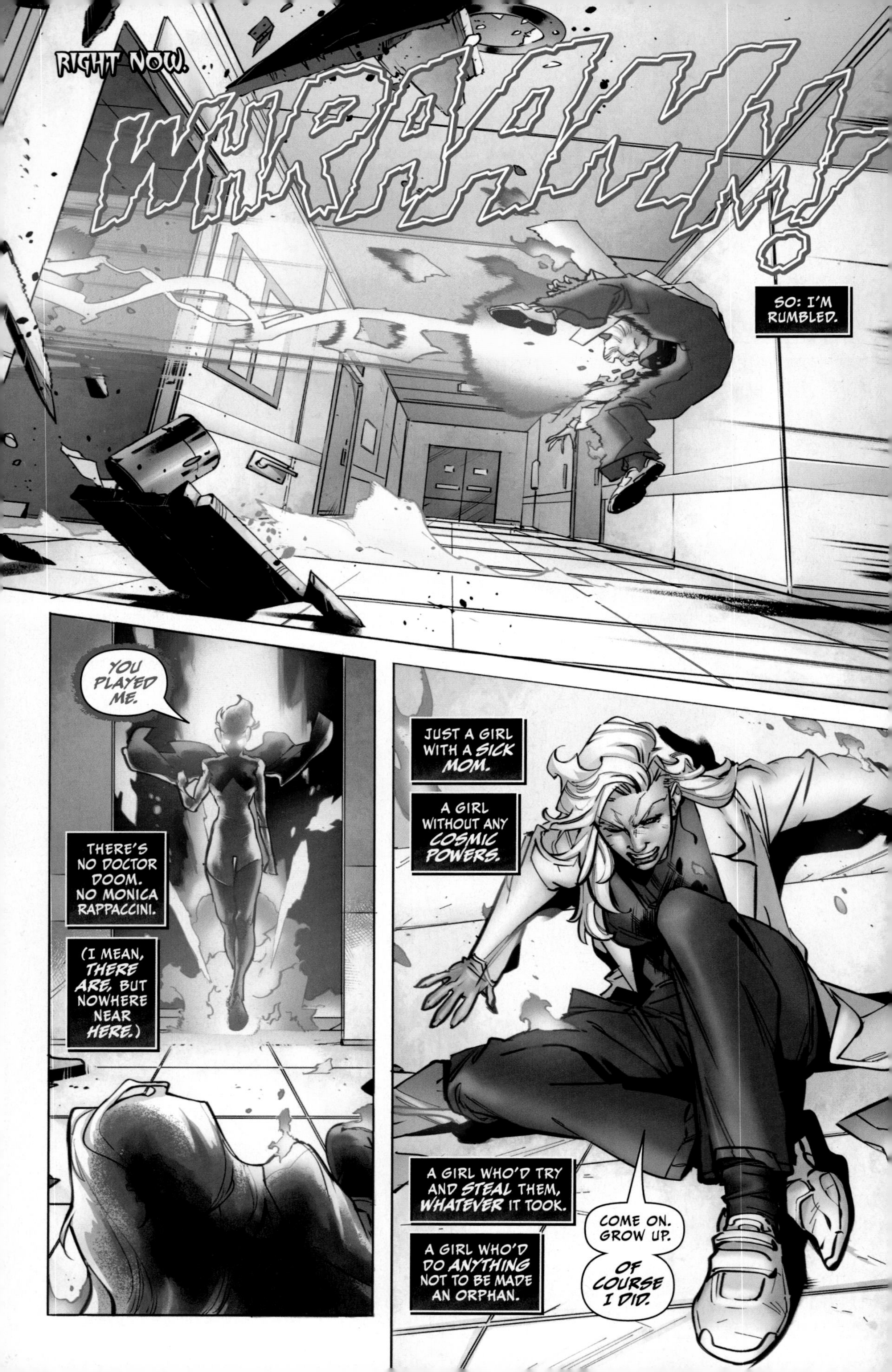

RIGHT NOW.
WHRAAAAM!
SO: I'M RUMBLED.
YOU PLAYED ME.
THERE'S NO DOCTOR DOOM. NO MONICA RAPPACCINI.
(I MEAN, THERE ARE, BUT NOWHERE NEAR HERE.)
JUST A GIRL WITH A SICK MOM.
A GIRL WITHOUT ANY COSMIC POWERS.
A GIRL WHO'D TRY AND STEAL THEM, WHATEVER IT TOOK.
A GIRL WHO'D DO ANYTHING NOT TO BE MADE AN ORPHAN.
COME ON. GROW UP.
OF COURSE I DID.

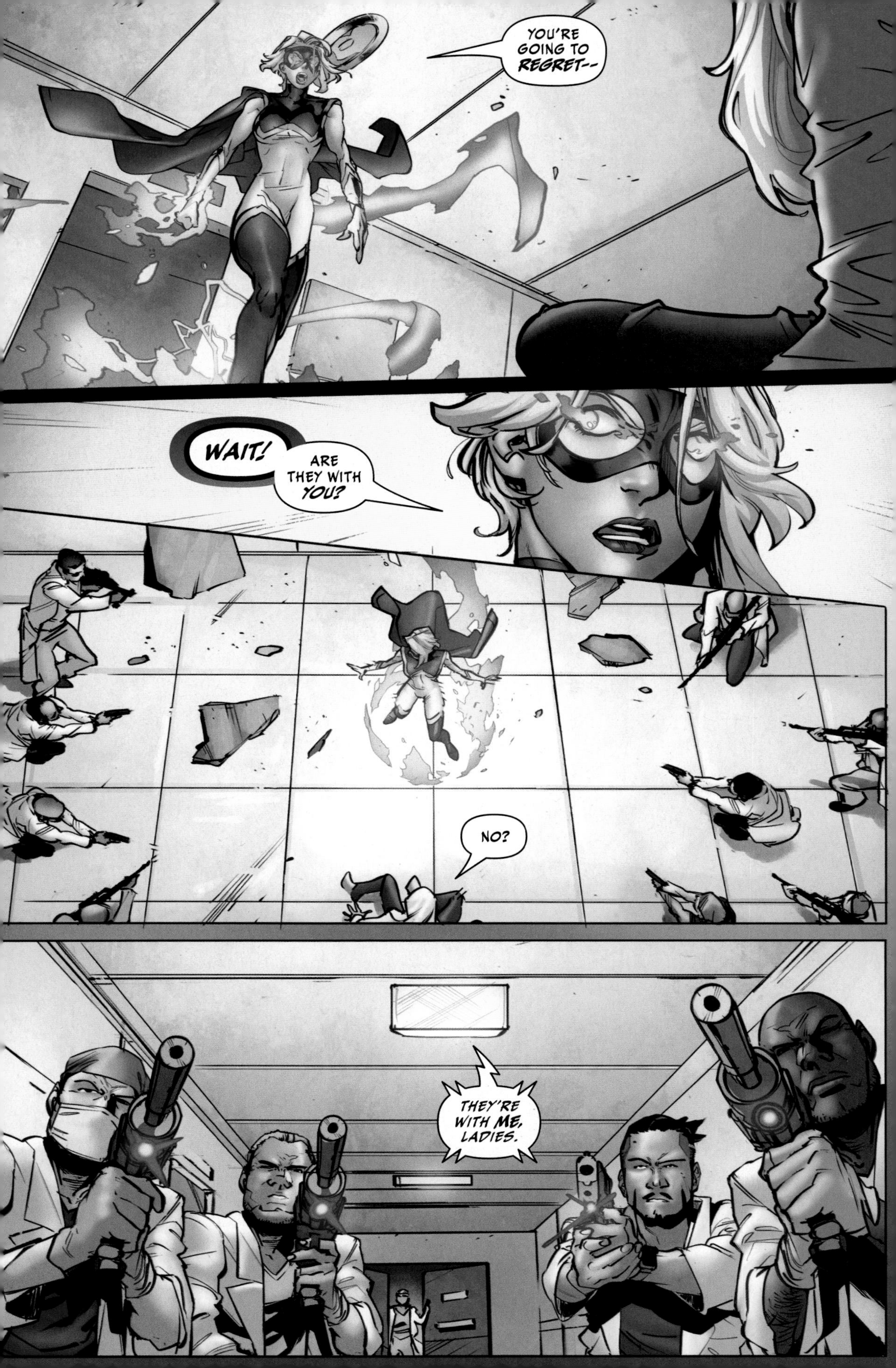

YOU'RE GOING TO REGRET--
WAIT!
ARE THEY WITH YOU?
NO?
THEY'RE WITH ME, LADIES.

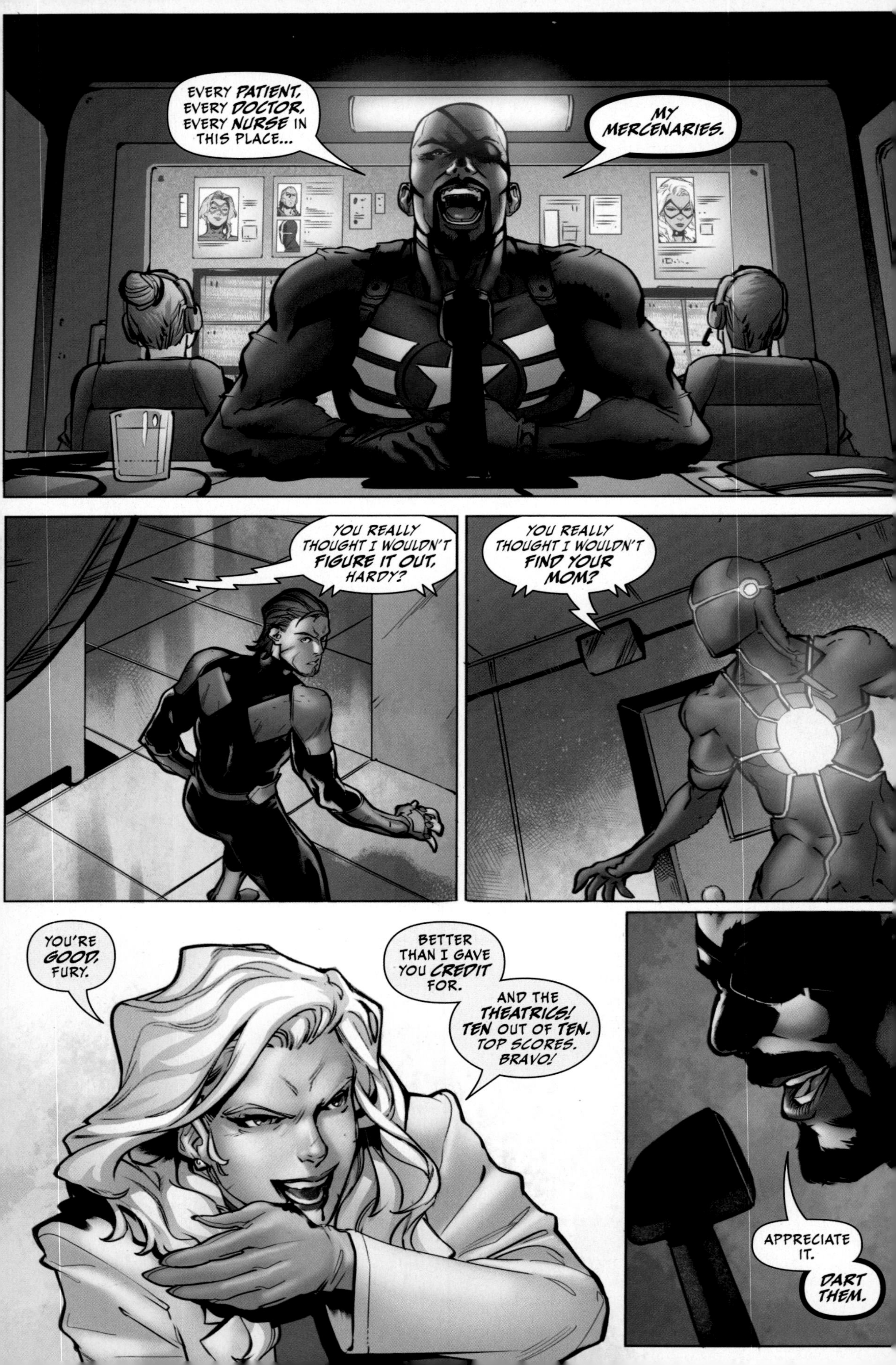
EVERY PATIENT, EVERY DOCTOR, EVERY NURSE IN THIS PLACE...
MY MERCENARIES.
YOU REALLY THOUGHT I WOULDN'T FIGURE IT OUT, HARDY?
YOU REALLY THOUGHT I WOULDN'T FIND YOUR MOM?
YOU'RE GOOD, FURY.
BETTER THAN I GAVE YOU CREDIT FOR.
AND THE THEATRICS! TEN OUT OF TEN. TOP SCORES. BRAVO!
APPRECIATE IT.
DART THEM.

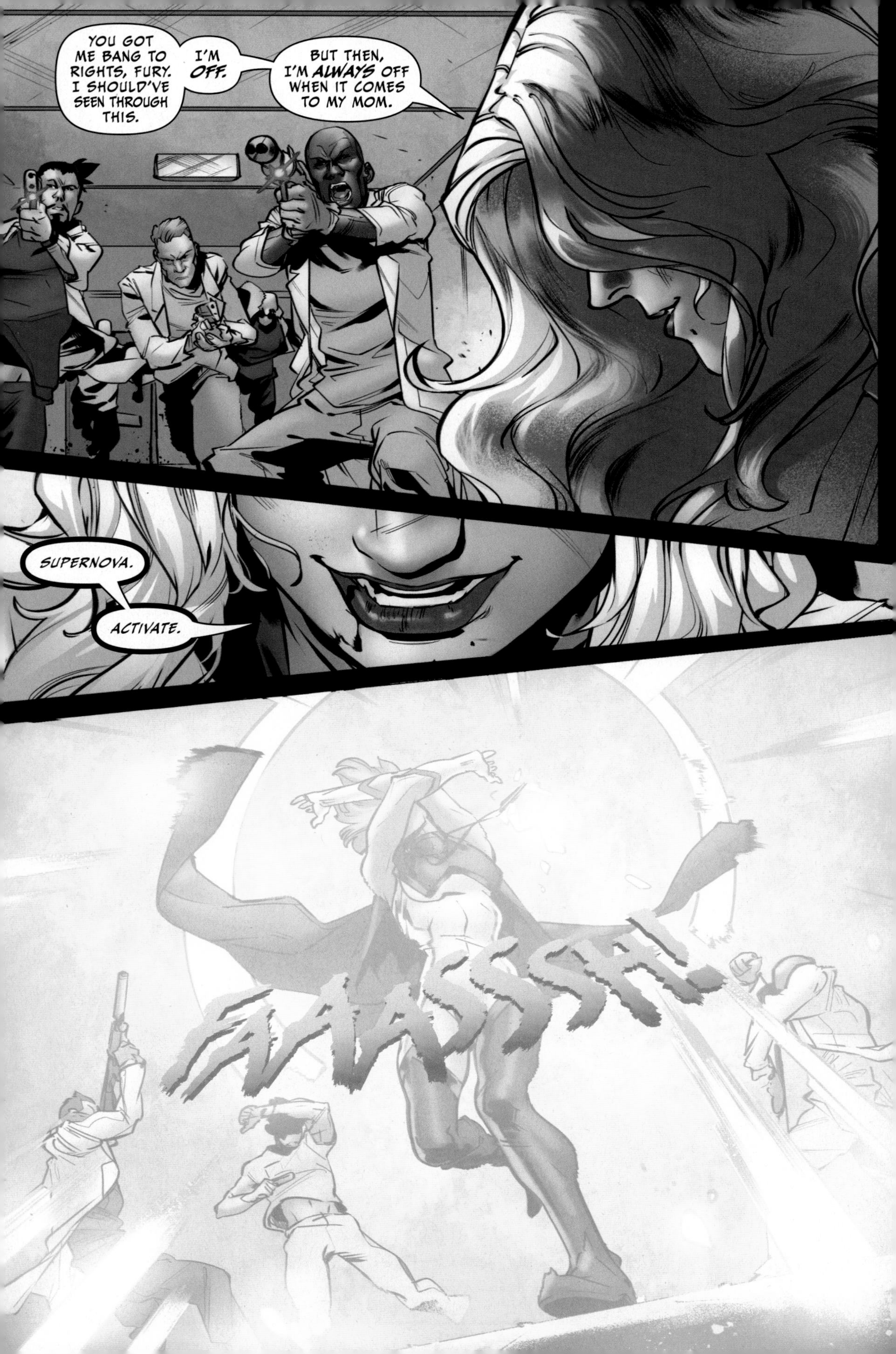
YOU GOT ME BANG TO RIGHTS, FURY. I SHOULD'VE SEEN THROUGH THIS.
I'M OFF.
BUT THEN, I'M ALWAYS OFF WHEN IT COMES TO MY MOM.
SUPERNOVA.
ACTIVATE.
FAASSSH!

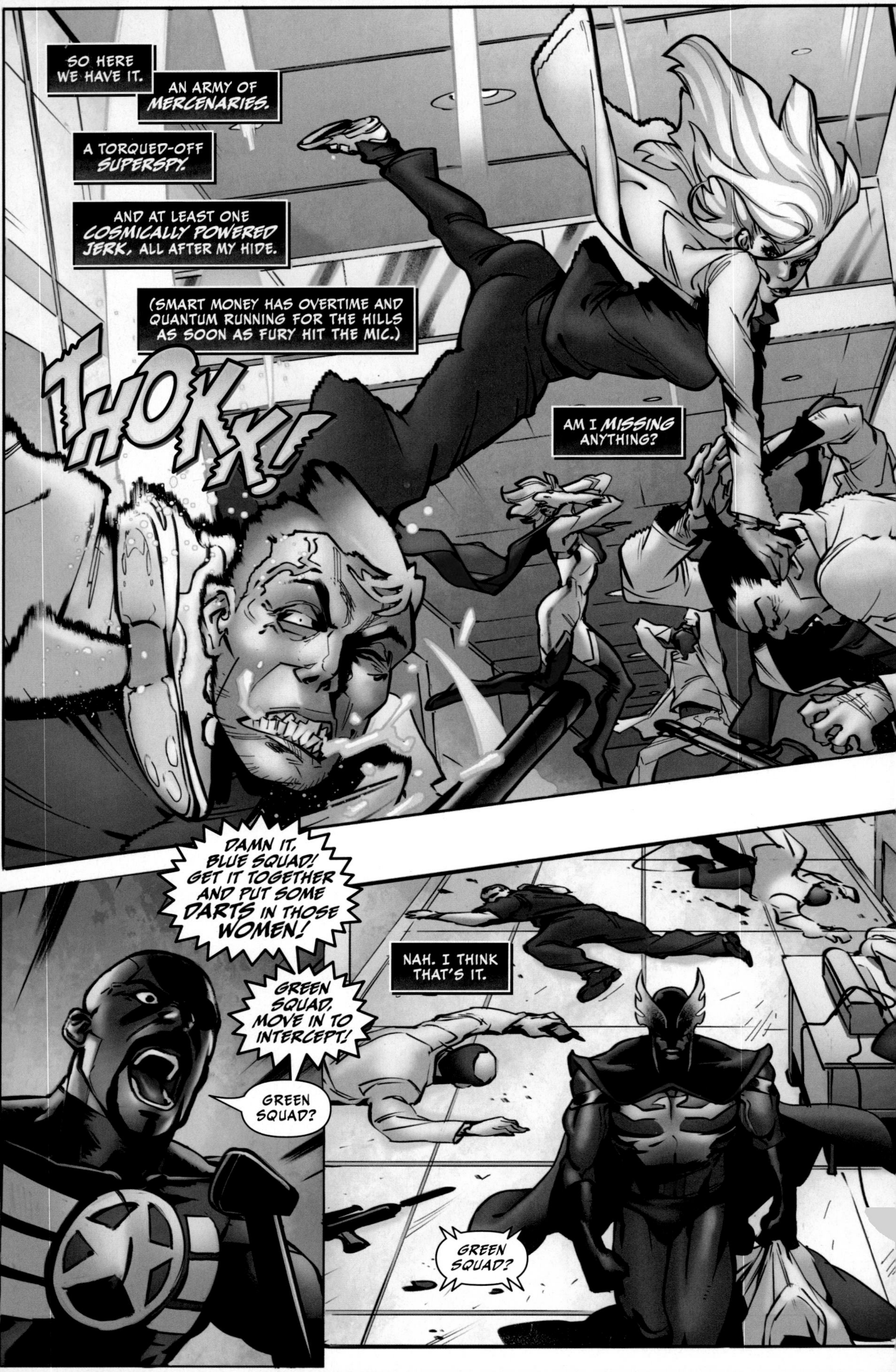
SO HERE WE HAVE IT.
AN ARMY OF MERCENARIES.
A TORQUED-OFF SUPERSPY.
AND AT LEAST ONE COSMICALLY POWERED JERK, ALL AFTER MY HIDE.
(SMART MONEY HAS OVERTIME AND QUANTUM RUNNING FOR THE HILLS AS SOON AS FURY HIT THE MIC.)
THOKK!
AM I MISSING ANYTHING?
DAMN IT, BLUE SQUAD! GET IT TOGETHER AND PUT SOME DARTS IN THOSE WOMEN!
NAH. I THINK THAT'S IT.
GREEN SQUAD, MOVE IN TO INTERCEPT!
GREEN SQUAD?
GREEN SQUAD?

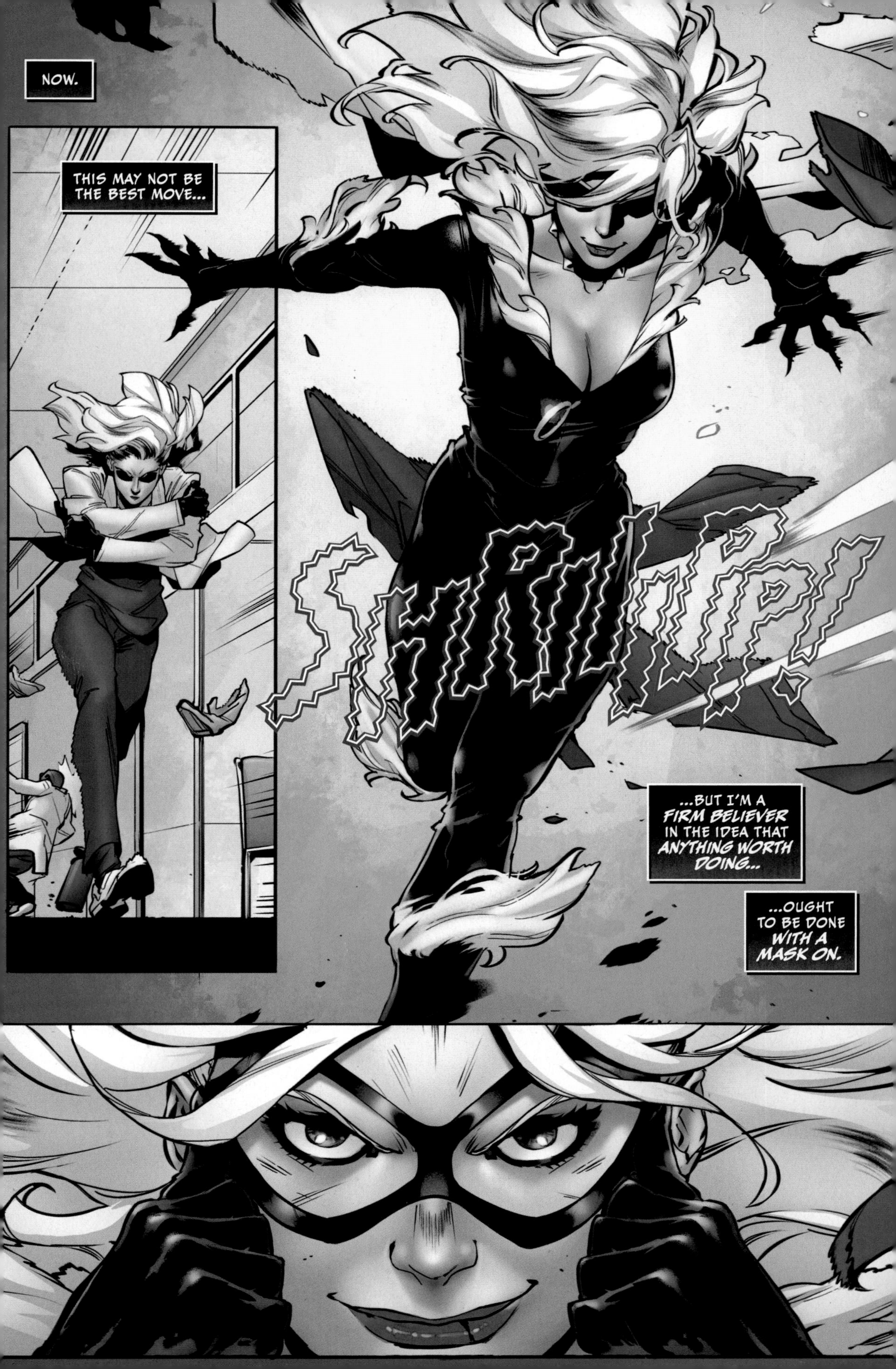

NOW.
THIS MAY NOT BE THE BEST MOVE...
SHRUNP!
...BUT I'M A FIRM BELIEVER IN THE IDEA THAT ANYTHING WORTH DOING...
...OUGHT TO BE DONE WITH A MASK ON.

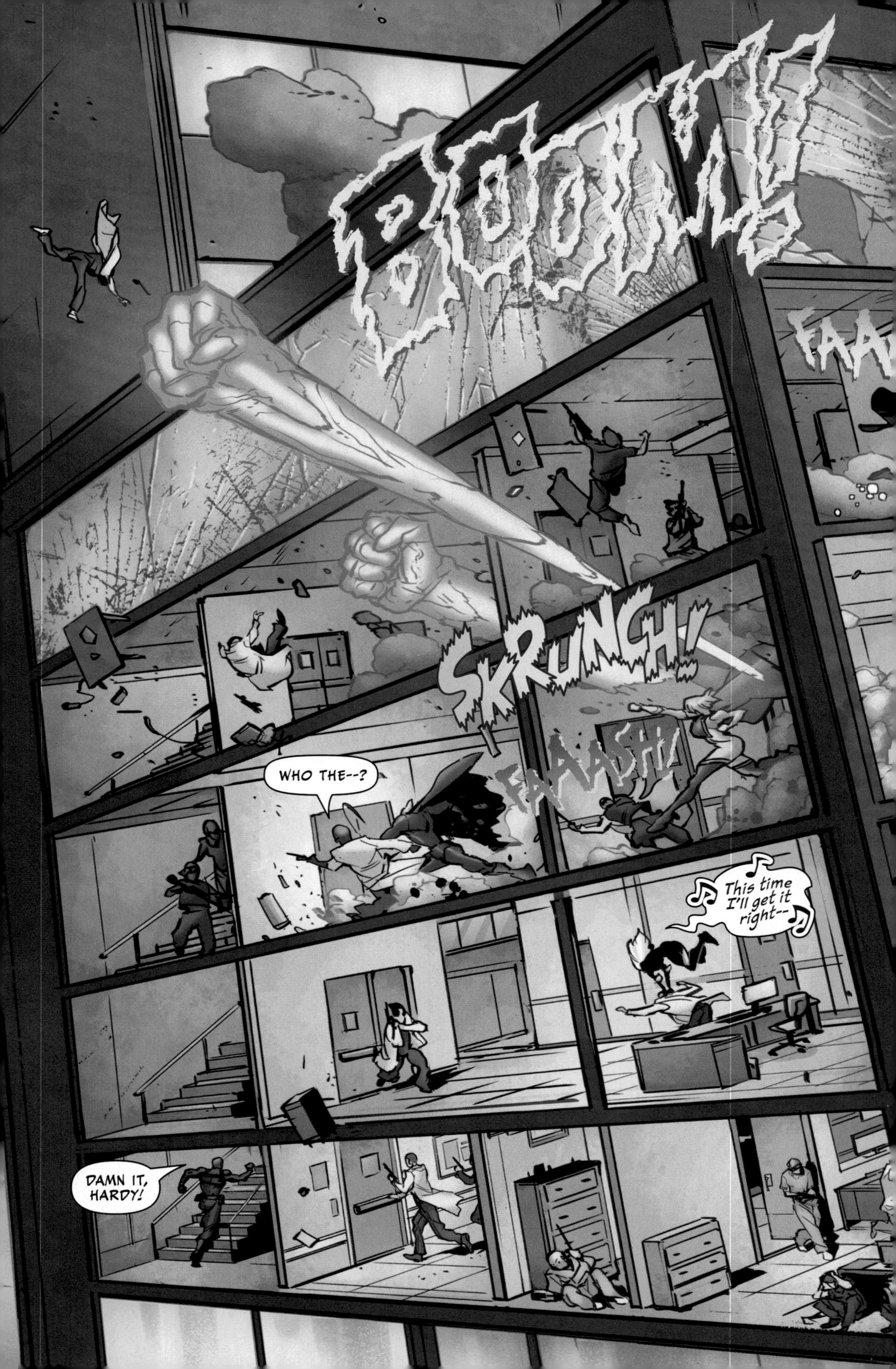
SKRUNCH!
FAAASH!
WHO THE--?
This time I'll get it right--
DAMN IT, HARDY!

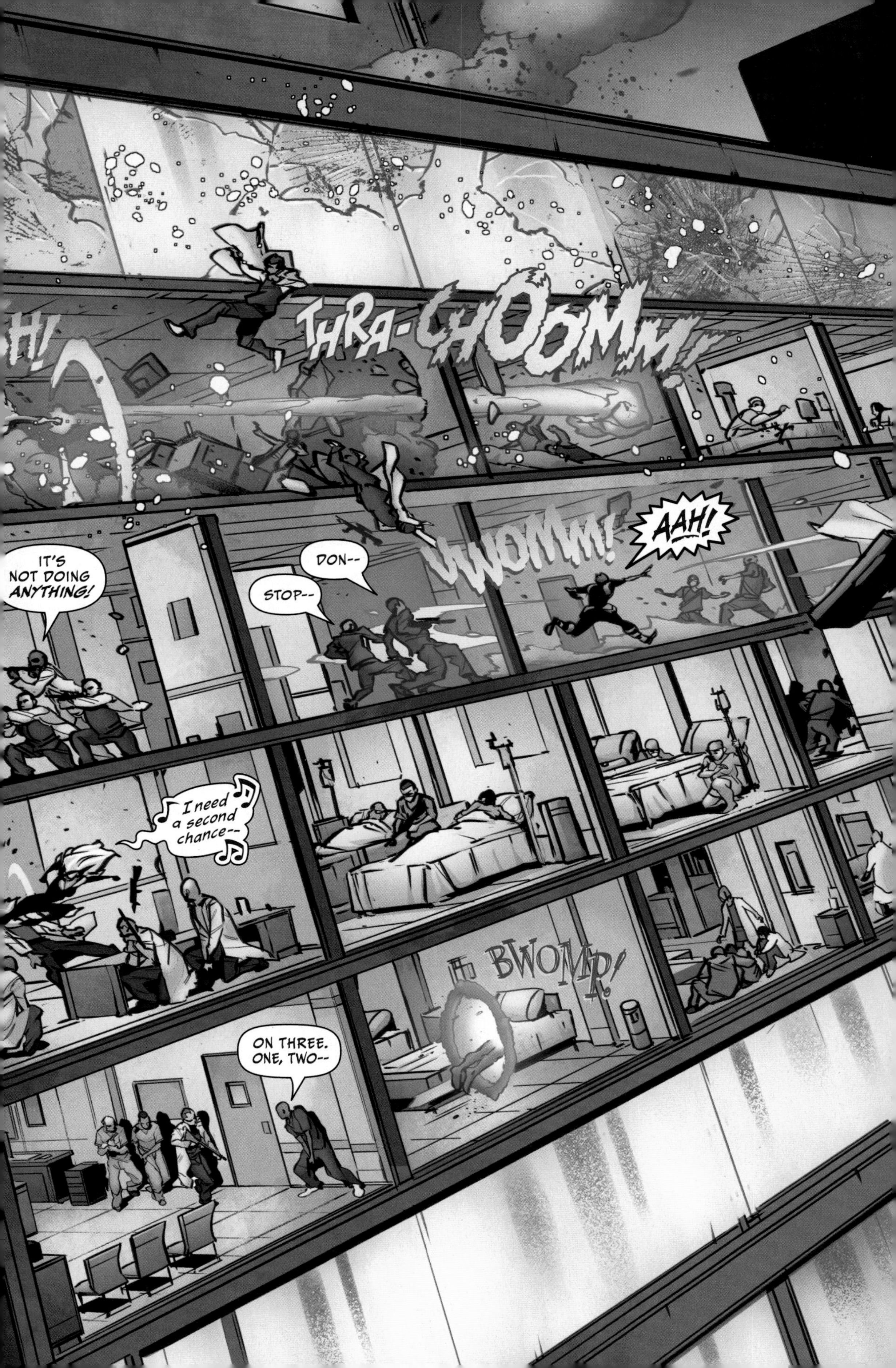

THRA-CHOOMM!
IT'S NOT DOING ANYTHING!
DON--
STOP--
WOMM!
AAH!
I need a second chance--
BWOMP!
ON THREE. ONE, TWO--

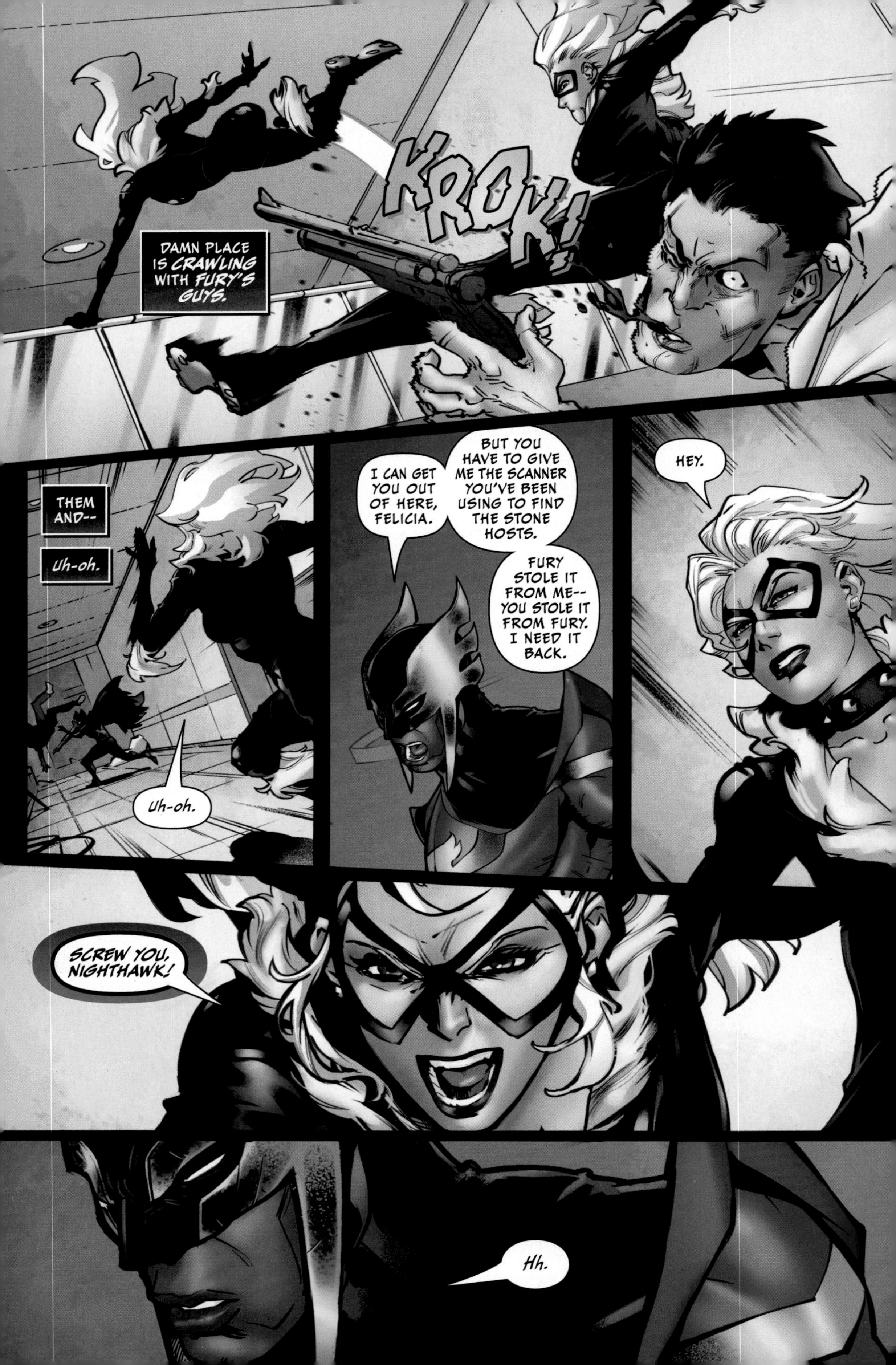
KROK!
DAMN PLACE IS CRAWLING WITH FURY'S GUYS.
THEM AND--
Uh-oh.
Uh-oh.
I CAN GET YOU OUT OF HERE, FELICIA.
BUT YOU HAVE TO GIVE ME THE SCANNER YOU'VE BEEN USING TO FIND THE STONE HOSTS.
FURY STOLE IT FROM ME-- YOU STOLE IT FROM FURY. I NEED IT BACK.
HEY.
SCREW YOU, NIGHTHAWK!
Hh.

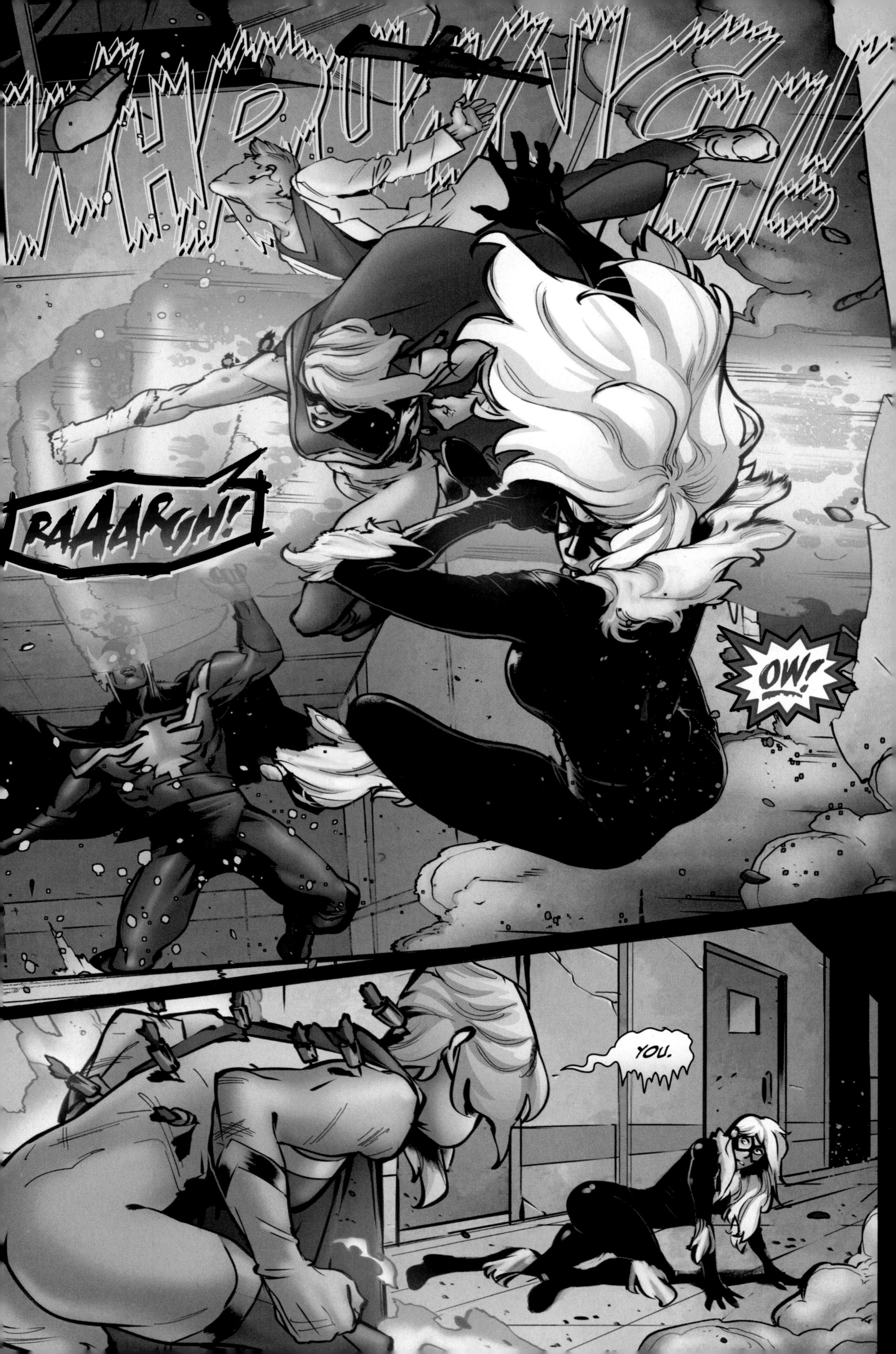
RAAARGH!
OW!
YOU.

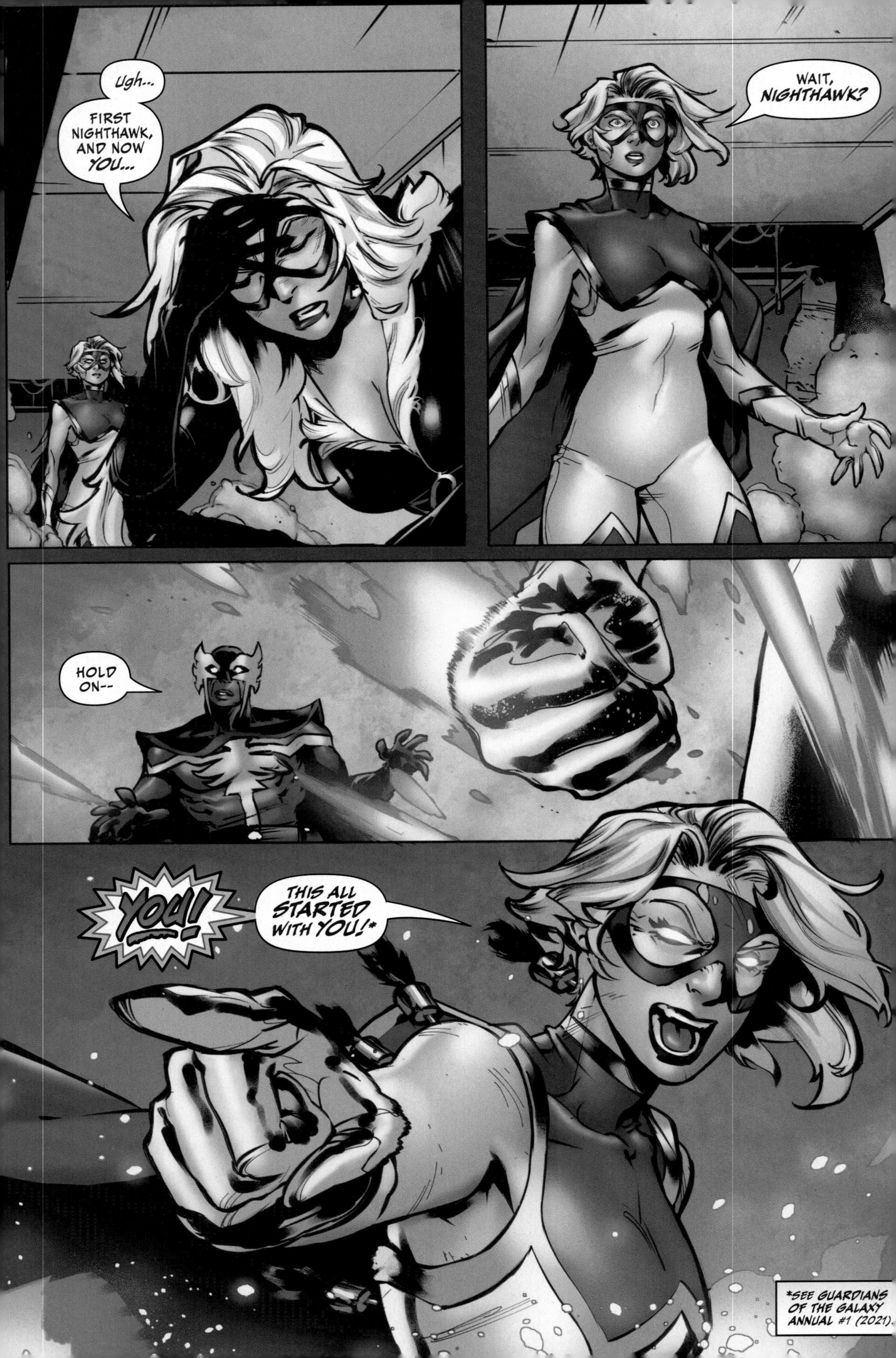
Ugh...
FIRST NIGHTHAWK, AND NOW YOU...
WAIT, NIGHTHAWK?
HOLD ON--
YOU!
THIS ALL STARTED WITH YOU!*
*SEE GUARDIANS OF THE GALAXY ANNUAL #1 (2021).

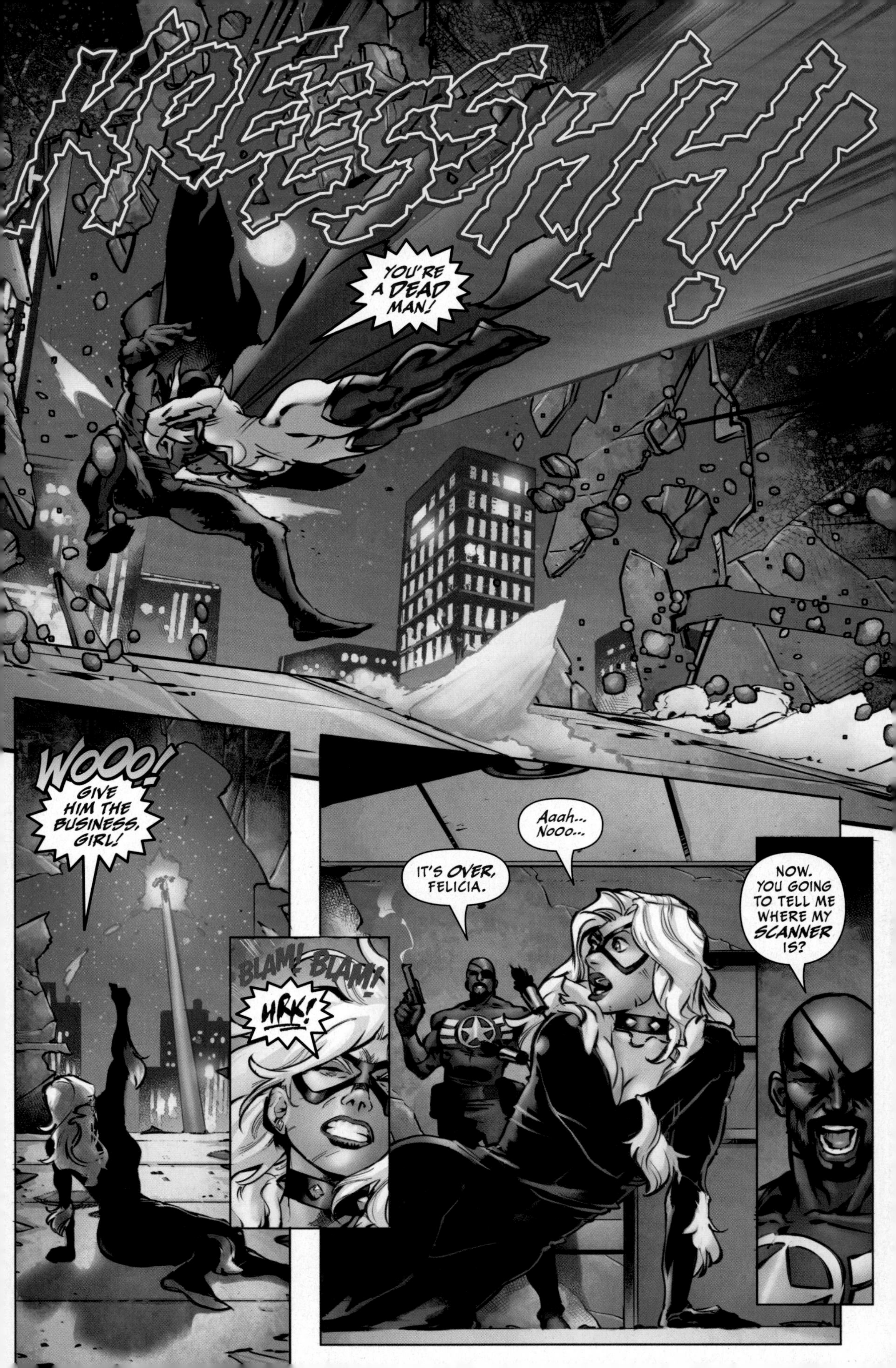
KROOSSHH!
YOU'RE A DEAD MAN!
WOOO! GIVE HIM THE BUSINESS, GIRL!
BLAM! BLAM!
URK!
IT'S OVER, FELICIA.
Aaah... Nooo...
NOW. YOU GOING TO TELL ME WHERE MY SCANNER IS?

TRASHED IT LAST NIGHT AFTER OUR THRILLING CHASE.

I GOT *THREE* OF THEM TOGETHER AND ENDED UP WRECKING A *HOSPITAL*, AND I'M JUST A SIMPLE (IF GORGEOUS) CROOK.

BUT, *YOU? NIGHTHAWK?* NAH.

NO ONE NEEDS GUYS LIKE *YOU TWO* GETTING *THAT KIND* OF POWER.

WELL, THIS IS TURNING INTO A TOTAL *DEBACLE...*

BUT AT LEAST I GOT *YOU.*

Pfff. PLEASE.

LISTEN, FURY. YOU GOT A MOM?

CHAC!

NOT ANYMORE.

WELL I STILL DO.

AND THAT'S *BECAUSE* OF WHAT I DID HERE, TODAY.

YOU THINK I *DIDN'T KNOW* THAT THIS WOULD PROBABLY END WITH ME GETTING *PINCHED?*

IT WAS *WORTH* IT.

YEAH. AND IMAGINE IF I HAD SPRUNG MY TRAP *BEFORE* YOU GOT A CHANCE TO FIX YOUR MOM UP. *THAT* WOULD HAVE BEEN A REAL SHAME.

WAIT, WHAT--?

I *KNOW* WHAT IT'S LIKE TO LOSE A MOM, FELICIA.

AND I ALSO KNOW THIS:

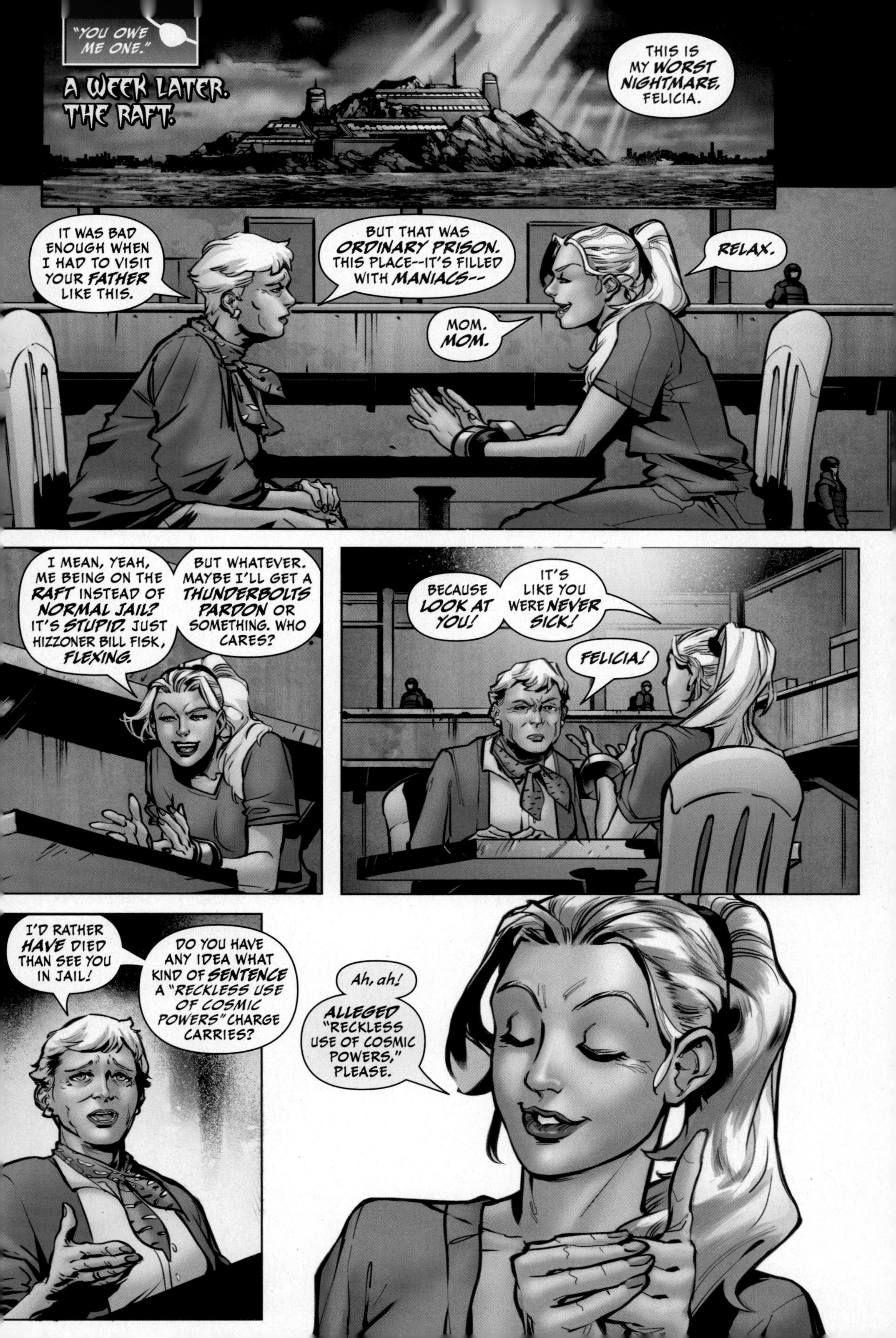
"YOU OWE ME ONE."
A WEEK LATER. THE RAFT.
THIS IS MY WORST NIGHTMARE, FELICIA.
IT WAS BAD ENOUGH WHEN I HAD TO VISIT YOUR FATHER LIKE THIS.
BUT THAT WAS ORDINARY PRISON. THIS PLACE--IT'S FILLED WITH MANIACS--
RELAX.
MOM. MOM.
I MEAN, YEAH, ME BEING ON THE RAFT INSTEAD OF NORMAL JAIL? IT'S STUPID. JUST HIZZONER BILL FISK, FLEXING.
BUT WHATEVER. MAYBE I'LL GET A THUNDERBOLTS PARDON OR SOMETHING. WHO CARES?
BECAUSE LOOK AT YOU!
IT'S LIKE YOU WERE NEVER SICK!
FELICIA!
I'D RATHER HAVE DIED THAN SEE YOU IN JAIL!
DO YOU HAVE ANY IDEA WHAT KIND OF SENTENCE A "RECKLESS USE OF COSMIC POWERS" CHARGE CARRIES?
Ah, ah!
ALLEGED "RECKLESS USE OF COSMIC POWERS," PLEASE.

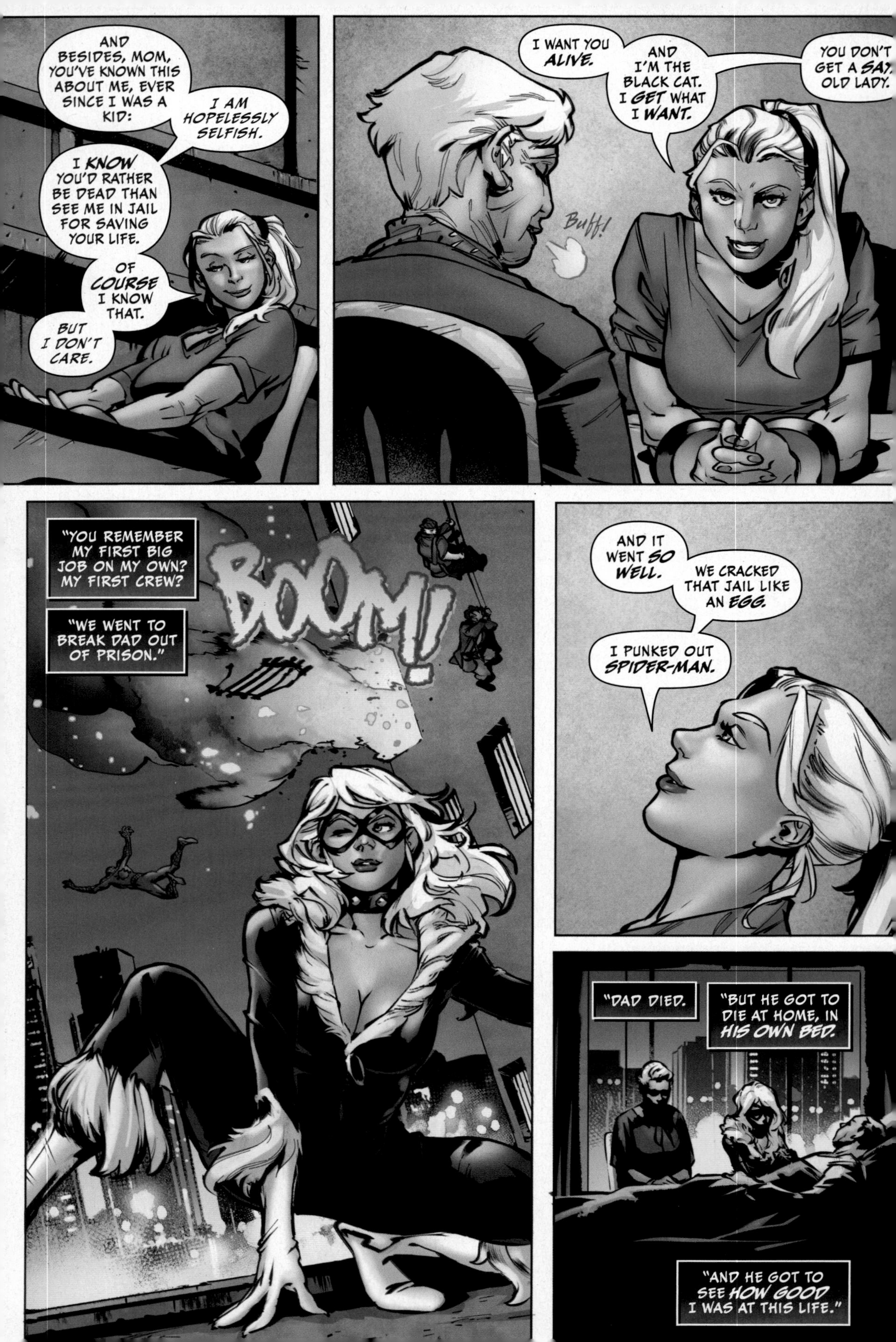
AND BESIDES, MOM, YOU'VE KNOWN THIS ABOUT ME, EVER SINCE I WAS A KID:
I AM HOPELESSLY SELFISH.
I KNOW YOU'D RATHER BE DEAD THAN SEE ME IN JAIL FOR SAVING YOUR LIFE.
OF COURSE I KNOW THAT.
BUT I DON'T CARE.
I WANT YOU ALIVE.
AND I'M THE BLACK CAT. I GET WHAT I WANT.
Buff!
YOU DON'T GET A SAY, OLD LADY.
"YOU REMEMBER MY FIRST BIG JOB ON MY OWN? MY FIRST CREW?
"WE WENT TO BREAK DAD OUT OF PRISON."
BOOM!
AND IT WENT SO WELL.
WE CRACKED THAT JAIL LIKE AN EGG.
I PUNKED OUT SPIDER-MAN.
"DAD DIED.
"BUT HE GOT TO DIE AT HOME, IN HIS OWN BED.
"AND HE GOT TO SEE HOW GOOD I WAS AT THIS LIFE."

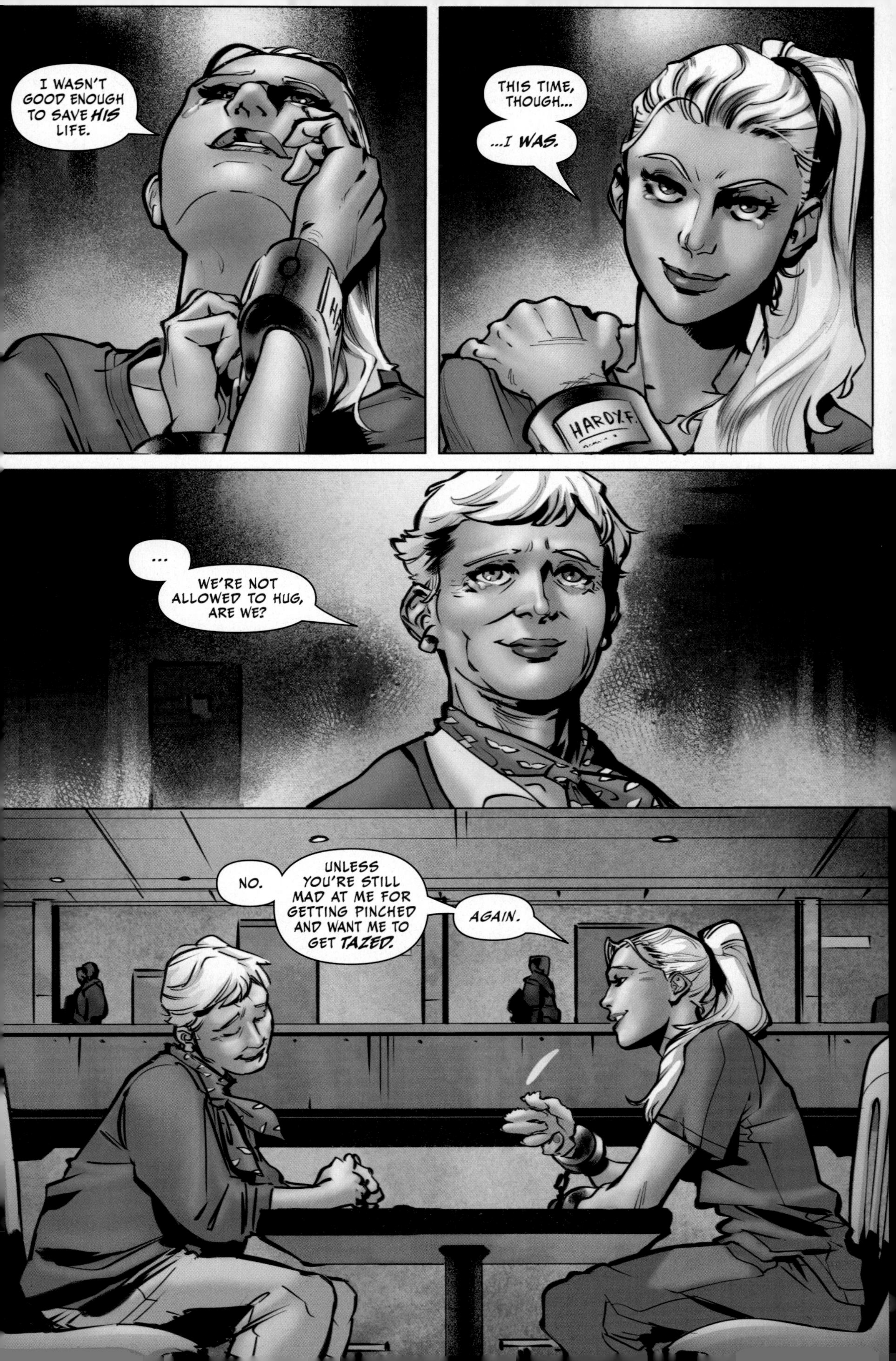
I WASN'T GOOD ENOUGH TO SAVE HIS LIFE.
THIS TIME, THOUGH...
...I WAS.
HARDY.F.
...
WE'RE NOT ALLOWED TO HUG, ARE WE?
NO.
UNLESS YOU'RE STILL MAD AT ME FOR GETTING PINCHED AND WANT ME TO GET TAZED.
AGAIN.

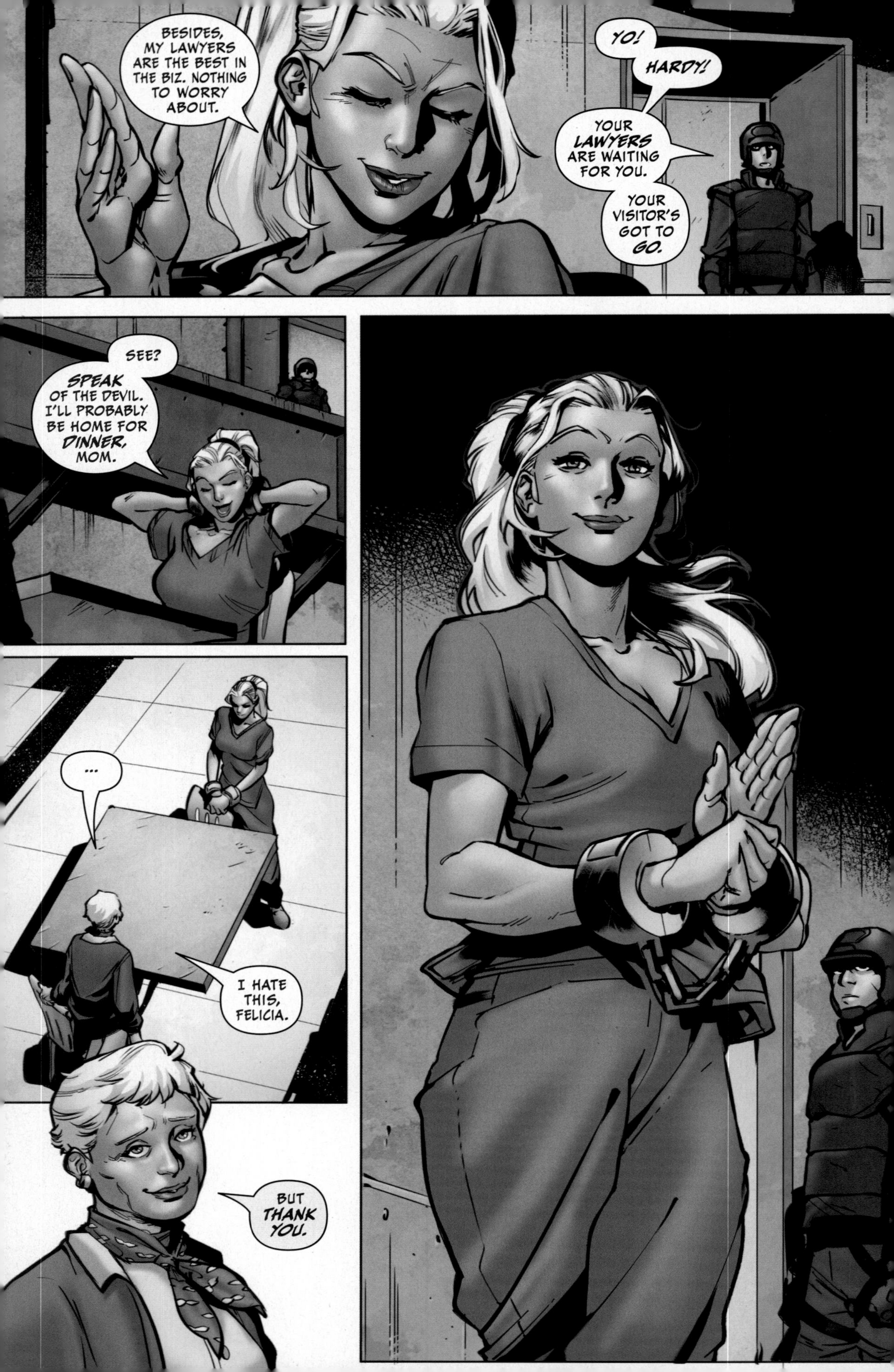
BESIDES, MY LAWYERS ARE THE BEST IN THE BIZ. NOTHING TO WORRY ABOUT.
YO!
HARDY!
YOUR LAWYERS ARE WAITING FOR YOU.
YOUR VISITOR'S GOT TO GO.
SEE?
SPEAK OF THE DEVIL. I'LL PROBABLY BE HOME FOR DINNER, MOM.
...
I HATE THIS, FELICIA.
BUT THANK YOU.

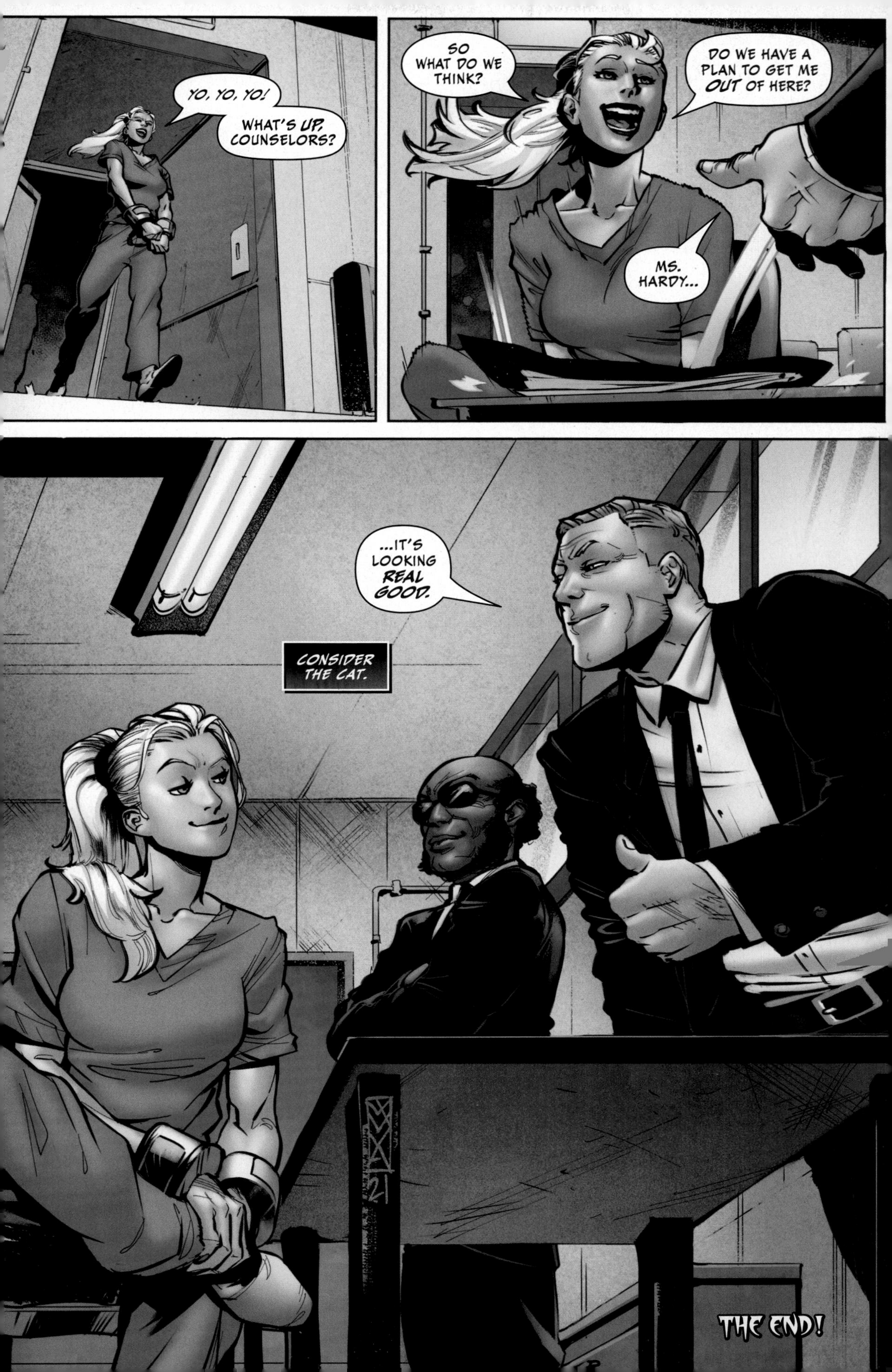

YO, YO, YO!
WHAT'S UP, COUNSELORS?
SO WHAT DO WE THINK?
DO WE HAVE A PLAN TO GET ME OUT OF HERE?
MS. HARDY...
...IT'S LOOKING REAL GOOD.
CONSIDER THE CAT.
THE END!

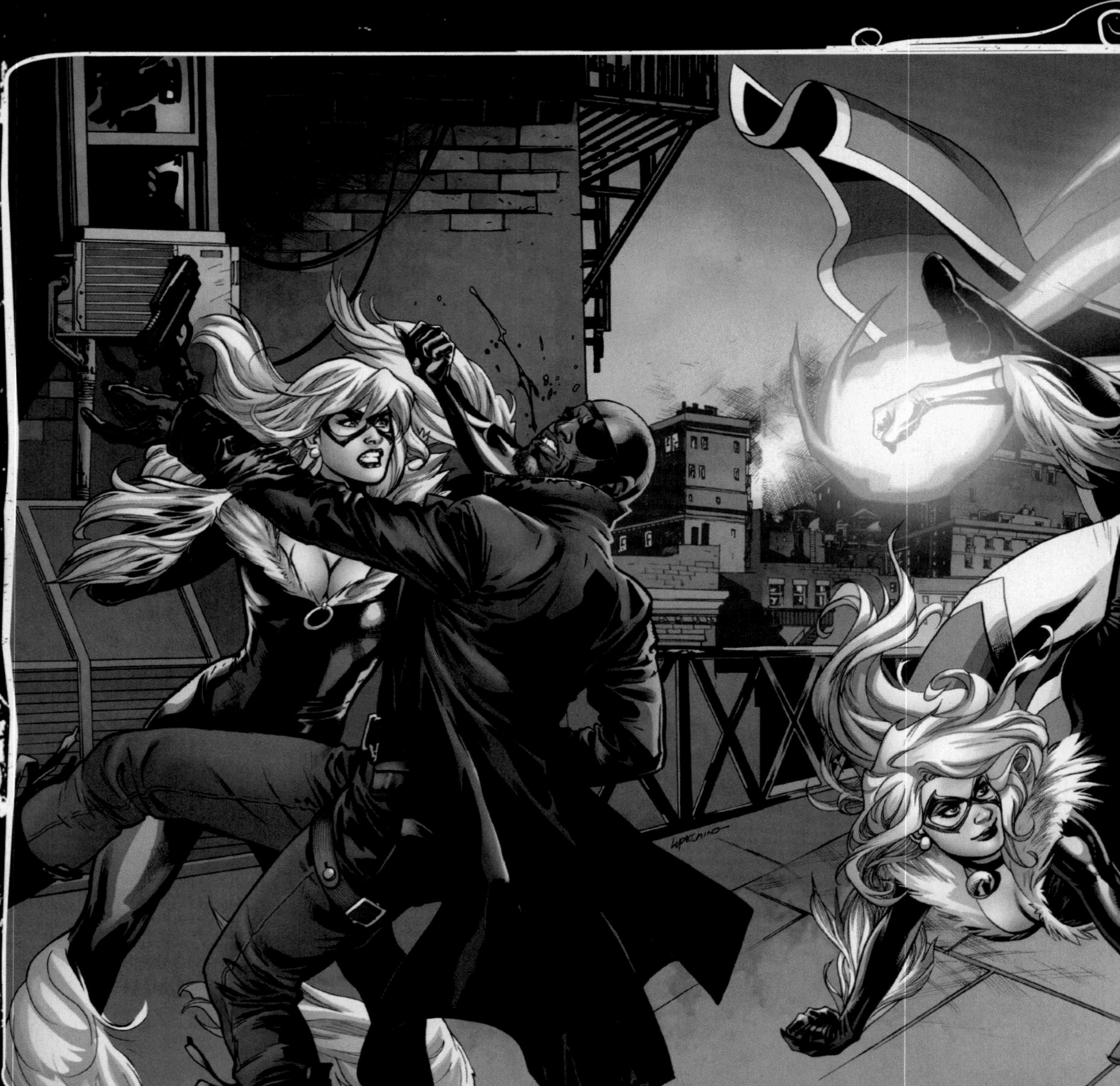

Black Cat #8-10 connecting variants by **EMA LUPACCHINO** & **BRIAN REBER**

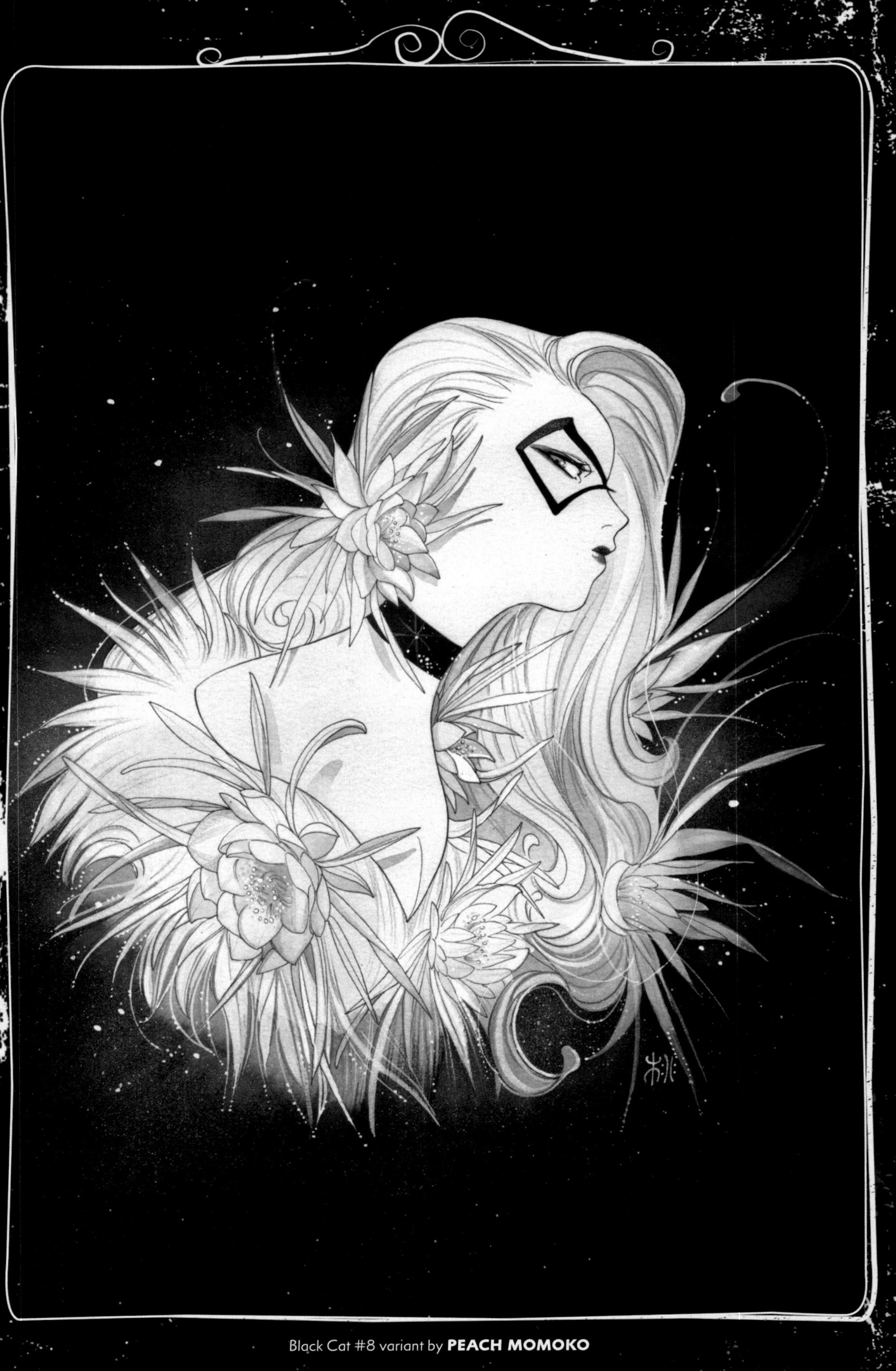

Black Cat #8 variant by **PEACH MOMOKO**

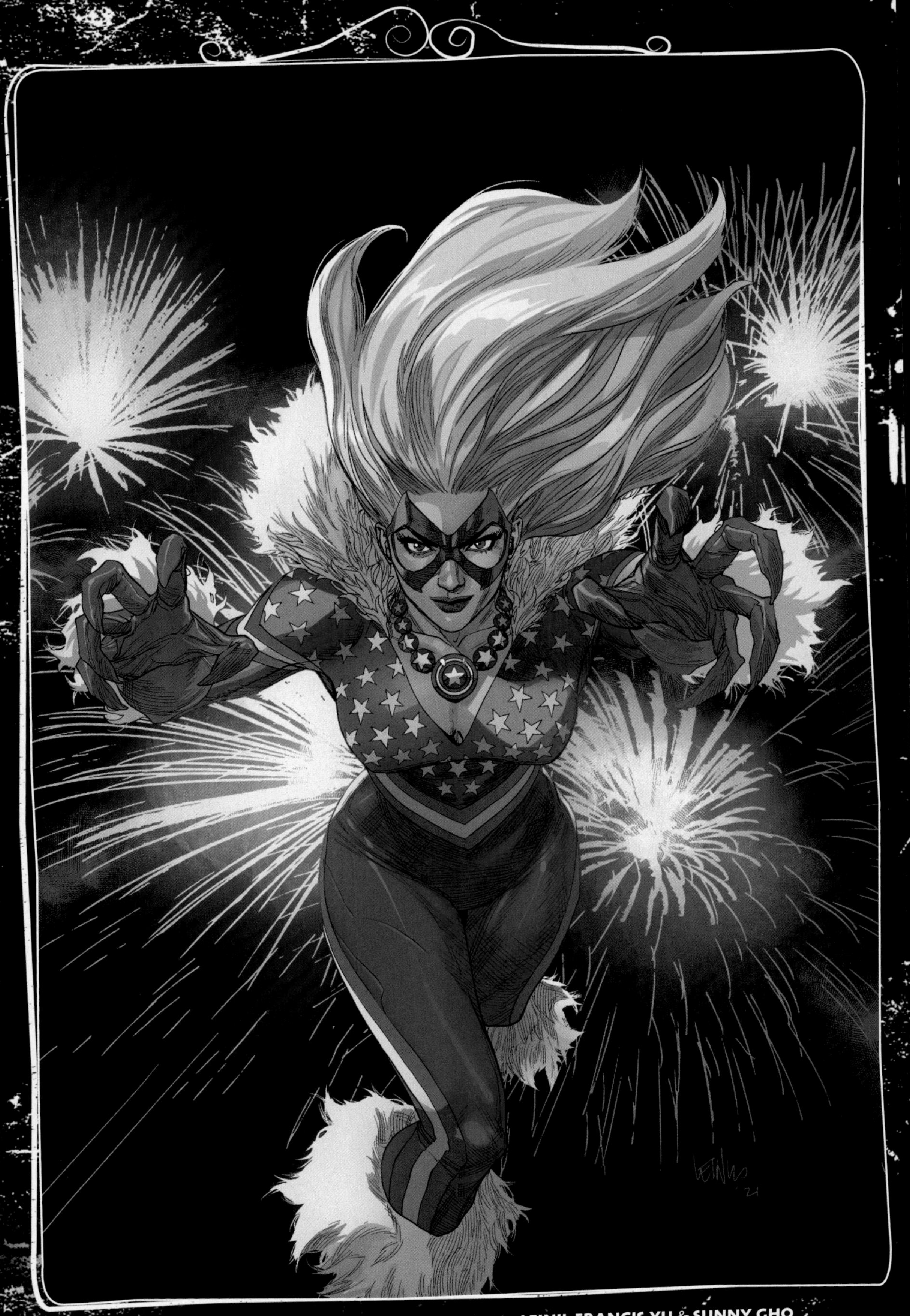

Black Cat #8 Captain America 80th Anniversary variant by **LEINIL FRANCIS YU** & **SUNNY GHO**

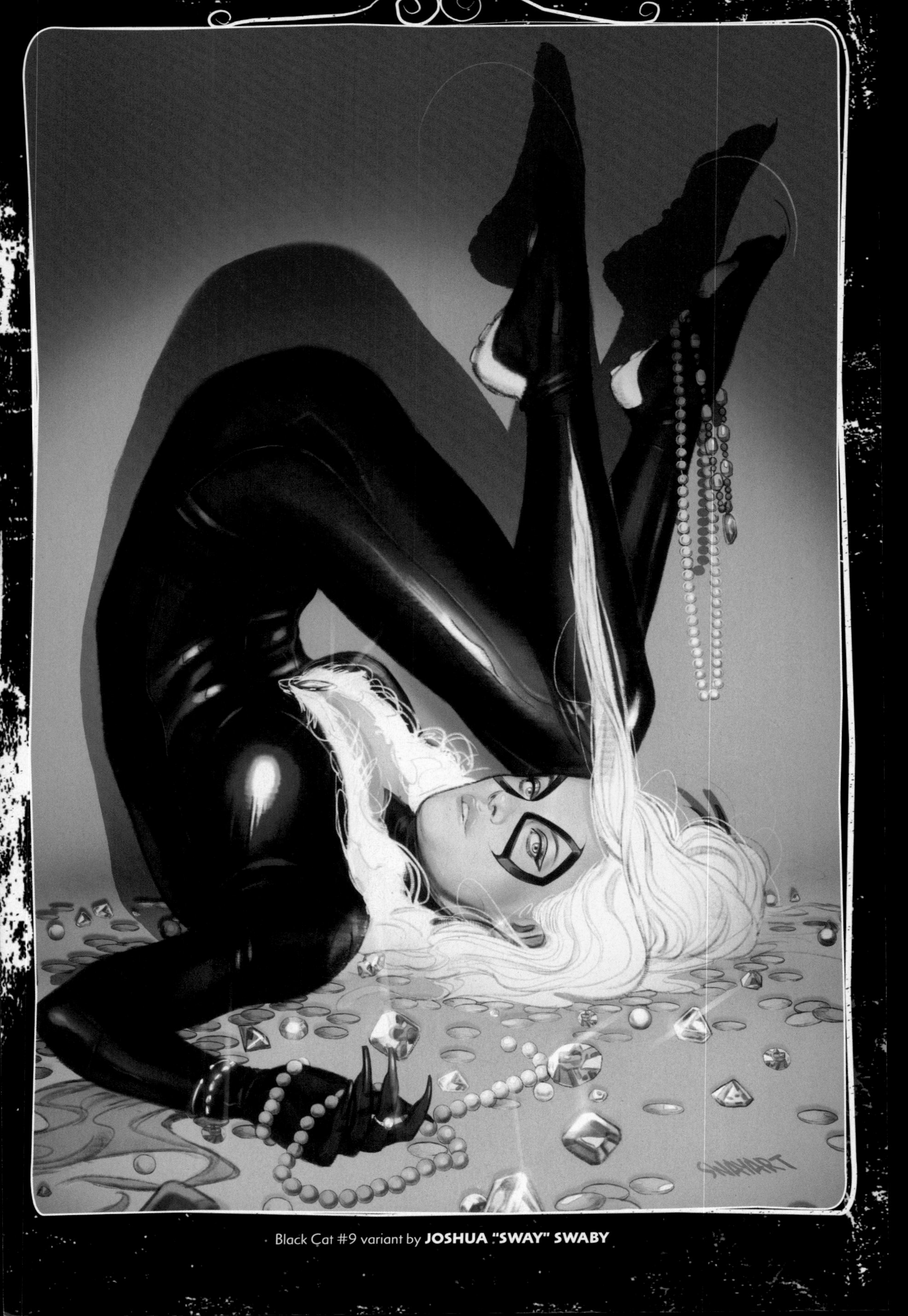

Black Cat #9 variant by **JOSHUA "SWAY" SWABY**

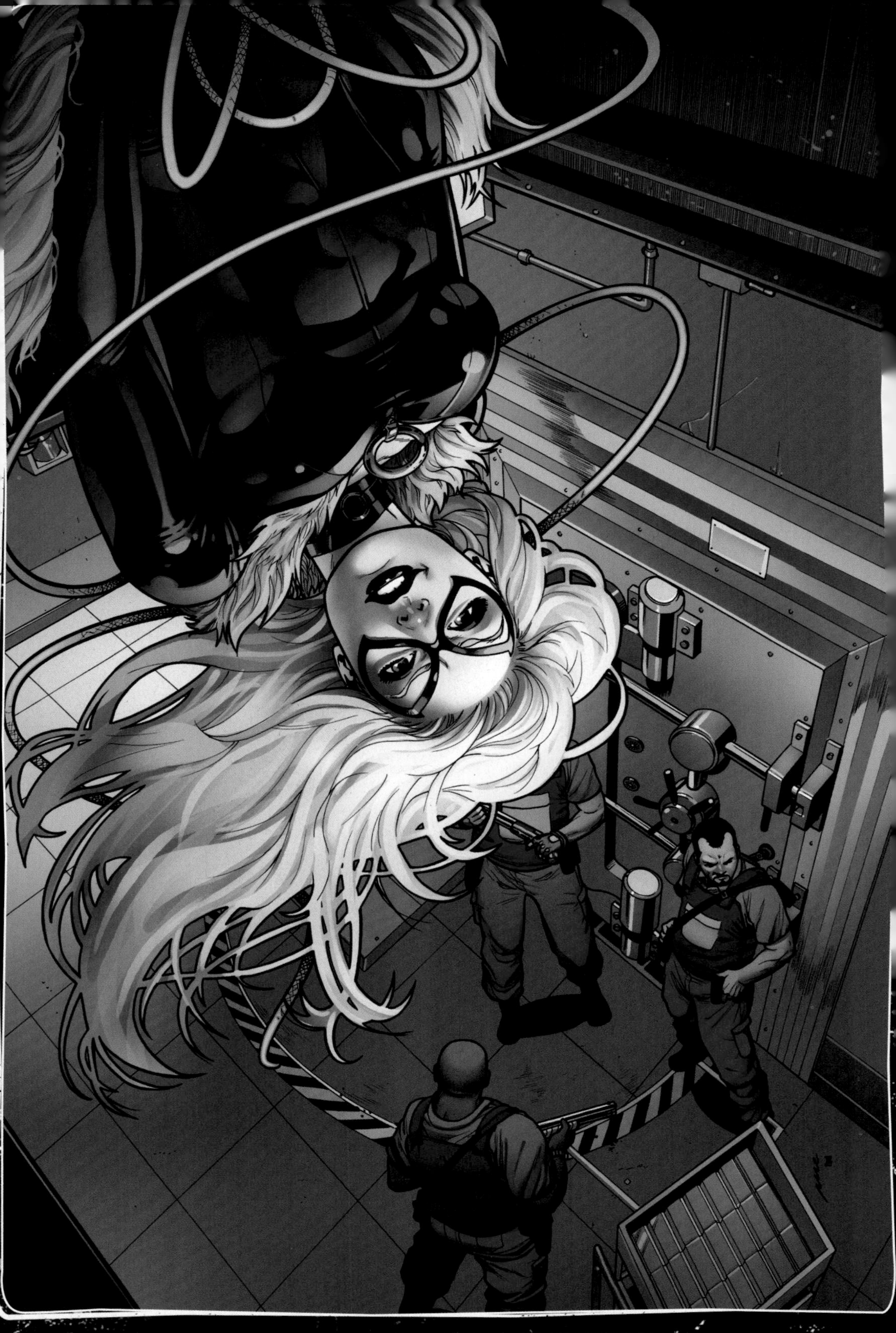

Black Cat #10 PEPE PÉREZ & FRANK D'ARMATA

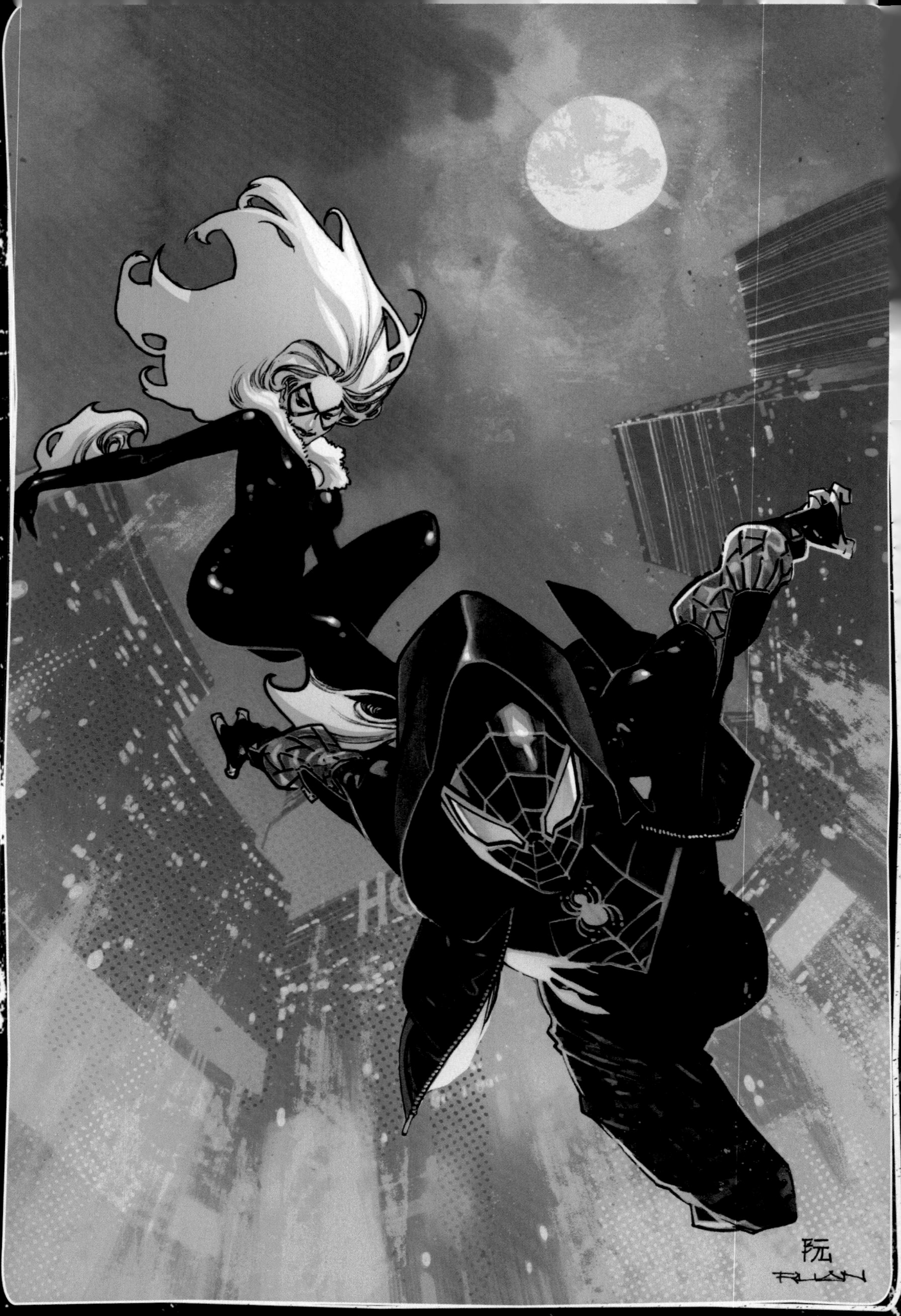
RUAN

Black Cat #10 Miles Morales: Spider-Man 10th Anniversary variant by **DIKE RUAN & DAVE McCAIG**

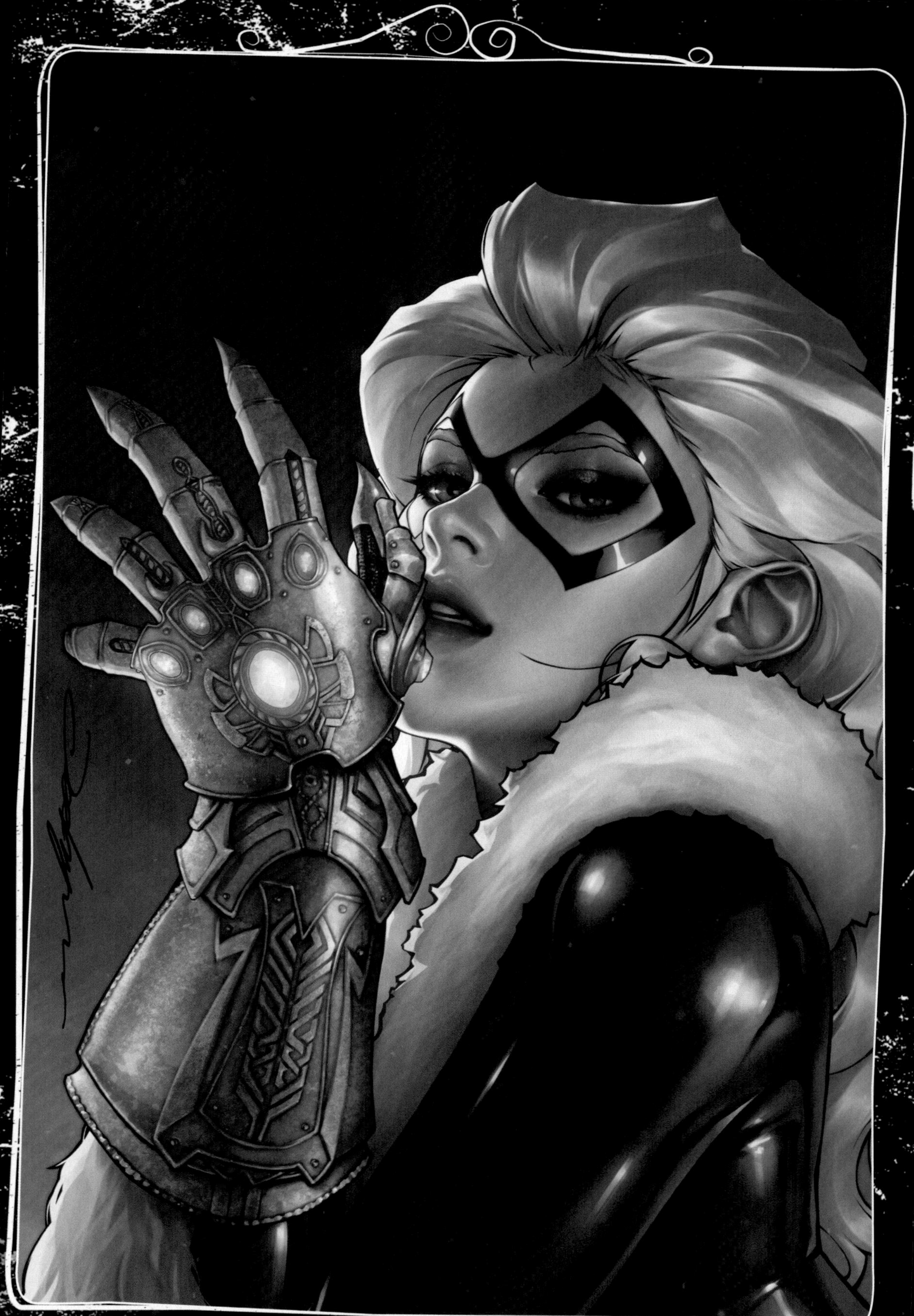

Giant-Size Black Cat: Infinity Score variant by **JEEHYUNG LEE**

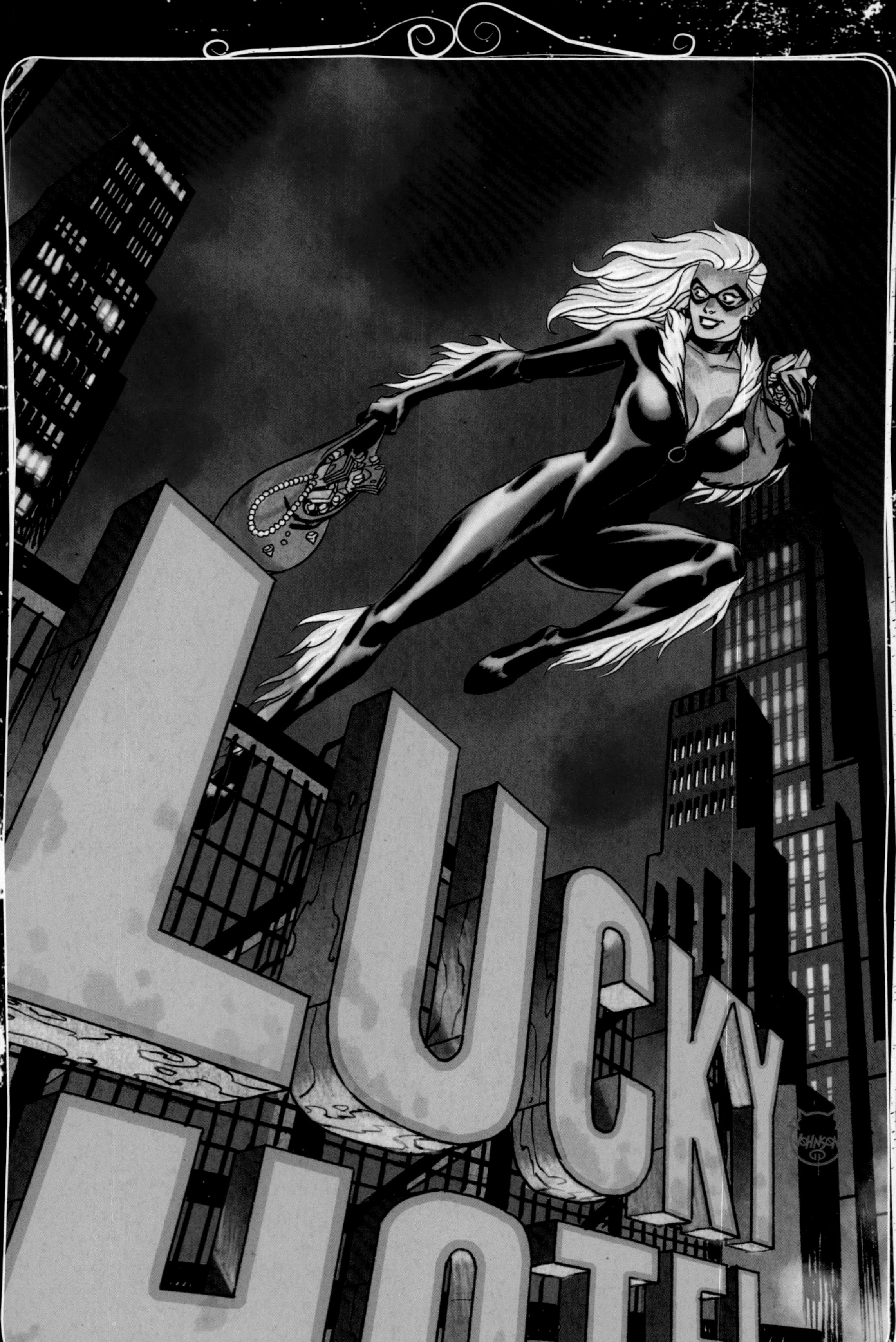
LUCKY

Giant-Size Black Cat: Infinity Score Lucky variant by **DAVE JOHNSON**

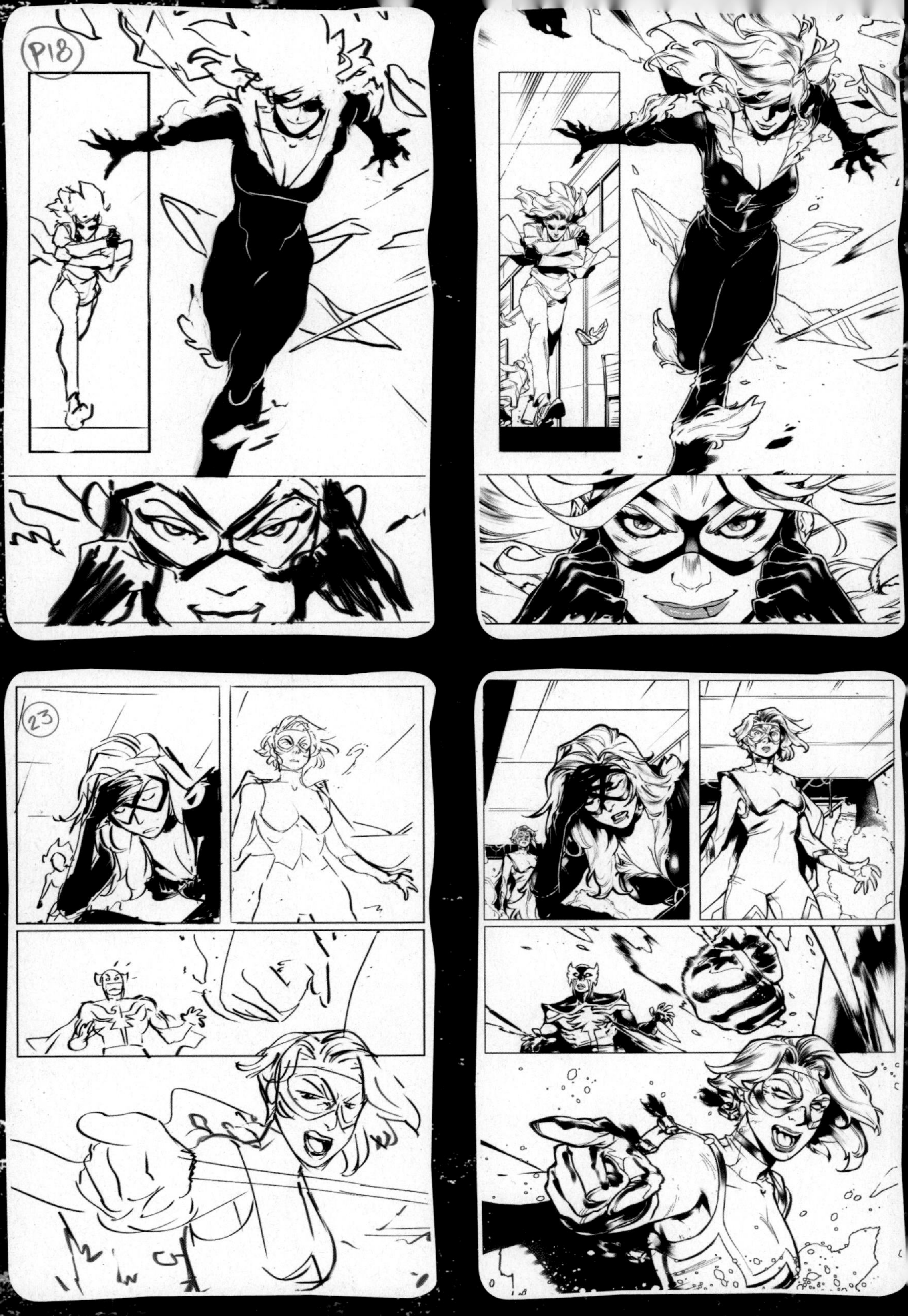
P18
23

Giant-Size Black Cat: Infinity Score #1, pages 18 & 23 layouts and inks by C.F. VILLA

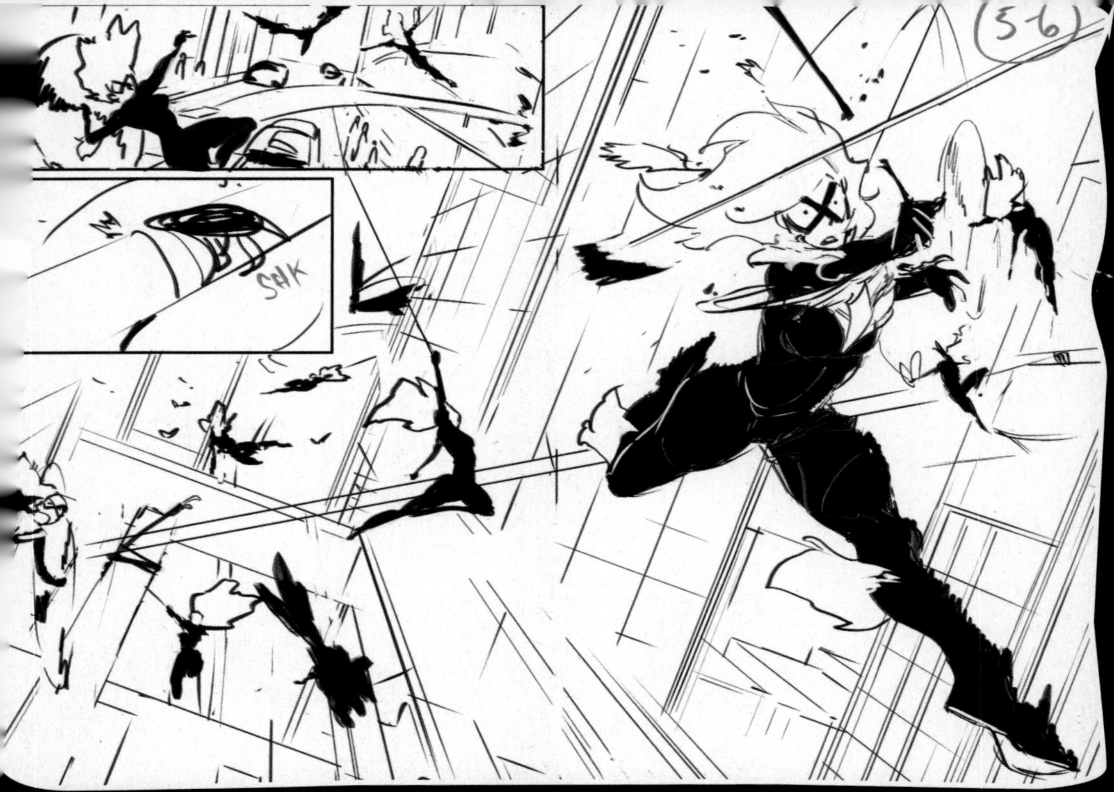
SAK

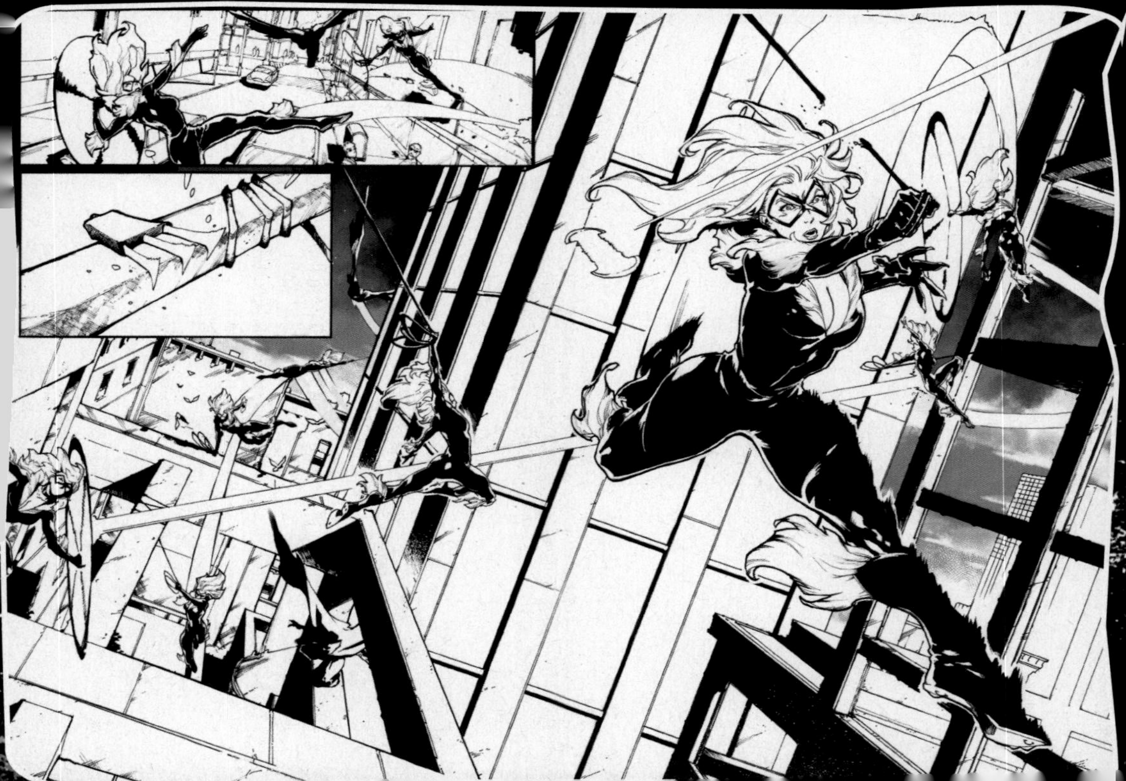

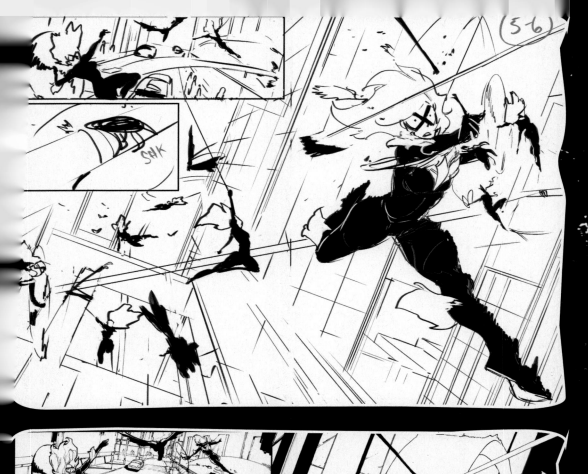

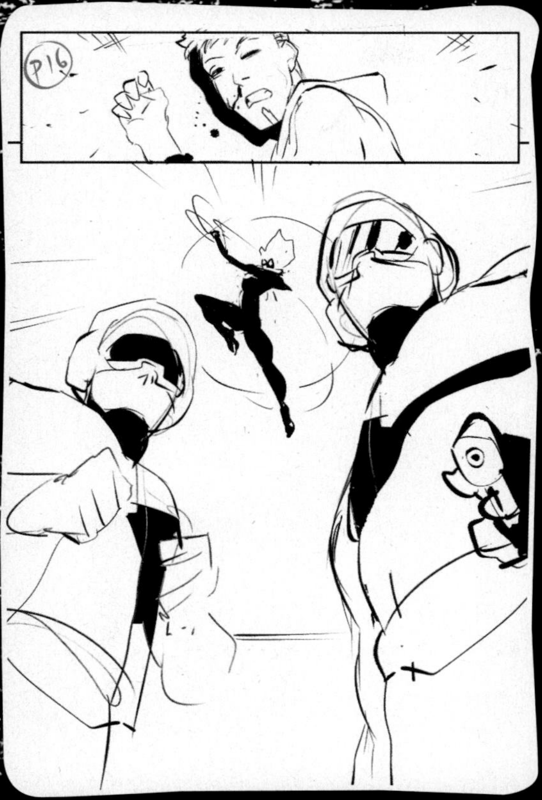
P16
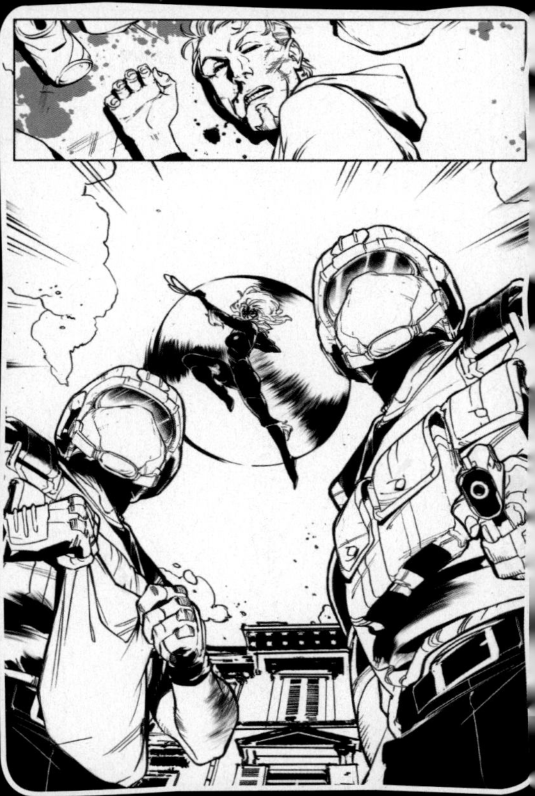
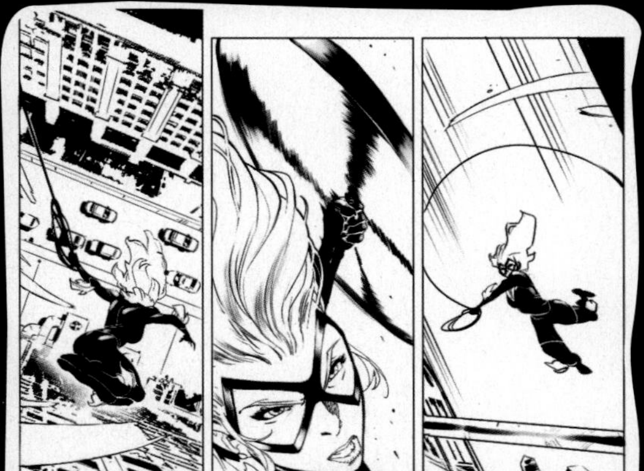
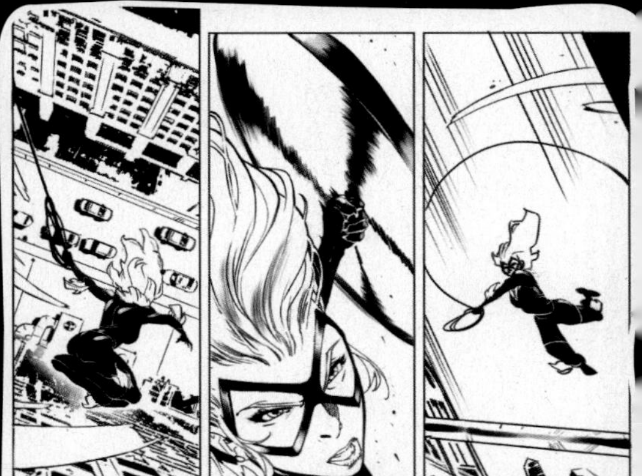

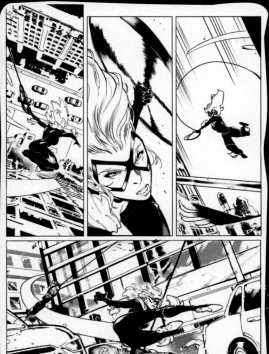

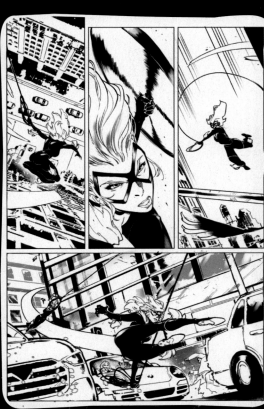

#9, page 16 and #10, page 4 layouts and inks by **C.F. VILLA**

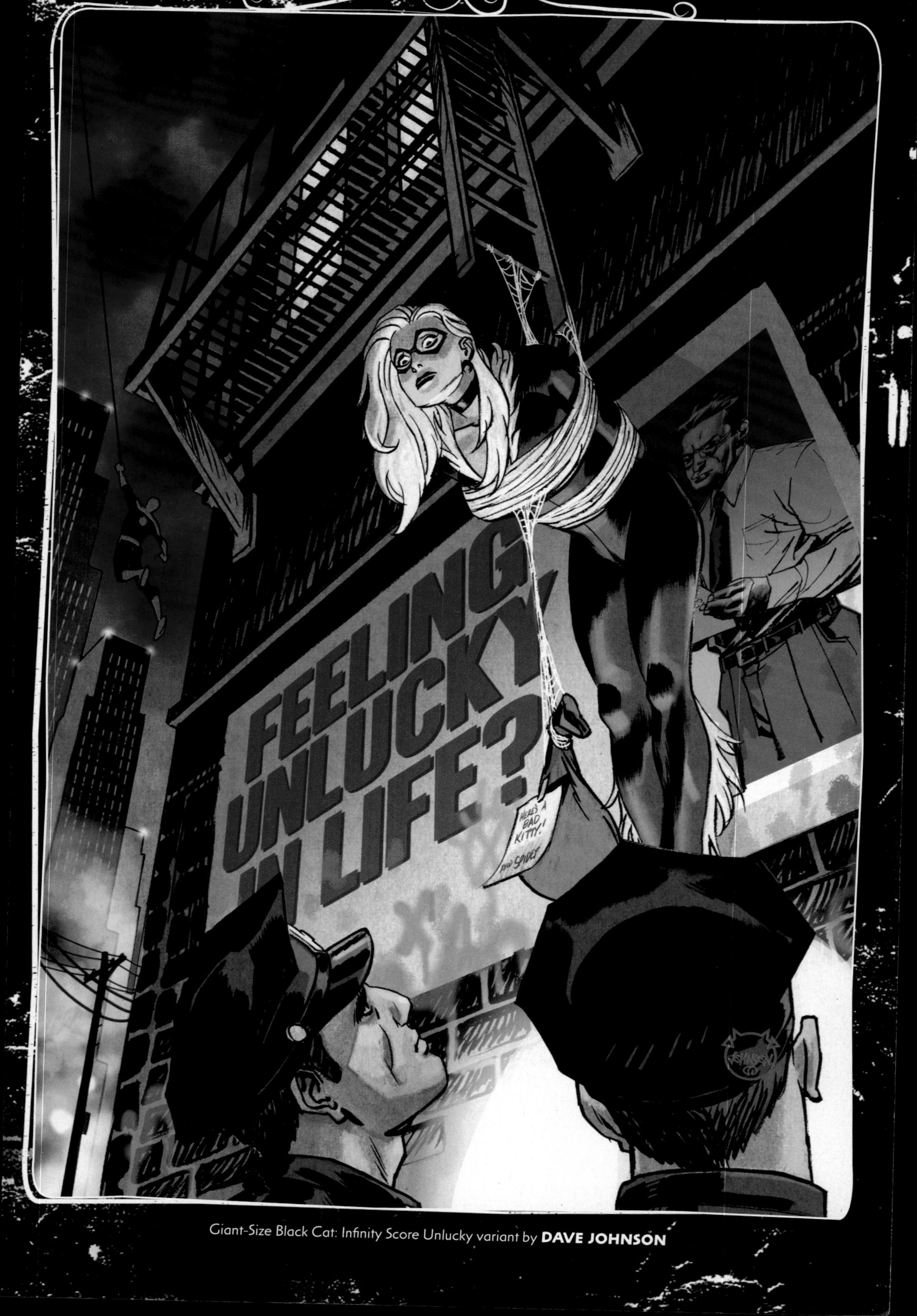
FEELING
UNLUCKY
LIFE?
HERE'S A BAD KITTY!
SPIDEY

Giant-Size Black Cat: Infinity Score Unlucky variant by **DAVE JOHNSON**